GREEN CHILI
AND OTHER IMPOSTORS

FoodStory
Nina Mukerjee Furstenau, series editor

GREEN CHILI
AND OTHER
IMPOSTORS

Nina Mukerjee Furstenau

University of Iowa Press *Iowa City*

University of Iowa Press, Iowa City 52242
Printed in the United States of America

Design by Nola Burger
Text: 11/15 Whitman | Display: Akzidenz Grotesk; Zeitung Pro

Printed on acid-free paper

Library of Congress Cataloging-in-Publication Data
Names: Furstenau, Nina, author.
Title: Green Chili and Other Impostors / by Nina Mukerjee Furstenau.
Description: Iowa City: University of Iowa Press, [2021] | Series:
  FoodStory | Includes bibliographical references and index.
Identifiers: LCCN 2021005208 (print) | LCCN 2021005209 (ebook) | ISBN
  9781609387983 (paperback) | ISBN 9781609387990 (ebook)
Subjects: Furstenau, Nina. | Women, Bengali—Biography. | Cooking—
  India—Bengal—Foreign influences. | Cultural appropriation—Nutritional
  aspects—India—Bengal. | Cooking, Bengali—Foreign influences.
Classification: LCC TX749.F87 2021 (print) | LCC TX749 (ebook) | DDC
  641.3—dc23
LC record available at https://lccn.loc.gov/2021005208
LC ebook record available at https://lccn.loc.gov/2021005209

The pen-and-ink illustrations of chilies throughout and the illustrations
on pages 2, 38, 41, 45, 55, 83, 151, 184, 196, and 214 are reproduced with
the kind permission of artist Mohan Banerji. Photographs on pages 15, 80,
and 121 were taken by the author. The epigraph to chapter 8 is drawn from
original text by Vidya Balachander and is reprinted with permission. The
poem "The Traveling Onion" in chapter 14 is reprinted with permission of
the author, Naomi Shihab Nye.

For Terry

Let agreeable things be given away.
Let agreeable food be eaten.

—*The Mahabharata of Krishna-Dwaipayana Vyasa*

CONTENTS

ACKNOWLEDGMENTS

I BEGAN THIS BOOK as a Fulbright-Nehru Global Scholar in Kolkata, India, and I thank the Fulbright program, generally for its mission of international education as a force for peace and personally for allowing me the wonder of being in India for nearly nine months of research. I cherish knowing the Fulbright administrators in Kolkata, especially Shevanti Narayan, Sumanta Basu, and Sima Bhattacharjee, as well as my program host, Jayanta Sengupta at the Victoria Memorial in Kolkata. My husband, Terry, and I are happily grateful to Dipankar Dasgupta and Krishna Sarbari Dasgupta for their many kindnesses and experiences of adda.

I cannot thank my family in India enough, most especially for their warm welcome and their help with my rather frequent questions: Susmita Mookerjee, Tapan and Nandita Chowdhury, and Suchitra Mukherjee in Kolkata and Rajat Chowdhury in Bhandarhati as well as Anuradha, Rahul, Basudha, Mahika, and Rajat Banerji in New Delhi. My heartfelt gratitude to my artist uncle, Mohan Banerji, who created many of the wonderful illustrations for this book, and Sheila Banerji for their continuing love and support. And a tip of my hat to our intrepid niece Paula Green and her super note-taking abilities during her visit with us in India.

Many, many people took the time to talk with me about Indian food, connected me to those I needed to see, and let me taste wonderful things. I am grateful to Brunnel Arathoon and Anthony Khatchaturian, Kastura Bandyopadhyay, Paula Banerjee, Sharmistha Banerjee and her lovely parents, Dipen and Ria Banerjee, Subir and Haimanta Banerjee, Bela Rani Devi and her family, Oindrilla Dutt, Bomti Iyengar, Monica Liu, Shireen Maswood, Salmolie Mukerjee, Bijoy and Asha Mukherjee and their daughter Prakriti, Srikanta Pramanik, Utsa Ray, Priyadarshini Ghosh Shome, Jael and Flower Silliman, Sandhya Singh, and many more.

My deep thanks to my agent in India, Preeti Gill, editors Aienla Ozukum and Kanika Praharaj at Aleph Books, and director James McCoy and editors Susan Hill Newton and Holly Carver at the University of Iowa Press. You are all amazing.

In Kolkata, I will never forget my introduction to the cultural life of the city that informs this book and the yoga retreat at the beautiful Balakhana Estate in Maheshganj, and I thank my friends Benigna Chilla, Milena Chilla-Markhoff, Ellie Choudhury, Samanta Duggal, Anita Kanoi, Shreya Kanoi, Rebecca Lindland, Jael Silliman, and our hosts in Maheshganj, Kalpana and Ranodhir Palchouduri, for the delightful experience.

A huge tip of the hat to my intrepid recipe testers—you were amazing!—David Baker, Kandace Davis and the gang of five—Lisa Burke, Carol Migneron, Jane Small, Caroline Tice, and Jill Wehmer—Le Greta Hudson, Kim "Naki" James, Kate Lebo, Jessica Martin, Laura McHugh, Jill Orr, Katherine Reed, Sharmini and Dahnya Rogers, Lynn Rossy, Cathy Salter, and James Prakash Young. I hope that you will come over sometime for a feast I create.

I cannot thank my early readers enough: Rahul Banerji, Jill Orr, and Jayanta Sengupta. It was a huge honor to have your perspective. As always, I send my heartfelt gratitude to my writing circle: Anne Breidenbach, Jennifer Gravley, Laura McHugh, Jill Orr, and Allison Smythe.

And to my family, Sachin and Sipra Mukerjee and Terry, Nate, and Anna Furstenau, thank you, thank you, thank you for keeping my spirits up and putting up with my crazy transcontinental life while I researched this work.

AUTHOR'S NOTE

NOT LONG AFTER I ARRIVED in the City of Joy, I was described as a fish returned to its water, although occasional sidelong looks offered a mildly different assessment. To be sure, I felt I was swimming in benevolent seas, happily chortling between meals. Though fully aware that the imagined India of my childhood in Kansas and my sandals-on-the-ground, dust-between-my-toes self in Kolkata were not always in alignment, my time there birthed this book, one distilled version of the possible. The foods that I highlight in *Green Chili and Other Impostors* are markers of shifts in the culinary story of Bengal as noted by the journey of a Bengali girl from Kansas, not a comprehensive history of the heritage foods of the region. Like you, my experiences sieve the world.

Some iconic ingredients in India, thought to be native, journeyed far and wide to arrive there, sailing under the colors of foreign ships, exchanged by very early travelers, or possibly catching a lift with an energetic bird. When does an adopted food become a keenly held tradition? The flavors of the subcontinent, transformed by cooks and caring, feasts and fasts, and thoughts on food as medicine, enveloped multitudes and eras. Other ingredients left the subcontinent and were adopted, assimilated, and performed heroically elsewhere in terms of taste, health, and nutrition.

This book is a recipe for you to test on the tongue and in your heart. The foods on your plate—the infinitely tender sensory moments of savoring—reveal history as almost nothing else can. Check out the textures. Assess the aromas that rise. I have followed these recipes and relished the results. The dishes created are pukka: absolutely first class or, more modestly, solid and genuine and tasty. See if you agree.

If I had held a crystal up to the Indian sun during the three seasons I lived on the subcontinent, its refracted light would have revealed what I sometimes missed: a flower peeking from a crack in a busy street, a shrine embedded in a sidewalk tree parting foot traffic with not one bit of trash tangled in its roots, dust motes tumbling through slanting rays at sunrise to slip into the homes of numerous small animals secreted away: everyday brilliance. With or without the crystal to illuminate these details, my time did reveal that though I am no longer in India, my spirit swims there free.

In this book, I chose Indian place-names over British-imposed ones. Mostly, this is because I am referring to current times. You will notice that I use Kolkata instead of Calcutta almost always unless I just couldn't help myself in order to pin the passage to the era of the British East India Company or the Raj.

I mostly use British and Indian terms instead of U.S. terms, so you'll see biscuit instead of cookie and custard instead of pudding. But sometimes I use the U.S. word, such as squash instead of gourd or eggplant instead of aubergine. It's a mash-up of intrigue, my choices.

You can substitute some ingredients throughout the recipes. For instance, if you do not have tamarind paste on hand, you can use lemon juice, though it will offer a different complexity on the tongue. Dried spices such as ginger and garlic are options, if needed, to replace the freshly mashed versions in the recipes, and ready-made ginger-garlic paste is available in jars at groceries for a shortcut. I strongly advise you to use fresh green chilies when specified because they create a different flavor dimension than dried red chilies or cayenne. For the fish, I was hard-pressed to find bekti, rui, and bummalo in Missouri and found that one-inch-thick tilapia, carp, steelhead trout, or black sea bass worked well, though should you get any Indian freshwater fish varieties, definitely use them.

In a specially loving way, I talk about nolen gur in several spots throughout this book. It is a fleeting winter delicacy, a syrup made from the sap of date palm trees, which are tapped much like maple trees, albeit much farther off the ground, and their sap is then boiled down to a subtle delicious syrup. Jaggery, while also made from the sap of palm trees, is a coarse brown sugar made by evaporation of the sap; it can be stored much longer than nolen gur ever could. If need be and if a molasses-like flavor is acceptable, you can substitute a simple syrup made from jaggery.

As I was on my journey to research this book, I rediscovered a known fact: impostors by definition are not what they seem. Left to our own devices, all of us put down roots to make space for ourselves, situating our stories within a larger cultural umbrella until we become part of the whole.

GREEN CHILI
AND OTHER IMPOSTORS

Introduction

SATISFYING OUR HUNGERS

Well!...But why have you come to India?

—Garcia de Orta, *Colloquies on the Simples and Drugs of India*, 1563

RANI FOUND ME SQUINTING UPWARD into mango trees, my eyes trained on the succulent orbs just out of reach. I never wavered even when the leaves shifted and the sun glinted through, blinding me temporarily. The smooth, fiber-free flesh of langra, one of fifteen hundred mango varieties happily fruiting in India, had an unmatched taste; when ripe they were so luxurious you could spoon the fruit out of their skins like custard. It was 1966, and I was visiting my grandparents in India from my home in the United States, where there were no mangoes like this. My grandmother Rani's trees were dwarfs that sat beside tasty papaya and custard apple trees. Her garden, complete with a small fishpond, was a wonderland.

There are almost 350,000 acres of commercial mango trees grown where Rani lived in the state of Bihar, now Jharkhand, each bearing an average of two to three hundred mangoes per season in their mature years. Even so, each year Rani acted swiftly at just the right moment before visiting monkeys could

Mango tree at Rani Villa.

feast, and the fruits, swaying in enticement, were plucked from their rhythmic dance with the wind to be left unmoored in a bucket. Jars of golden chutney soon glistened in her kitchen.

Mangoes and slow heat, both sweet and tart on the tongue, the last jar of her fruit that seemed to so effortlessly distill the Indian sun, opened and consumed, and what was passed down through generations stopped short. It was a kindness not to know when or by whom the final spoonful of my grandmother's green mango chutney was swallowed. No one knew her secret, her recipe was shuffled into a drawer, if ever written down, and though Rani had preserved a flavor, a kitchen, and a life, I felt sealed out, grasping for connection.

My grandmother reached the trees I stood under by skirting the small fish-pond in the garden as well as the family tulsi mancha, the terra-cotta planter for basil revered in Bengali households. She made sure to light the diya lamp each day to protect the household, using homemade cotton wicks my uncles rolled against their legs. The aromatic tulsi, a powerhouse of ancient India's Ayurveda medical system, is thought to be a gateway between heaven and earth, and the fragrance of basil, as well as the thought of langra, might well have done the trick and opened divine doors. The garden was fruitful, the mangoes sublimely delicious.

Those mango trees may well have been the instigator for my life's work in food story. A perfumed garden can be far-reaching. In 2018, I gladly and humbly accept a nine-month Fulbright-Nehru research grant to study the heritage foods of Bengal. I arrive in Kolkata, and much as I did as a child staring up at the mangoes just out of my reach, I gazed around me in wonder at the rich food tales and trails reaching back to antiquity in northeast India. This book is the result of those tales as they unfolded to me over three seasons in my family's homeland.

~~~~~

Before I contacted every Bengali relative I could to find the favorite foods of my grandmother and her recipes-for-goodness'-sake, before I knew much about the care and synergy required to get these foods to my plate, before I booked a seat to Kolkata or worried overmuch about the state of my language skills there, the foods of my family's table were simply flavors I enjoyed. But I could feel this shifting.

I have to say, straight off, I am presently fifty-nine years old. No matter what comes of this tale—no matter how you might want to roll your eyes and ask, What took her so long, why is this happening, wouldn't this be better left to private conversations in the home?—keep in mind, just like you, the first story I ever heard was the one that told me who I was, where I belonged, and to whom. Babies everywhere, gazing in wonder at the hatching world, take it on faith. What is perfectly true is that I was born to Bengali parents while they were living in Thailand, I grew up in a sturdy catalpa-leaved town in southeast Kansas in the United States, and my family's Bengali homeland means I own certain stories that were vastly different from those told to other babies around me.

It seems, too, that my American Midwest home was the one predestined for me even though, in 1962 according to the 1960 census, I was one of just 12,000 immigrants from India in the U.S. at the time, almost all of them *not* in Kansas. In that same 1960 census, self-reporting replaced enumerator reporting for most Americans, and Indians faced with boxes to check for race ticked "etc.?"—and, yes, there was a question mark, as if the U.S. was uncertain about the existence of other races—or "white" for their category. All through my teen years, I always hesitated on forms with boxes that didn't seem to fit. Once, I handwrote "India" below the list as a kind of defiant protest and then couldn't stop myself thereafter, always writing in the white space where I wasn't allowed. It took until the 1980 census, the year I graduated from high school, for the category of "Asian or Pacific Islander" to be an option. Though my feeling of belonging seemed steadfast, this was an inconsistency and I needed to connect the dots.

Like you, the story I was told early of who I was seemed snug—a Bengali girl in Kansas—but soon, without Indian culture to surround me, it was as if I wore an ill-fitting coat: the collar itched, the seams felt badly sewn, and eventually that coat shook itself free and I was left with a newly pieced-together version. Seams had come undone in fifth grade softball, they frayed in seventh grade as I roller-skated, and then they sort of gave up as I became a forever fan of county fairs, ice cream, and pickup trucks. I was a product of two cultures and extraneous at times in both. But life emerged as it does, slowly, and in a form less foreign than might have been imagined in the beginning.

I began to uncover the source of my comforts and discomforts as I grew. To find out why life outside our front door lacked the music of the lilting Bengali language, the brushing sound of silk or soft cotton as women walked, and the aroma of cardamom anywhere, I became a code breaker. I intently listened to my parents speaking their native Bengali and found, often, that food story linked my world in Kansas with Bengal.

I noticed when certain dishes were made according to the weather. When cool rains came through Kansas and neighbors talked about craving chicken noodle soup or a mild version of chili con carne, my parents talked about khichuri, a stick-to-your-ribs wonder made with rice and lentils, a sprinkling of vegetables in my mother's style, and butter. Spring in Kansas meant a postponed killer humidity, vigor, and growth in the farms all around. Winter wheat, tender and green, swayed in the fields; beets, broccoli, lettuce, and more emerged in gardens. And suddenly I knew what barsha, monsoon season, in Bengal might be like. There a long stretch of heat and humidity was rewarded with the monsoon rains, and when the temperature eased and muggy weather transformed into rain in Kansas, my father longed for the comfort of my mother's warm, simply made khichuri. Other times, my code breaking wasn't so straightforward.

It took me years, for instance, to connect the delicate dessert payesh with a treat to be had during the autumn festival celebrating Lakshmi, divinely feminine and powerful goddess of prosperity, and not just my father's late November birthday. And I never knew then that summertime korola was not, in fact, a blood purifier, which I swore it was every time I had to eat it, but a squash that Bengalis relished specifically for its bitterness as it not only helped subtly balance all the other flavors of a meal but was also considered good for your health.

These stories of food and the seasonal rains linked me to land I was not part of, space I had not lived in. Everyday things teased my memory from early occasional trips to India: wooden bowls filled with ripe mangoes, a garden with a fishpond, vegetable sellers calling out, and lizards lazing on white walls. Like Lakshmi and her annual descent to earth at the full moon in the month of Aswin, mid-September to mid-October—when she goes around asking "Kojaguri?" or "Who's awake?"—I was not quite awake to all my history. And, as in the Midwest, food that grew from the land in Bengal became another code, not only the showcase for the mix of nutrients from a particular soil but evidence of a place, a pointer to the heart of a culture and what made a family tick. The centrifuge of food and the land it emerged from moored everyone from the farmer to the club member sipping sweet-salty lime soda on a veranda in Kolkata to me in the American Midwest 8,100 miles away.

I tried to explain myself once to an unsuspecting friend, getting only so far in my thoughts. If you look at a cell under a microscope, it's easy to see it as a permeable filter of its environment. "We're like that. We take in, we send out," and I jabbed her arm. We grow accustomed to partnering with our place on earth. In that rhythmic back-and-forth of air, food, and water, we become generous without effort, constantly giving back. Part of the whole.

This I knew: the deepest murmurs I could recall paid no heed to my knowledge of these things or lack of it. It took years, really, to connect the dots to the vibration in this exchange, to see rebirth. In my twenties, especially when the earth boomed in thunder, when the hum of insects at dusk gathered speed, or when the swoop of an owl as I stepped through the woods raised the hair on my scalp, there were hints of a communal hum underlying everything, but then the notion faded.

Years later, bending into the wind, I pedaled my bicycle faster and heard engorged droplets hit gravel like a drumming in my sternum. In another vibration unforgettable and resounding, arctic ice sheared away from melting masses on a journey in Alaska. There were monks chanting to night skies in travel memories of incomparable Himalayan vistas and the bells that rang at monasteries there. My mother's hands featured in memory, pat, pat, patting round disks of roti into place. Her bread rose into air-filled pockets and with a light whoosh settled onto a plate, pat, pat, pat, while sunlight slanted through the air and turned the bread to gold. All these bass notes rising, lifting, burrowing down.

Everywhere the thrum, strained by air, building edges, leaves, and blades of grass, echoing from farms to the most congested of cities, not merely repetition but partly the voice of all it touched: Thoreau's voice of the wood. Inward hearing is groundswell when let loose in space, and no matter that my childhood fields were now alleyways, that my warm-season grasses were soon to be street sweepers brushing the pavement with straw brooms. Sound has ever made silence audible.

I tap, tap, tapped down a stairwell, finally alert, and sensed the one common language of the world. At the heart of it, this was what drew me east.

I found a code.

~~~~~~

In August, I watch clear yellow butterflies coast past my farmhouse window in Missouri, heading to Florida south of the frost line. The diminutive lemony cloudless sulphur, *Phoebis sennae*, butterfly migrates for sustenance through the winter, for welcoming petunias, lantanas, morning glories, impatiens, and zinnias. The taste of azaleas, too, with their deep red elongated flowers, makes the butterflies ecstatic. I imagine happy prancing, the cloudless sulphurs making use of the taste sensors on their feet, dancing for the food of their gods.

In Kansas growing up and even more recently on my Missouri farm, I watched all forms of life move over our planet—walking, trotting, buzzing, and flying for survival and perhaps for their souls. The idea of a migration of my own to the homeland of my parents in Bengal, then back to mine in Missouri, stayed in my mind.

I seek the kernel of connection between traditional foods, what they offer in taste, in health, and in cultural significance, and the health of my world. Opening a jar of homemade apple chutney from the refrigerator instead of one of my grandmother Rani's jars of green mango chutney that I crave, spooning out a serving next to my dal, I resolve to follow the clues on my plate deeper into my two nations—heartland America and India.

Food story can so swiftly fade. I gaze through the window at warm-season grasses, tassels blowing in the hot breeze, and think of the Osage and the Otoe-Missouria, the people of the big canoes, who lived on this land just 135 years ago. Their food history, recorded by storytellers and women stooped over fires, sustained people on our rolling hills for more generations than those of the families here now. On any given day, especially after a strong rain, arrowheads and stone cooking tools still nose up through the mud along our farm's creek beds. This land, where shamans danced and wives and daughters cooked for their families, fed generations, but their foods do not appear in my kitchen and likely never will. Acorn flour is not something I learned to make; I have no persimmon or pawpaw. It strikes me that I know nothing about their daily lives and culture because of the loss of their foodways. No mistake, this loss is a world heritage loss and, for most, the Otoe-Missouria have disappeared.

It is so around the world. Indigenous and traditional crops were an important source of food and fiber for every culture. Often, these crops evolved to tolerate fluctuations in temperature and rainfall and resist disease and pests. I walk outside just off the porch and step on an acorn. My foot curls away from the lump, its self-evident protective shell right in front of me. Steadfast. Seemingly here to stay.

In indecorous haste, however, plant diversity everywhere is disappearing. As of 1999, according to the Food and Agriculture Organization of the United Nations, some 75 percent of our plant genetic range since the early 1900s has been lost. My local grocery typically offers five or six varieties of apple in their season. Five or six. Allowing for overlap in naming, Tim Hensley tells us, 14,000 apple varieties were grown by Americans in the nineteenth century. There is more. This narrowing of nurtured and early wild crops is accompanied by a drop in the nutritional quality of the plants we do cultivate. One of the basic reasons: we have tired soils.

I gazed across my Missouri acres at the tall grasses, their straw-like color contrasting with the crisp green fescue crowding the pastures. Their roots hold them in topsoil much reduced from the time of the Osage and the Otoe-Missouria. In 1936, Franklin Roosevelt said, "The history of every Nation is eventually written in the way in which it cares for its soil." It feels like a false sense of security, then, our high use of fertilizers, irrigation, and plowing. A self-restoring soil ecosystem beats a possible Dust Bowl any day.

Limited variety in food meant fragility throughout history, whereas a biologically varied system carries the ability to restore its own equilibrium. True for the human body as well as the planetary body of Earth. Personal equilibrium means health in the old ways of Ayurveda, and it became part and parcel of eating in Bengal. What is left of that system of eating given the fusion of cuisine in India, its changing soils and agricultural system, its suspect waters in which all-important freshwater fish swim?

Looking down at my plate, I feel a tug and an echo. A lesser diner might be disconcerted by this, but as I push my fork into substitute apple chutney, my imagination conjures a scoop of sweet, sour, and slightly spicy green mango chutney with chunks of fruit. Even without actual familiarity with the preparation of Rani's preserves, I know them deeply: my teeth bite into the just-right give of the fruit, my tongue registers the balancing flavors that nature provided and Rani used. It is not the last-ever taste. Regeneration is possible. I am not too late. And, at this, the planet with its thin crust of topsoil emanates a happy hum: my earth, sealed, soils in place, worth saving.

I walk through the woods on my farm to the mailbox and pull out a book, *Bangla Ranna*, from New Delhi. The words written in 1982 by Minakshie DasGupta hold Bengal on the page. East as well as West Bengal, Anglo-India Bengal as well as long-ago Bengal. I flip through the pages and begin to see the pattern of Rani's kitchen. There is a recipe for green mango chutney. Not quite hers. Two tablespoons of sugar couldn't be enough. Mango murabba, a preserve using slaked lime as a rub on the fruit, makes me frown. Rani had done that. Her green mango chutney seems tantalizingly close. I bend my head and read the two recipes again. A little more of this, a bit less of that. I step quickly over a pile of the acorns that hurt my feet. Here. Rani did this combination. Two recipes could work together. Yes.

There she is.

Finding Rani
Green Mango Chutney

Makes about 2 ½ cups

The best mangoes for this recipe are green with a seed that has not yet grown hard. However, I used the unripe green mangoes with already-hardened pits available in U.S. grocery stores as a substitute and they worked. If using sweet ripe mangoes, decrease the sugar to ½ cup or to taste.

6 large green mangoes
½ teaspoon slaked lime
⅛ teaspoon salt
3 cups water
1 cup sugar
2 whole dried red chilies
4 inches cinnamon stick, broken into 2–3 pieces
6–8 whole cloves
6–8 green cardamom pods, peeled, seeds extracted (about ¼ teaspoon)
2 tablespoons raisins, soaked in water and rinsed
Salt to taste

Pit the mangoes, peel them, and cut them into large pieces about ¼-inch thick. Prick the pieces with a fork, coat them in the slaked lime, and soak them in water to cover for 6–8 hours. Remove the mangoes, wash them in several changes of water, and place them in a pan with enough water to cover. Add the salt. Bring the mango and water mixture to a boil, then remove from heat and drain. Dry the mangoes slightly by patting with a paper towel. In a deep saucepan, bring 3 cups water to a boil. Add the sugar. Remove the foam that forms on the surface as the syrup simmers. Add the mangoes and chilies and continue to simmer. Add the cinnamon, cloves, and cardamom seeds. Add the raisins. Add salt to taste if needed. Mix well. Simmer the mixture in the sugar syrup, stirring occasionally, until the mangoes are soft and the syrup is quite thick, 60–75 minutes depending on your preferred thickness. Remove from heat. Cool. Store in a glass jar in the refrigerator for up to 3 months or, to store longer, can with a pressure cooker.

Chapter One

TEN MEN IN A TRAIN CAR,
TO SAY NOTHING OF THE CHEESE

The Bengali seems to have always had a sweet tooth.

—K. T. Achaya, *Indian Food: A Historical Companion*, 1994

I AM SITTING ON gritty concrete steps staring into the eyes of a goat. A surprisingly slow blink is my reward. Granted it is a stately if placid-gazed brown and white Anglo-Nubian, a British breed of goat that originated in the nineteenth century after crossbreeding with the lop-eared Indian ones, and it lies resplendently across the train station steps. I decide that the goat would be at least a little agitated if groups of men carrying cheese had already raced by to catch the fleeting stop of a train.

Reassured that I hadn't missed the whistle-stop yet, I take a minute to gather my courage. Cheese from India is not often noted by the culinary world. Yet here I am, getting ready to board a train full of cheese heading into Kolkata. Sleuthing for cheese, an urge born out of love of the cuisine of Bengal, soothes my itch to know more about my family's home ground. It's a way to savor connections here after a lifetime in the American Midwest and to test how traditional culinary delights fit the modern global palate. A Fulbright-Nehru research grant enables my curiosity to hunt for the essential flavors that drive the cuisine of Bengal.

I have seen photos of trains moving through the Indian countryside with their car doors wide open, people sitting in the openings. Never did I imagine being in one of those openings, the wind blowing my hair back, the scent of cheese in the air. I obviously underestimated the scope of my early dreams of coming back to India.

Thousands of pounds of cheese, from many villages surrounding the mega city, traverse the train lines daily to meet the demands of Kolkata's sweet tooth. When I mention sweet desserts and cheese in my Midwest home in the U.S., my friends look perplexed. But Bengal abounds in dreamy dairy-based desserts such as sandesh, rosogolla, chomchom, and many more. The quest for their source material begins here.

It may be an Old World idea to make your cheese at home and let it dry in a cloth tied to your kitchen faucet. But my mother did it this way for years in Kansas, making sweets and savory dishes as I grew up. I learned early to wait before squeezing excess water out through the cloth so I didn't burn my fingers. I learned how heavenly it was to pinch off a bit and sprinkle it with sugar. I was baffled: nobody I knew made cheese in their kitchen.

In Bhandarhati, it is a different matter.

The tall walls of the train station nearest to the village cinch back trees doing their best to reach over the gates, and though these trees shade the Anglo-Nubian goat, I am in the sun. I shift. The goat straightens, delicately pulling back its front hoof.

A woman walks by with a basket, glancing over her shoulder at me as she sedately makes her way. The colorful scarf tied around the contents of the basket undulates each time she turns to steal a glance. Joining a train full of men and cheese in search of the origins of iconic Bengali sweets is unusual, judging by the fluttering.

Questions arise, and one, "Tomar kache koto chhana ache?"—"How much cheese do you have?"—needs to be asked very soon. I contemplate saying this

Anglo-Nubian goat, Belmuri station.

out loud, pronouncing the *a* vowels correctly, on a moving train with its doors open to the wind.

It seems that I actually do say it out loud to my goat friend. The people in the ticket line twenty feet away begin to stare openly. I try to look as if I had not just leaned a bit too close to a goat. Instead of dwelling on the probability that the people in line are now referring to me as "machela je chagol er songaei kotha bolae"—"woman who talks with goats"—I cross the tracks to be in the right spot to catch the Kolkata train, stepping nimbly around clusters of cheese in baskets hooked together by hemp ropes. The obstacles, left by early-bird cheesemakers, are ready to load onto the 12:45 p.m. train. There is more, much more cheese to come.

When I left my cozy kitchen in Missouri, I had not dreamed of chasing a train full of cheese, but we do not always know our dreams. Unlike my beloved cloudless sulphur butterflies, heading to Florida each fall across our farm, I am after more than a haven: I am seeking the origins of much-loved heritage flavors and the wonder of how they evolved to suit the modern global palate. I want to get closer, too, to deciphering the bass notes of my family's homeland. In the village of Bhandarhati in Hooghly District, the soft ricotta-like cheese, chhana, integral to Bengali sweets is in abundance, but this was not always the case, or so I am told. Sensing a mystery, I am here to find out more.

All India knows Bengal for its sweets with their chhana base. I think of the cheesecake restaurants in the U.S. with their large upholstered booths. Bengal takes a similar base ingredient of soft cheese and expands it into an array of confections celebrated across India. It's the stuff of legend and, in 2018, one of the sweets became a fictionalized biopic film, *Rosogolla*, made about its origins and the life of Nobin Chandra Das, who reputedly developed the Bengali favorite. This, after a court case was held between the neighboring states of Odisha and Bengal over who could claim the original.

One of my first memories of my visits to India as a child was of sandesh, an iconic chhana-based dessert: soft and sweet with a lifting aroma of fresh milk made into tender cheese and specially formed into shapes, often shells. Plates of these treats were on a tray next to milky tea. And if I wasn't careful, I would take far too many.

The members of the Krishna Chandra Ghosh family in Bhandarhati have made cheese for generations. Their cheese joins the train, as do cheeses from three or four small villages in the surrounding area, to culminate in about 300 to 400 quintals of cheese a day being sent to the city of Kolkata. One quintal is just over 220 pounds, enough cheese to raise concerns about the arteries of Kolkata's citizens, considering that this is but one cheese train. And one cluster of villages. Other trains route through different villages each day laden with chhana, chugging away to bring in the base product needed by city sweet makers for the delicate sandesh, rosogolla, chomchom, roshmalai, and so many more sweets of Bengal.

At the Belmuri station, more and more cheese baskets arrive. The concrete platform seems mostly empty, then erupts into action. Men with long wooden poles, bak, usually made of bamboo, carry their cheese in what looks like a quickstep over the tracks. They carry three eight-pound baskets of chhana on each end of their bak, forty-eight pounds of cheese, and balance it over one shoulder. As they walk, lined baskets dripping whey hang down to their shins and gently bounce.

Suddenly surrounded by cheese, the gathering men and I board the train that, having slid to a pulsing pause in its rush down the tracks, gathers itself and moves on with a mild zoooooooooooosh and a barely perceptible tug. In the compartment, there is so much cheese that people are standing in tight clusters or lying down on high bunks to be out of the way. I move to the open doors and the wind pushes my hair off my forehead. It feels exhilarating to be moving across the land with pounds and pounds of cheese. One of the men on board shrugs when I lean over to ask my central question.

"I can't tell you how much is here," he says in Bengali and smiles, "only what I bring."

This turns out to be more than fifty pounds, and as he departs at the Howrah station in Kolkata, his bak bends low with cheese baskets nearly brushing the concrete.

<center>~~~~~</center>

I had begun the day bearing recording devices and a nervous disposition. My research has attracted the interest of filmmakers, and there were camera people coming along for a possible documentary segment. There was a sound technician and lots of wires to clip microphones where no microphones had been before. After over an hour, as filmmakers Gautam Bose, Sangita Paul, and Sanjeev Chatterjee and I drew closer to the village of Bhandarhati, the driver leaned out of the car and asked for our host's house. There was no hesitation. Even from an hour away, the Chowdhury house was well known. Built in the 1930s by the grandfather of the current resident, Rajat Chowdhury, it was a melon-colored beauty of Bengali arches and verandas, interior courtyards, and cane chairs overlooking a lake with cormorants and songbirds making the trees sing. Its gates were open when we arrived. Later there would be omelets, tea, and conversation, with cool breezes and softly rotating ceiling fans, but first Rajat sent us on our way to the cheese-making Ghoshes, a family of skilled chhana makers and owners of seven crossbred Jersey cows.

I met Tumpa Ghosh outside her house. Older women watched from a few of the doorways and teenagers on bicycles pedaled past over the brushed-clean path as we walked to where the cows were kept. Tumpa's sari gently swished and though I wasn't taller than she was, my tennis shoes made me seem so. Trees hung over the walkway and shaded our path. Bhandarhati was a quiet place that morning.

~~~~~~~

The Ghosh family has been sending cheese to Kolkata to serve the sweet tooth of the city for sixty years or more, no one remembers exactly. Some families in Bhandarhati milk cows, some make the chhana, some do a little milking and a little cheese making, buying extra raw milk from trusted neighbors. Tumpa's family does all this. Their cows provide about ten liters of milk a day, and they purchase forty or fifty more. Each morning, Tumpa stirs the milk over an open fire behind their house and her mother-in-law, Sumitra, separates the curds and whey using the "mother" whey she has tended for sixty years, always leaving a potful to carry forward for the next day's work. Neither woman uses thermometers or gauges, unlike the modern chhana-making plants starting to pop up in Bengal. Tumpa and Sumitra test the temperature to make the chhana by feel and sight.

This morning, after spreading a clean cloth on the ground for her work, Sumitra rhythmically swirls the mother whey into the newly heated milk waiting in a linen-lined metal bowl. I stand watching, trying to remember the complicated chemical reaction happening, the one that involves the concept of micelle that holds the milk's casein protein in suspension to curdle it, but those thoughts dissolve for me into an elegant woman's sure movements with a small wooden-handled pan.

Sumitra coaxes the curds away from the whey by gripping her small pan with three fingers on the handle and two on the metal and pouring a bit of the mature mother whey into the milk in circular motions. Her deft motions as she does this dip and swirl, dip and swirl, dip and swirl make me rock back a little on my heels, lulled. Finally, she rises from her squatting position and the microphone clipped to my shirt records my sharp intake of breath. Her fore-arms tense and her fists clench to pull up the linen, releasing the whey below it in a sucking whoosh. No one else seems awestruck by this daily transforma-tion, but I marvel as, without seeming effort, Sumitra moves the eight pounds of fresh chhana to a nearby basket.

Without fanfare, Sumitra bends to tie a knot at the top of the fabric encas-ing the newly formed cheese. I want to applaud, but I find I can't look away from her quiet, unhurried, and careful patting of the fabric. Despite the chha-na's coming jostling by bak, then train, then bak again to the Kolkata chhana market or directly to a sweet-maker's shop, like an artist particular about the finishing touches on a masterpiece, Sumitra gently lays the damp linen knot ends down like petals.

~~~~~

Most credit the Portuguese, though some also mention the Dutch, in Kolkata with the tradition of making what they called cottage cheese, but I feel chhana most resembles ricotta in texture. But could its provenance be true? India has been a dairy culture for millennia. In fact, it is the largest producer and consumer of milk in the world, though overall per person milk consumption levels are low due to India's large population and high rate of poverty. Unlike in the West, most milk in India is consumed not as a fresh drink but in the form of yogurt used in cooking or whipped into a drink, as khoa—milk cooked down to solids to be made into sweets—or as chhana for sweets and some savory dishes as well.

But for centuries, though many slowly simmered milk to reduce it to khoa and made sweets, it was considered bad form to curdle it, which complicates things regarding chhana. Ancient Aryan ideas deemed milk one component of the panchagavya, the cleansing Vedic material, and one of the five products of cows—dung, urine, milk, curds, ghee—so useful they were categorized as inherently pure. This made "breaking" milk into curds and whey with an acid frowned upon. But the fame of Bengali sandesh, rosogolla, chhanar-jilipi, and many other confections with chhana at their base proves there were some who dared to separate milk and then went further to make sweetmeat magic happen.

Indeed, it could have been the Portuguese who helped lift the taboo in India on deliberately splitting milk. When Europeans arrived in their ships in the second half of the seventeenth century with an avidity for spices and the like, the traders left behind some enticing things. Cottage cheese was relished and, apparently, the Portuguese curdled to their hearts content. Soon, Ahsan Jan Quaisar tells us, the Portuguese numbered 20,000 in the Kolkata area, and besides baking breads for use at English or Dutch factories and private homes, they ate cheese.

This makes me pause. The magic of sandesh, a kneaded and shaped sugar-chhana mixture with a delectable heart-stealing taste, and rosogolla, made by boiling balls of chhana in syrup for a spongier texture, is due to Portuguese influence? I have a history of failing to make good sandesh and trying again anyway because I am unashamedly in love with it. Though things usually go badly for my cheese, it is with a sense of betrayal that I think of all my efforts over the years to create the quintessential Bengali sweet and it is… Portuguese?

With relief and a harrumph from my inner sandesh warrior, I note that the process of making chhana is mentioned in the *Manasollassa*, written in the twelfth century—well before the Portuguese rounded the Horn of Africa to get more quickly to the spice trade.

The *Manasollassa*, "delight" or "refresher of the mind," a Sanskrit verse version of fashionable wit and wisdom written by King Somesvara III, who ruled from 1126 to 1138 in southwest India, covers medicine, magic, veterinary science, precious stones, vehicles, the art of acquiring and ruling a kingdom, elephants, painting, music, dance, literature, women, fish, plants, and cuisine, according to Colleen Taylor Sen in *Feasts and Fasts: A History of Food in India*. Women and food rank a bit too far down the list from my perspective, but the king, annoyingly, is not available for comment. Among the hundred-plus dishes mentioned by Somesvara, many of which exist today, there is something suspiciously like chhana. "Milk was split by adding a souring agent and draining the whey through cloth to make curds (chhana); the curds were blended until smooth, mixed with sugar and fried in small balls," Sen says.

Before getting overly relieved—and believe me, this is highly tempting even for a transplanted Bengali—I find more. K. T. Achaya, in *Indian Food: A Historical Companion*, says that it is doubtful that what we think of as sandesh today was mentioned in the early literature (that is, by my liege, King Somesvara III), that it is likely sweetened khoa, rather than chhana, that was made in the king's day. Then, too, there have been extended debates over who *within* the Indian citizenry discovered cheese and where these iconic cheese-based sweets originate. In November 2018, articles in the *Hindustan Times* and others carried headlines like "Bengal Wins the Rosogolla Battle, Authorities Say Sweet Didn't Originate in Odisha." Another article in the *Indian Express* by Priyanjana Roy Das says that "some foods can divide us and one of them is rosogolla."

One other cheese, bandel, India's only indigenous Western-style cheese, is likely directly due to Portuguese influence. In Kolkata's New Market you can buy a fresh roundel. Its taste is wholly unlike chhana, its texture is dry, a little crumbly, and it has a salty, smoky flavor. This cow's milk cheese is highly aromatic and, depending on your nose, strong.

Bandel aside, my lineage hails from a land of bitter debates over famed desserts (and, yes, Bengal won rosogolla, though hearts are broken in Odisha). But pause here for just a moment. Rosogolla is Bengali, confirmed in *a court battle over a cheese-based confectionery*. So thank you, Somesvara, king of many things and one of them my chhana-loving heart. The Portuguese may have made cheese making less of an ill-omened thing to do, giving confectioners a new substance with which to work, but Bengali ingenuity made the results stellar and the geographical indications registry of India says so.

〜〜〜

After almost nine months, when I am back in my Missouri kitchen, I take up making yogurt as a tribute to the taste of it in India. It dawns on me as I glance at my homemade yogurt, another ancient specialty in India, this time involving deceptively calm fermentation within milk, that I am actually seeing a type of war of the worlds and had seen it many years ago, too, on the windowsill of my grandmother's house in India. All seemed quiet with the whole milk in her bowl, but underneath the creamy white surface that was slowly thickening in the Bihar heat, there was mayhem.

In the cultures of milk, as Andrea Wiley says in her book of the same name (meaning the dairying communities in the world), fermentation is a process that produces lactic acid found in such sour foods as pickled cucumbers, kimchi, and yogurt as well as alcoholic wine and beer. To make these foods we love, as Robin Sloan explains in *Sourdough*, it's a bloodbath. Vast cultures rise and fall, armies of bacteria convert carbohydrates into acids in what could be seen as a diabolical process: an organism converts (read "eats") a carbohydrate, such as a starch or a sugar, and transforms (read "crushes") it into an alcohol or an acid.

Who knew the metabolic process was so aggressive? In my kitchen, the cooling yogurt, which I greatly enjoy blended with peaches in August, or maybe strawberries, or bananas, seems so innocent.

I love the braided historical complexity of milk that Andrea Wiley presents. Consider that it is one of two foods on the planet created just to be eaten. It could be debated whether the other, honey, counts because bees do not make it within themselves but use plant pollen. Everything else, flora or fauna, has to be killed before it is consumed. Perhaps this was one reason why milk is considered a pure food in India, where its purity transports it to the realm of the sacred. If you consume milk or foods cooked with it, the sanctification rubs off.

If you think the culture of milk in the U.S. is vastly different in its story, think again of the biblical references to the land of milk and honey, the lasting idea of milk's wholesomeness, iconic children's books with images of large and docile cows, the association of milk's whiteness with purity. It gets complicated, this connection between milk and purity. Even its physicality in India is fraught because much milk on the market in fact comes from water buffalo, whose status is anything but sacred but whose milk is much richer in butterfat and fetches a better return economically. While belief systems might seem curious at times, it is probably true that we humans behave in ways that ultimately enhance, rather than diminish, our well-being.

And sometimes these behaviors take on political, nation-building roles. Early cow protection laws in India, using the trope of the Hindu sacred cow, served not only to generate more milk for a citizenry ready to break free of colonizers and be better nourished, they also showed resistance both to the British (and earlier Muslim) rulers and their predilection for beef and to those who could see the cow's main purpose only as a source of meat or milk, leaving out dung and its uses valued for millennia in India.

Food is resistance, we've seen it time and again. A daily dose of what's good for you and good for cultural imagination, too.

Through Andrea Wiley, I learn that India ranks among the cultures of milk that include northern Europe and its subsequent populations in North America (looking at you, Wisconsin), Australia, and New Zealand as well as the nomadic populations of Central Asia and East and West Africa. Even so, across India only an average of 20 percent of people can digest milk after weaning age. In the United States, recent research indicates that the average is closer to 75 percent, with the average of European Americans at 90 percent and African Americans, Native Americans, and Asian Americans at a mere 10 to 25 percent.

Esteem for fresh milk has not meant uncomplicated digestion.

It's an unresolved mystery, why this is. Humans are built to stop producing lactase, which digests the milk sugar lactose, at weaning. But across the world, after dairy animals were domesticated 8,000 years ago, the genetic mutation for lactase persistence throughout life grew. But not in India.

I gaze at my slowly forming yogurt and consider that biology works both ways—we shift things around to make our environment more comfortable, changing the ecology to suit us at times, and our environment reciprocates.

Fresh milk was mostly made into yogurt and ghee in India, and the process of making these removes almost all the lactose from the end result, as well as increasing the life span of the milk. With yogurt, the practice of heating milk and letting it sit at warm temperatures encourages fermentation by bacteria such as lactobacillus, which converts lactose into lactic acid and yields the end result of yogurt. Depending on how long this process goes on and the quantity of bacteria present (warriors all), most of the lactose will be removed. Butter made from churning these curds produces buttermilk to drink as a by-product, and in India it is then heated and the remaining solids removed, forming ghee, also very low in lactose.

The oft eaten sweet specialties in Bengal, mostly made from chhana by dosing milk with mother whey like the Ghoshes do or by adding acid such as lemon or vinegar to cause the milk curds to separate from the liquid whey, are low in lactose. Conveniently, it dissolves in the liquid whey that is drained off.

With these tasty products, little *fresh* milk was drunk in India, and the population never had to develop a biological tolerance for digesting lactose as adults. For descendants of other dairying communities in the United States and elsewhere, fresh milk was a significant source of dairy and more lactase was necessary to digest it. Presto, the human body adapted.

Despite differing digestive lineages, India and the United States produce and consume the most milk in the world, and though thousands of years apart in milk history, they share milk mythology. It's mother love, it's nurturing, it's pure and protective, and in India, because of its status as a pure food, it supersedes many food codes that ground Hindu social interactions. Neat trick, that.

To make the most of my yogurt made from mayhem, I toss together a lassi, first tasted in my grandmother's kitchen but often yearned for when spied at street vendor carts whenever I visited Bengal as a child. India, with its ancient food-as-medicine focus, never neglected a food's effect *on the body*. Traditionally, lassi is made with fresh homemade yogurt, salt, and spices such as a small amount of roasted ground cumin seeds to enhance its digestive properties. Even so, I never underestimate the basic sweeter recipe as an excellent cool drink for hot summer days.

Lassi

Serves 2

1 ¾ cups plain yogurt
6 cubes ice, crushed
½ cup chilled water
2 teaspoons sugar
Pinch of salt

Mix all ingredients in a blender, or use an electric mixer or a hand whisk, and blend until frothy. That's it, drink up! Ah, but there are options. For a salty version, add ⅛ teaspoon salt plus ¼ teaspoon ground cardamom, ½ teaspoon roasted cumin seeds ground into a powder, or a few strands of saffron to the yogurt-ice-water mix and omit the sugar. For sweet mango lassi, blend ½ cubed ripe mango, 3 tablespoons sugar, ¼ teaspoon ground cardamom, ¾ cup plain yogurt, and ¾ cup water until frothy. If you add ice cubes, reduce the water by ¼ cup or to the thickness you prefer.

As yogurt continues to be prepared, lassi continues to be drunk, and pastoral and idyllic chhana making continues in Bhandarhati, in Kolkata some chefs are busy making their modern mark. In 2019, in a kitchen at the Salt House sporting stainless steel, Chef Auroni Mookherjee and his team, known for delectable foods that mesh traditional Bengali flavors in Continental forms, work in tandem, mixing fresh chhana with a scoop of mascarpone into an ultrasmooth and creamy "cheesecake" base. Assisting, Chef Milon zests both Italian lemon and Bengali gondhoraj lebu into the mixture, releasing a simultaneous citrus and floral zing into the air. I poke my nose near the misti doi, traditionally a steamed or baked sweet yogurt dessert now to be used as a top layer, to catch its gentler aroma. Later, Chef Auroni dips mounds of sandesh into the misti doi and coats them until they glisten. The finished dessert sits atop a flourish of pistachio cream and a crumble of buttery shortbread-like naan khatai biscuits. Scrumptious nolen gur, a simple winter delicacy made from the date palm tree that is like maple syrup in consistency, is swirled over the entire creation.

"You're taking parallel memories of flavors in your mind and applying them to a dish," Chef Auroni says. I am barely able to stop staring at the dessert long enough to nod. To me, it is as if a beam of light has landed directly on the cheesecake, beckoning. I rouse myself long enough to spoon up a bite.

"That connection between your palate and your memory bank is a library you can keep accessing." Busy accessing, my mouth full, I fervently agree.

Chef Auroni says his cheesecake pays homage to the para'r mishti dokan, the neighborhood sweetshop, a Kolkata institution. I would agree that he has created a distinctly Bengali flavor profile with nuances of the West, if I could speak around the flavors exploding in my mouth. For me, however, these flavors are more than the neighborhood sweetshop. They evoke my grandmother Rani, who mastered chhana as a teenager. And though Rani had never heard Clifton Fadiman refer to cheese as "milk's leap towards immortality," she herself becomes immortal as I remember watching my mother squeeze lemon, as

Rani did, into milk, watching her step back out of the steam as she poured the whey through a colander lined with cheesecloth, watching her tie the bundle of fresh curds to the kitchen faucet to drip-dry into the sink, and, finally, after finishing, pushing hair that I know had been bothering her behind an ear.

Sandesh holds stories—cultural, individual, and agricultural—that develop for me over mealtimes around a lacquered wooden table in Kansas. But here at Chef Auroni's table is a development born of the land it is from. Though India goes underground in southeast Kansas for me except in the kitchen, its flavors continue to sift through the cluttering aromas of the hamburgers and pot roasts of the American Midwest in my memory. Sandesh, rosogolla, and misti doi magically appear for dessert, made by my mother's hands, as I grow up. But while my family was away, another type of underground food story in the face of busy lifestyles is emerging in Bengal: traditional flavors transmogrified into new creations.

Sandesh and Nolen Gur Cheesecake

Recipe courtesy of Chef Auroni Mookherjee
Serves 8

SANDESH LAYER

2 cups freshly made chhana (recipe to follow) or ricotta

½ cup mascarpone

½ teaspoon gondhoraj lime (or key lime) zest

½ teaspoon lemon zest

3–4 tablespoons sugar

MISTI DOI LAYER

1 quart whole milk

8 tablespoons sugar

2 tablespoons water

1–2 tablespoons plain yogurt with active cultures

6–8 naan khatai biscuits (recipe to follow) or store-bought shortbread

PISTACHIO CREAM

½ cup pistachios

¼ cup heavy cream

½ cup condensed milk

½ cup nolen gur or simple syrup made of jaggery (recipe follows)
3–4 tablespoons cold butter (optional)

To make the sandesh layer, mix the chhana or ricotta, mascarpone, and lime and lemon zest with an electric mixer or beat vigorously by hand until smooth. Gradually add the 3–4 tablespoons sugar to the mix; sweeten to your taste. Set this mixture aside in the refrigerator and let it chill for a few hours.

While the sandesh is in the refrigerator, make the misti doi layer. Heat the milk in a heavy pan. As it begins to boil, add 4 tablespoons of the sugar, reduce the heat slightly, and simmer until the volume reduces by half. In a small pan, add the remaining 4 tablespoons sugar to the 2 tablespoons water. Heat the sugar water until the sugar melts and turns golden brown. Add this caramelized sugar to the thickened milk and gradually boil the mixture down for another 15 minutes over low heat. Remove and cool the mixture to lukewarm. When it is warm to the touch but not hot, add the yogurt and mix thoroughly. Set aside to continue to cool and thicken.

Crumble the naan khatai biscuits or shortbread. Set aside. For the pistachio cream, mix the pistachios, cream, and condensed milk in a blender until they resemble a smooth pastry cream. Set aside.

To plate, coat egg-sized sandesh roundels in misti doi, place each one atop a dollop of pistachio cream and crumbled naan khatai biscuits or shortbread, and drizzle nolen gur or, for a stronger molasses-like taste, jaggery syrup over the top before serving.

You can try this recipe as a traditional cheesecake. Press the crumbled biscuits or shortbread (mixed with 3–4 tablespoons cold butter so they will hold together as a bottom crust) into a round cake mold, then spoon the chhana mixture over them and smooth to level. Add the misti doi, which should be thickening but still pourable, in a layer over the chhana mixture. Add the pistachio cream on top and put the entire cheesecake into the fridge to set for 1–2 hours. Slice into pieces and drizzle nolen gur or jaggery syrup over the top before serving.

Simple Jaggery Syrup

Makes ½ cup

1 cup jaggery
¾ cup water

Crumble or chop the jaggery into small pieces. Place it in a small pan with the water, and bring to a hard simmer on medium heat. Continue to simmer until the jaggery dissolves and the volume reduces by a third or a half, depending on how thick you like your syrup. Cool before serving.

Chhana

SIMPLE SOFT CHEESE
Makes about 2 cups

1 gallon whole milk, as fresh as possible
½–¾ cup lemon juice
Cheesecloth

In a heavy stockpot, bring the milk to a full boil, and when it starts to rise in the pot, add the lemon juice a little at a time until the milk separates. Strain the curds from the remaining liquid whey and place the solids into the cheesecloth. Squeeze out as much water as possible with your hands, being careful as the liquid will be very hot. Hang the cheesecloth around the kitchen faucet to drip for 6–8 hours, or tie it to a wooden spoon placed over a pot and slide it into the refrigerator for 6–8 hours to do the same.

Naan Khatai

Makes 12–14 biscuits

4 tablespoons unsalted butter at room temperature

½ cup powdered sugar

1 cup all-purpose flour

Pinch of salt

1 tablespoon semolina

¼ teaspoon baking soda

½ teaspoon ground cardamom

10 pistachios, finely chopped (optional)

Preheat oven to 350° F / 180° C. In a large mixing bowl, combine the unsalted butter and powdered sugar and beat with an electric blender for 3–5 minutes or 15 minutes with a hand whisk until the butter-sugar mixture is light and fluffy. Add the flour, salt, semolina, and baking soda. Mix well. Add the ground cardamom. Mix and turn onto a clean surface and knead for 1–2 minutes. Make 1-inch balls and flatten them slightly with your palm. If you are not using the biscuits for nolen gur cheesecake, top each one with a few chopped pistachios and press gently before baking.

Place the naan khatai on a baking sheet covered with parchment paper or a light coating of vegetable oil and bake for 15 minutes or until they just begin to turn golden brown on top. Remove from oven and allow to cool completely on a rack. Slide the cool naan khatai off the sheet and store in an airtight container.

Chapter Two

WHEN LIFE HANDS YOU UNCOMMON LIMES

It is a fact that there are some Portuguese so pig-headed
that they would rather die than acknowledge that we have here
any fruit equal to that of Portugal; but there are many fruits here
that bear the bell…and the limes vastly better.

—Garcia de Orta, *Colloquies on the Simples and Drugs of India*, 1563

A SOUR FEELING EMERGES as I look at my paperwork for a return trip to Kolkata. My research has taken me only so far—goats guarding train steps, temples, feasts, kitchens—and I need one more migration to finish my thoughts on the page. A visa necessitates a birth certificate and a passport with enough pages for official stamps. I put it all together for a visa for a person of Indian origin, and then I stump the system.

What to do with someone born to Indian parents, now U.S. citizens, who no longer have their last Indian passports from sixty-plus years ago, who were not issued Indian birth certificates in 1928 and 1941 as this was not yet done there, and who were living in Thailand when I was born? A tourist visa is an easy option, but something about that seems off after living in Kolkata on my Fulbright research grant for nearly nine months, especially when I think of my family. I want acknowledgment that I could belong to India if I chose, but my temporary migration to the homeland of my family seems stalled. It does not seem to matter that I had handwritten "India" to identify my category of human on every job or college or other application form I filled out in Kansas ever since I was old enough to fill in the blanks for myself. A **NOREPLY** email and then the Cox and Kings assistants on the phone tell me with regret that I need to cancel my application and start over. I am too foreign, even for India.

~~~~~

What constitutes foreignness? Do the words we mispronounce tip the scales? "*Cal*-cutta," I say, trying for "*Kol*-cut-ta." Do the comforts we cling to reveal us for who we are? When I'm not feeling well, keema and fragrant rice can rouse me, while some of my friends in Kansas might say the same for American mac 'n' cheese. The in-between of the world—emerging along margins like these willy-nilly—is not a good fit with bureaucracy. I look in a drawer and see a recipe for misti doi in my mother's handwriting and I know that scrap of paper will not prove my heritage. Instead of pondering this, I go to the kitchen. A chopping board, two limes, sugar, and a glass await.

Sometimes doing nothing at all to a food is reward enough, no chef interventions needed. The food is what it is—no matter that it traveled a bit to get to your kitchen, or that it was once considered exotic, or that it had no transport papers. Take the lime: its flavor sweeps the palate in Bengal, much as it does in Thailand and Latin America. Distinctive and integral, lime wasn't something I realized as being intrinsically Bengali until its flavor hit me metaphorically over the head.

During a hot day in Kolkata, after fifteen minutes of waiting at one of the city's numerous coffee shops near Hindustan Park, I casually tilt my chair back to look into the kitchen. At least three young men in identical brown shirts huddle around a glass, my glass. There is a lot of quiet discussion, furtive looks, vigorous stirring. I scoot back down and look away, apprehensive.

But the drink that finally arrives is tart, sweet, and sublime, and instantly a vital taste of Bengal comes into sharp focus. Cool and aromatic, the fresh lime soda eases down my dry throat, expanding my esophagus in relief, and disappears much too quickly from my glass. Afterward, I clink the two cubes of ice left, my eyes trained on the bottom of the glass, in silence.

Fresh lime soda is a drink so ubiquitous in the city that no one remembers to mention it to me when offering refreshments. It's almost always an option. With unknowing ease, the omnipresent lime offers a world of history and an iconic flavor profile essential to most meals in Bengal. While geography, the seasons, and history shaped the flavors of eastern India to a great extent, gondhoraj lebu (the sultan of limes or the aroma king in some translations) is the wind beneath the wings in kitchens throughout the region. Plus, it likely made the world's first lemonade. If you can't find gondhoraj limes, marut or key limes will do.

Nimbu Pani

FRESH LIME SODA

Makes 1 refreshing drink

3 tablespoons fresh-squeezed lime juice

3 tablespoons simple syrup

1 cup water or soda water if preferred

Salt to taste

Pinch of fresh-roasted ground cumin seeds (optional)

Fill a tall glass with ice. Add the lime juice to the glass, then add the simple syrup. Fill the glass with water or soda water (my favorite), salt to taste, and, if you like, garnish it with a pinch of fresh-roasted ground cumin seeds.

To make simple syrup, add 1 cup white sugar to 1 cup boiling water and stir until dissolved. Cool. Store in refrigerator.

To roast cumin, heat a small pan on the stove and add 1 teaspoon whole cumin seeds. When the seeds start to turn a darker brown and smoke, shake the pan vigorously for about 20 seconds. Remove from heat before the seeds burn. When they are cool, use a spice grinder or mortar and pestle to grind them into powder.

Find your lime soda sweet spot and create your favorite sweet, salty, or savory concoction. Add white and black salt to the ground cumin seeds, or try amchoor—dried sour mango powder—black pepper, dried ginger, cayenne, turmeric, asafetida, or mint.

Humans just seem to need sourness. Or maybe we need the balance of brightness and acidity that keeps other flavors from being too cloying. The tak or sour note in Bengal is usually a balancing flavor in food, not served alone, and Ayurveda, a medical science of ancient India that deems food as medicine, says that it cleanses and balances inside and out, that the humors of people need balancing, too.

Even before the cheese train expedition and my experience with the station goat, I am alert for the distinctive flavors of Bengal, the ones that drive its cuisine. I step into sweetshops whenever possible, self-sacrificing as I am, searching for as many creative uses of chhana as I can find. But there is more to Bengal's bounty, and citrus is one of India's standouts.

It turns out that the ubiquitous lime is a pivotal taste. Lime has pucker, but its power lies in its acidity, which mostly hits well below 7 pH, depending on how ripe the fruit is allowed to become. Acidity creates saliva in the mouth, generated to protect the teeth, making citrus literally mouthwatering for humans. In my kitchen, lemon or lime juice, vinegar, and wine serve the taste for acidity, but so do tomato, achar—pickled relishes—and fermented dairy such as yogurt. Thinking of all the dishes in Bengal that use these doppelgängers for acidity, I realize anew the art of balance in cuisine. My grandmother Rani's green mango chutney had this acidity, synced with sweetness and a little kick of piquant pepper, and it lives long in family memory.

Taste is an intimate sense and Rani stays close for those who ate from her kitchen. As Diane Ackerman writes in *A Natural History of the Senses*, there's no way to taste at a distance. If you have ever had the occasion of finding something too sour, too bitter, or seemingly too far along the way to putrefaction in your mouth, you will agree that taste buds loom large. Those times never end well.

But in reality, taste buds are exceedingly small for the amount of power they have. The average adult has about 10,000 taste buds or taste receptors. These are grouped inside papillae, the small bumps you can see on your tongue, which in turn are comprised of the 50 to 150 receptor cells that actually

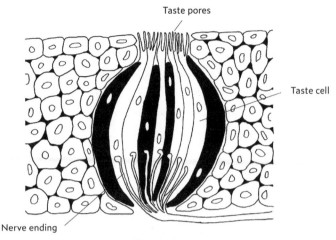

Taste pores

Taste cell

Nerve ending

Taste bud.

process taste. These tiny, tiny cells process by theme: salt, sour, sweet, bitter, and umami. And our bodies have a yen for all of these.

The day I am in the coffee shop, I am smitten by nimbu pani. I continue to stare at my empty glass, and the cool, tart taste and floral aroma of gondhoraj lime linger to tweak my senses. The sun slanting through the front windows of the shop causes me to close my eyes against the glare. The moment lets me seal in the flavor and I breathe in deeply, only later noticing that the waiter stands to the side, anxious, watching me closely. I place my glass on the table, smile, and hear a deep exhale, mine and also his, as he slips away.

~~~~~

All citrus in the world journeyed outward bound from Asia. What an eye-opening flavor lime, lemon, and orange must have been for early Western visitors. In the sixteenth century, travelers noted the abundance of citrus trees and marveled at fruit they had never before seen. François Bernier carried a stock of limes with him for refreshment while writing *Travels in the Mogul Empire* in 1670. In *Oranges*, John McPhee explains that citrus became the rage in the West, and in fact its spread kept pace with some of the major journeys of civilization. There were no oranges, for example, in Peru until Pizarro took them there. The seeds the Spaniards carried to the Western Hemisphere came from trees that had entered Spain as a result of the rise of Islam.

Limes and lemons fanned out from India and southern Asia, and still the largest production of these citrus comes from the subcontinent. In early times, the two citrus siblings were not as clearly differentiated as they are today in English. In Spanish, the word "limón" refers to both limes and lemons even now in the Americas, although in Spain the word "limas" is used for limes and limones for lemons. But when Muslims ruled Spain, limón was a generic word, and only after the time Columbus sailed did lima come into common usage. Limes were well traveled and helpful for all kinds of reasons—besides being a deterrent against scurvy for sailors and a hindrance for the plague in Paris due to the qualities of limonene in their skins, they also provided a balancing, bright flavor for all.

But in Bengal, the very particular gondhoraj lime never made it much beyond its alluvial beginnings. Not for it did the allure of the high seas prevail. It heard no call for adventure. No daring dreams held sway. While gondhoraj left a strong mark on many heritage recipes of the region, the small orb remains little known outside India.

In my Kolkata kitchen, making nimbu pani is a simple process. Squeeze a little lime or lemon juice into a glass, add sugar and water and maybe some roasted cumin seeds or black salt, and stir—but first I had to learn a thing or two about limes.

"Not the Italian lemon," my neighbor of a grandmother's age says as I asked which citrus to buy after explaining my coffee shop experience with gondhoraj. The large yellow citrus she calls Italian has notes that zing but don't match gondhoraj in aroma.

Italian Sorrento lemons are everywhere in the market, and I spy *Citrus latifolia*, the Persian or Tahitian lime, the one I was used to seeing in my grocery store in Kansas growing up: large, juicy, adaptable in cooking everything from cilantro-lime prawns to chicken piccata. The common Indian lime, looking almost exactly like a key lime from Florida, abounds. I realize as I walk the market looking at limes and lemons that while they have long been my tarty friends in the kitchen, I have never thought much about their distinct aromas and *levels* of tartness. Plus, there is the color issue.

Walking in front of the heaping market stands of produce at Lake Market in Kolkata, I am skeptical of the speckled gondhoraj I see. I lean in close, sniffing: nothing. I roll a lime over in my palm: mottled. I make a fist and squeeze: super hard.

In Missouri, limes at the grocery are always evenly green, but I come to understand that speckles are not rejected here. That green limes are, in fact, underripe. When I try to quietly pick through a pile for solid green limes, the vendor merely asks what quantity I want, pushes a random half kilogram of speckled specimens into my market sack, and looks up expectantly.

"Ara ki?" "What else?" he asks. I rock back on my heels and look at the display of every vegetable in season, at fruits I have never eaten, take a deep breath, inhaling the sharp aroma of the fish market across the street, and, ignoring the scuffing sound of leather sandals sliding against the pavement as others walk too close behind me, point three times. I receive bounty: a curvy snake gourd, a long thin eggplant with skin colored a feathery purple, and a green coconut for consumption of its juice on the spot.

Here's what I did not know, emerging as I did from the plains of Kansas: all citrus types stay green until ready to be picked. Oranges, too, even though their name implies otherwise. Limes and lemons are extremely cold sensitive, and in their tropical lands of origin, of which India is the epicenter, they sport colors other than an even-toned green. A lime is partially yellow for one of two reasons: either it's ripe and less acidic, or other fruits or leaves blocked its access to sunlight while still on the tree.

What I also didn't know is that citrus is botanically a berry. A special kind of berry called a hesperidium. And it is monoecious—meaning both sexes are in the same blossom. It literally can stand alone. In fact, all citrus are hybrids that emerged from their base in South and East Asia out of just three primary ancestors: citron, pomelo, and mandarin orange (*Citrus medica, Citrus max-*

ima, and *Citrus reticulata*). Due to this ancestry and in an amazing-to-me and stealthy fashion, all citrus can grow from each other's rootstock.

My aromatic favorite, the gondhoraj lime, is likely a cross between a lime and a mandarin. It's in the Rangpur lime (*Citrus limonia*) family from what is now Bangladesh and joins cousins such as the Canton in South China and the Hime in Japan.

Though the gondhoraj lime declined to gallivant about the world, it flourishes with a swashbuckling verve on plates in Bengal. Once, tempted by the beauty of the aroma and the fact that a tiny serving bowl at a homey Bengali restaurant offered three quartered pieces of a small gondhoraj lime nestled sweetly as a foil against glossy perfect green chilies, I took the bait. I bit into a green chili, yes, I did. Then, immediately, I groped for the lime. The heat did not abate, but there was temperance. Thankfully, temperance.

~~~~~

Limes and lemons have a colorful history almost everywhere. After visitors to India saw limes and, no doubt, the fresh nimbu pani made there, a Western lemonade version appeared in Europe after a drop in the price of West Indian sugar in 1630. Lemonade came first to Rome and later to Paris. Limonadiers

served the delightful drink there at Paris sidewalk cafés but also from tanks that men carried on their backs to all the nooks and corners of the city.

This was a stroke of luck for Paris that may have foiled the bubonic plague. The disease was generally thought to have been spread through Europe by the fleas that infested gerbils aboard trade ships; once the ships docked, the fleas jumped to the European rat population. Humans and rats in urban centers transmitted the deadly disease between each other via bacteria. But oddly and wonderfully, in Paris, in 1668, the cycle of the plague was interrupted.

French limonadier.

The plague, dormant for a decade, had returned to France in the mid-seventeenth century—and it was already in Normandy, Picardy, Soissons, Amiens, and Rouen. It was threatening Paris. Between 1665 and 1666, only a few years earlier, London had lost more than 100,000 people to the plague. Vienna was decimated (80,000 dead), Prague (80,000 dead), and Malta (11,000 dead); almost no European city was spared. Except Paris in 1668.

Since the 1650s, when hardier varieties of citrus trees—not the resolutely regional gondhoraj lime—reached Italy, Romans had been treated to lemonade from tanked-up street vendors. Seeing this, Cardinal Mazarin, chief minister to the king of France, realized that the popularity of the drink could mean something new to tax and brought limonadiers to Paris.

Limonene contained in citrus fruit is a natural insecticide and repellent. The most effective part is the limonene-rich peel. Even today, the U.S. Environmental Protection Agency lists fifteen insecticides in which limonene is the chief active ingredient. In the days of the plague, citrus peels from the limonadiers were piling up in Parisian trash, the abode of Parisian rats. The rats were not deterred by the new taste of lemon and lime peels, the very thing that adds distinction to Bengali cuisine, but the fleas wouldn't have been able to survive riding on those French rats, by then loaded with limonene. What a stroke of bioluck that was.

Sailors had another reason to tout limes and lemons. On their great voyages after Vasco de Gama opened up the route to India, they needed limes to ward off the horrible wasting death of scurvy: livid splotches around the roots of their hair, weakness, fatigue, muscle ache, bruising, appalling breath, and more. As a sort of scurvy-protection way station, Portuguese sailors planted citrus heavily on the islands of St. Helena. Portuguese, Spanish, and Arab crews planted similar health centers on the African west coast, in the Azores, and in the Madeira island group. South Africans established their first citrus plantation in 1654 under the Dutch. And the British admiralty issued orders for regular rations of lime juice on all of His Majesty's ships, ever after making the name "limeys" appropriate for British sailors. Lime juice, too, was one of the five components of the arrack-based punch (likely from the Sanskrit pancha, five, for the five ingredients in the drink) during colonial times in India and prior. Nimbu pani and, later, fresh lime with soda were the rage in British India.

Long before that, though, citrus captured the imagination of the Romans, who depicted the Hesperides—the daughters of Hesperis and Atlas—crossing the Mediterranean from Africa in a giant shell bearing citrons, oranges, lemons, and limes in their arms as gifts for Italy. Though citrus actually reached the Italian peninsula via India, the thought of offerings via shell boat seems just dreamy enough for me.

The fanciful and sensory delight of citrus infiltrated everywhere. When the forces of Islam conquered a wide swath across the world from India to Spain in the sixth and seventh centuries, orange, tangerine, lemon, and lime trees tracked the path of armies. Think of it: men bent on war trailing scented groves of citrus, white blossoms like lace against the sky.

The Moors surrounded their Andalusian desert buildings with pools, cascades, and gardens full of citrus. Normans, after taking back Italy, tempted by the taste of citrus planted by the Moors, went native in Sicily. They literally would not go home. Poets wrote odes to lemons, ground was given over to groves of lime. Sweet orange and bitter orange scented the air. The Norman conquest of southern Italy was a scandalous love fest of citrus.

The oldest known reference to citrus appears in the *Vajasaneyi Samhita*, a collection of devotional texts in Sanskrit literature dated prior to 800 BCE, and there it was called jambhila. Citrus, consecrated to Ganesh in India, is held in the treasure god Kuvera's hands in Java. In China, by 1179, Hon Yen-Chih had named twenty-seven varieties of sweet-sour fruits in the orange-mandarin group in *Chu Lu*, the oldest known monograph on citrus.

Though citrus fruits are grown in more than 140 countries, India outstrips them all in limes and lemons, growing more than twice as many as even China at over 2.5 million metric tons in 2009 and nearly 4 million metric tons in 2020. In 2020, by the reckoning of the Food and Agriculture Organization of the United Nations, China, Brazil, the U.S., India, and Mexico led in the production of all citrus fruits. All that and without a declaration of Indian origin, think of it.

It's not all tonnage and production. Lime trees have a poetic history, too.

In the ancient world, citrus trees were coveted for their beauty long before anyone ever thought to eat their fruit. I imagine that their delicate flowering petals blotting out the sky and swoon-worthy aroma made this so. In a world without citrus, it's believable that one might stay in a foreign land just for the pleasure of lime.

Our citrus reference point goes back, then, some thousands of years. The power of it lay not just in its novelty, poetic odes, and pucker but in its balance and health properties. In the base texts of Ayurveda, food as medicine reigns supreme, and limes are one of the astringent fruits eaten for cleansing.

Though special, in Kolkata gondhoraj limes are lumped in with all limes and lemons in markets as nimbu, without specification. Gondhoraj really deserves better. It's not quite round. It's not juicy. It makes magic happen to drinks, to cumin, coconut, mustard, green chili, dal, the spicy mutton curry of kosha mangsho, and many fish curries. Kolkata phuchka, that delectable street food of hollow, crispy bread filled with a mixture of spiced water, tamarind chutney, chili, chaat masala, potato, onion, and chickpeas, would not be the same without gondhoraj limes. In cooking, the leaf can be thrown in for aroma, the zest for extra punch, and drops of the juice for a subtle wash with distinct olfactory pleasure notes. It should never be lumped in with other, if I may, lesser citrus.

And so, walking and sniffing as unobtrusively as possible, stepping past skins of discarded fruit and smiling absently at vendors who try to catch my eye, I peer instead at colorful citrus piled on tarps and boxes in Lake Market. Oranges are green, lemons thankfully yellow, limes both colorations, a mildly confusing vision of fruit gone color wild. Gathering my market sack of greenish lime orbs, I walk back to my apartment, nimbly stepping from shady patch to shady patch on the sidewalk. The gondhoraj keeps its fantastic aroma a secret on the journey, but once in the kitchen, a mere slice makes my nose perk up. I picked well.

Just as the terroir of *Vitis vinifera* grapes can make wine unique to a region, the tropical complexity of gondhoraj lebu pinpoints Bengal in as authentic

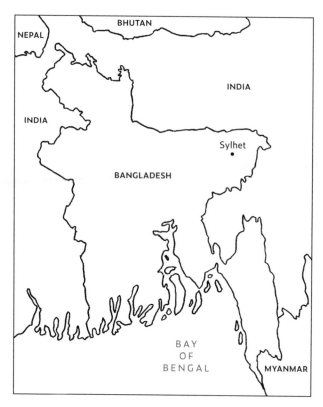

Bangladesh.

a certificat d'origine as you can get. The thought makes me pause. So many regions of the world are fighting to protect their iconic foods and their terroir. France's certificate of origin and Italy's denominazione di origine protetta— protected designation of origin—were established to mark foods as certified because they are rooted in a particular place. This guard against subterfuge by lesser products, in effect, brands a place and its food. What of India's hallmarks of cuisine? Bengal's gondhoraj has no legal protection. Grow one anywhere and it's yours to market as anything you like.

The only protection it has are the grandmothers who know a thing or two. And its own pickiness for certain soils.

The gondhoraj lime was born a border child between West Bengal and Bangladesh, likely in Sylhet and the hill tracts near Chittagong, and it is difficult to grow it anywhere else. There, where most of the soil is loose, unconsolidated, and alluvial, gondhoraj lime flourishes. The ambiance it loves is humid, subtropical, and marked with monsoons. Citrus roots don't like to stand in water, but they need a lot of it. Presto: gondhoraj lebu and eastern India, a Tinder match. The proof might just be summertime panta bhat—cilantro-lime rice—which can make converted followers even of those who lack knowledge of this special citrus or the way to pronounce it (gone-dor-aage).

It may be because the small green citrus fruits are picky about soil and temperature that gondhoraj lebu has not been mass-produced in orchards elsewhere. Many other limes are better known: the key limes of the Caribbean, Italian and Persian limes, Thai limes, and the regrettably named Kaffir limes, called marut by those wanting to avoid evoking this fruit's name-calling history. Kaffir, stemming from the Arabic word "kafir," which means "nonbeliever" or "infidel," was adopted by white colonialists to describe black Africans; its power as a slur only grew in apartheid-era South Africa. In Sri Lanka, an ethnic group called the Kaffirs retained a neutral understanding of the word, according to *Slate*, but everywhere else it is an injurious epithet.

These other limes may have more fame and more juice, but even so gondhoraj limes are coveted. Their scent—clean and citrusy like you would expect but with a surprisingly intense floral sweetness—could drive an entire cuisine.

And so it does in Bengal. From the sidelines.

For millennia, gondhoraj lime has been an enhancer after the cooking is done. You might say an enabler. Offered in quarters to be added as individual taste demands or made into pickles in spicy oils, this lime has been the plucky sidekick of garnishes. Tempering super-hot dishes with a squeeze, adding a lift to staples with a twist, the gondhoraj lime has been essential yet always just shy of the limelight. Restaurants in Kolkata wanting to mimic intimate family meals and entice the unsuspecting such as myself offer gondhoraj limes in a bowl shared with green chilies. They sit there on the table, their pale translucent flesh cut into quarters next to glossy green skins, in so innocent a pairing you'll want to reach for both. As gondhoraj lime tends to lose its aroma when heated, it's a fragrance best served cold.

But this wind-beneath-the-wings role may be changing as chefs in Kolkata highlight it, name it on menus, and celebrate its origins in Bengal, East and West. Online, in the *Times of India*, the *Telegraph*, and the *Economic Times*, chefs in Kolkata like Anjan Chatterjee of Oh! Calcutta and Joymala Banerjee of Bohemian talk about gondhoraj with nostalgia and offer it as a star attraction on their menus. Since 2013 or so, steamed bekti fillets in coconut-gondhoraj sauce, gondhoraj soufflé, and a virgin gondhoraj julep have appeared on city menus and achieved acclaim.

In the cuisine of Bengal and Bangladesh, lime lore is ever addictive. Over dinner in my Kolkata neighborhood, Shireen Maswood, born in what is now Bangladesh, remembers gondhoraj on the plate as well as in the glass. We nibble on tasty breads and sip lime soda as she recalls, "It was a particularly hot and humid afternoon and the hilsa season had begun. The menu for lunch was to be simple." As she says this, she indicates that her host may have been understating the delicious offering. The memory of the meal has stayed with her for decades.

Shireen called her host didi-bhai, older sister, a respectfully affectionate term, and the older woman teasingly called the younger Shireen didi-bhai in return. Her simple lunch turned out to be moong dal—the yellow split version of whole green mung beans—with gondhoraj lime, rice, aloo posto—potatoes with poppy seeds—and ilish maatch bhaja—pan-fried hilsa fish. All of it so tasty that at the time Shireen didn't pause to separate out the nuances, she just ate with acute pleasure and never forgot the sublime dal with its delicious lime flavor.

Moong Dal with Gondhoraj Lebu

YELLOW DAL WITH LIME

Recipe courtesy of Shireen Maswood

Serves 2–4

½ cup moong dal

¼ teaspoon turmeric

3 green chilies or to taste

2 tablespoons vegetable oil

¼ teaspoon yellow mustard seeds or nigella seeds

1–2 whole dried red chilies or to taste

1 teaspoon salt or to taste

½ teaspoon sugar or to taste

1 gondhoraj lime, sliced into rounds ¼-inch thick (key limes can be substituted)

Gondhoraj lime leaves (optional)

Wash the moong dal. Place in a deep pot and add water to cover. Bring to a simmer and skim the surface foam from the top. Add the turmeric and one of the green chilies, and continue to cook on a hard simmer until the dal is medium-thick, about 35–40 minutes. In a small saucepan or small wok, heat the oil over medium heat. Add the yellow mustard or nigella seeds and one or both of the dried red chilies according to your taste. As soon as the seeds start sputtering, add the mixture to the cooked dal. Add the salt and sugar, the two remaining green chilies, and water to the desired consistency—the dal should be like a thick soup—and stir. Discard the red chili or chilies used for tempering. Bring the dal to a boil. Place the sliced limes in the pot. Gently, without stirring, grab the pot and swirl the dal around the lime slices. Cover. Turn the heat off. Remove the lime slices after 30 minutes and discard them. If you like, garnish with gondhoraj lime leaves. Serve with rice.

~~~~~

The day I make Shireen's moong dal in Missouri, I slice key limes since gond-horaj limes are not available. The knife slices through the rind, a tangy scent rises, and a tiny droplet hits my thumb in a small connection. I lay the rounds onto the dal, swirl gently, trying to avoid submerging the islands, and cover the pan. When it's time to taste, I inhale deeply first. Citrus. Bright. Sharp. Dal. Deep. Earthy. My nose proceeds to inform me of all of this before my first bite. Nearly 90 percent of taste is aroma, and with this dal your nose will confirm this. The taste, though not from gondhoraj lime, is a close approxima-tion in the end. The burst of citrus lifts the dal out of the ordinary, makes it rather special, lighter on the tongue than usual; the heavy texture is lifted by aroma, and I can see what attracted young Shireen to this meal. On a hot day, what could be a better match and balance to the environment? The accom-panying cilantro-lime rice heightens the lime flavors just enough to keep you wanting more.

Panta Bhat

CILANTRO-LIME RICE

Recipe courtesy of Shireen Maswood

Serves 4

2 cups water

1 tablespoon butter

½–¾ teaspoon salt

1 cup long grain aromatic rice such as Basmati

1 teaspoon lime zest

2 tablespoons fresh-squeezed lime juice

½ cup cilantro, finely chopped

Heat the water in a saucepan. While it is heating, rinse the rice three or four times in water and then drain. When the water is boiling, add the butter, salt, and washed rice to the pan. Cover and reduce the heat to very low. Simmer until the rice is tender, about 20 minutes. When it's done, sprinkle the lime zest, lime juice, and cilantro onto the rice and fluff with a fork before serving.

In my Kolkata kitchen, I walk up to my fourth-floor flat in Deshapriya Park with a bag of the first limes I bought for myself. I roll the limes onto a cutting board and cut into one rind, only to be mildly disappointed with its dry-looking flesh. Had I purchased old dried-up limes with little juice left to squeeze? Is that why they weren't uniformly green? Just as I am considering this possibility, aroma stops me. That scent. Sweetly tart, very fresh, summer in one slice. It is potent enough that several drops and some of the abundant pulp are all that is needed to flavor the entire glassful I am craving. I add sugar and water, and since I had not made simple syrup beforehand, I stir a long time just like my brown-shirted waiter did at the coffee shop, until the large crystals of Indian table sugar mostly dissolve. I drink it up, pleased by its tartness, its tropical zing, and the scent on my fingertips that I do not bother to wash off.

I know there is more to this citrus than the sweet or salty lime sodas of summer, although those are my go-to favorites. And in case you think that I carry on a bit too much about fresh lime soda, that my foreignness in Bengal made me a zealot, understand that gondhoraj limes have been known to bring about robust yearning even from never-left natives. When I'm offered sweet, salty, or sweet-salty versions in restaurants in Kolkata, I always order the combination. Many times, I enjoy the masala option using roasted ground cumin seeds, and I find that the salty version has its own balance in the tart and sweet mix—satisfying and especially refreshing on hot days. But in my own kitchen, that hot day in Kolkata, I find the table sugar and skip the salt.

Chapter Three

A GRAIN BY ANY OTHER NAME

A bowl of rice will provide equal satisfaction
to a rich man and a poor man, to a saint and a sinner.
—"Lakshmi Revealed," *Deccan Herald*, 2009

ON A HOT SUN-FILLED DAY in Kochi, I sit with Chef Anumitra Ghosh-Dastidar at her Edible Archives booth at the Kochi-Muziris Biennale, an international art festival, and talk about lost rice.

"When I arrived to build up this display, I cooked a different rice variety every day" to understand each variety's basic nature, Chef Anu says. She did this with twenty-four varieties, and her menu board reveals the story behind her choices. Food as art that reveals the tale of land and communities is an idea I love. Plus, Edible Archives is trying to resurrect lost tastes—the rice varieties that got away.

One bowl served at Chef Anu's festival booth contains Kattuyanam rice along with roasted pumpkin, cauliflower, ridge gourd, mango, dal, cucumber salad, and mustard microgreens. Another combines Bengali Gobindobhog, a short grain rice with an aroma that makes you want to inhale deeply over and over, with ginger, green chilies, cumin paste, and the crunch of radish. The chef is after fresh flavors and contrasting textures. She is interested in reviving vanishing Indian rice strains. What is more, the Edible Archives project, born between Chef Anu and author, consultant, and caterer Prima Kurien, intends to curate the idea that each meal is an entry into an individual edible archive of the person eating it.

~~~~~~

Getting off the ferry from Vypin Island at Kochi, I see a line of pedestrians and people with small motorbikes waiting to get on. The "grand old trees" of Kochi, as the Malayalam poet K. G. Sankara Pillai wrote in "The Trees of Cochin," murmur "'ramarama,' 'maramarama' in the breeze / flapping ears, twitching tails, waving trunks." Maram means "tree" in the Malayalam language, and their murmuring has a lullaby feel—a sweet serenade for humans and perhaps self-comfort for the trees as well. They bow over the dock near the water to shade the entrance into one of the oldest port towns on the subcontinent. Here spices were traded for millennia. Here many Europeans and others first met Mother India.

If you look left or right, you'll see large spidery Chinese fishing nets reaching gently out over the water where they've been in use for six hundred–plus years. Fixed to land originally by hardened coconut trunks driven into the water, they have teak, bamboo, or, increasingly, modern wire poles that cantilever sixty-five feet over the channel, holding nets that stretch horizontally like a large hammock. The balancing weight of fishermen walking the outstretched poles causes the nets to lower into the water, while rocks as large as your head tied by ropes rise. The motion is slow and smoothly hypnotic due to days upon days of practice. Hundreds of smaller nets dot other banks in the region, but these giants are getting rare; only eight remained in 2019.

The elegant Cheena vala nets have existed in Kochi since perhaps 1350, brought some say by Portuguese traders from Macau, a Portuguese colony until 1999. Others say the Chinese explorer Zheng He introduced them on his

Cheena vala nets.

treasure voyages to Southeast Asia between 1405 and 1433. Though there are fewer of the giant nets every year, in addition to being picturesque they are still used daily to fish.

As tempting as it is to watch the hammock-like nets indefinitely, the idea of the biennale, an international art extravaganza held every two years, pulls me farther into town. This immersive artistic journey into the vision of the Malabar Coast, as well as beyond, has displays across Old Fort Cochin inside ancient spice warehouses with mustard-colored heat-baked exterior walls, through arched doorways and cool spaces that feel dim just for a moment after you duck in out of the sun, and in officers' quarters long since abandoned. Across the world there has been a surge in biennale festivals of art—fifty some—held in cities such as Beijing, Liverpool, Prague, São Paulo, Sharjah, and more. Here, the 2018–19 show displays works by seventy-six artists from India, Thailand, Cameroon, Indonesia, Austria, South Africa, China, Cuba, Brazil, Lebanon, Vietnam, and more. This port town, site of a great food exchange in Indian history, seems apt for the power of this art and for Edible Archives in particular.

"It all starts with the farmers," Chef Anu says. "Most of these rice varieties are not grown in a big way. Farmers just grow their small-small portion for their own consumption, or sometimes they sell it in the local haats or just to one another."

Over the course of a couple of hours, I mill about as Chef Anu interacts at her open-air display with cooks and pleased eaters: she finishes interviews, stirs pots, and discusses flavor pairings and textures. As I watch, the hot temperatures of that February day in Kochi rise further, and the nearly 98 percent humidity makes even cotton clothing feel sticky. Everyone decelerates. I make a slow-moving break for a table in the shade.

The creative idea behind Edible Archives showcases indigenous and lesser-known rice varieties and pairs these ancient grains with seasonal dishes. Bowls of what appear to be home-cooked foods pass by my table. The dynamic textures and colors of the rice are startling, intriguing. And, in fact, as I look down, my own bowl surprises me. There, nestled on one side, is Burma black rice, with a slightly nutty flavor and distinct texture that pair extremely well with yams made into a sour curry. The colors are beautiful, too.

"So, this black rice is not a sweet rice," Chef Anu says. "It has a sticky texture. In fact, if you eat only the rice, you will notice a very mild bitter aftertaste."

These attributes create the perfect balance with the strong flavor of the sour yams, she says. And she's right: the black rice can stand up to it, not be overpowered. The flavors complement each other and make another bite and then another necessary. The other rice in my bowl, a scented white rice nestled under a mild dal, has almost an opposite profile on the tongue.

"The dal is very mild. It will give you a creamy texture, but the flavor that will come through will be the flavor of the rice." I find this true, and the mix of these tastes and textures creates a satisfying but not heavy feeling.

The quintessential Edible Archives offering, Chef Anumitra says, is a one-bowl meal in which the six tastes identified in Ayurvedic writings—sweet, salty, bitter, sour, pungent, astringent—are perfectly balanced. Each of Chef Anu's bowls features indigenous Indian rice varieties, many of which are endangered.

The pairings in each bowl are "designed in such a way that all the flavors help spotlight the taste of the rice," the chef says. I find I like this idea of showcasing what has been a background element for many. Back in the U.S., I try to duplicate one of Chef Anu's bowls: Radha Tilok rice with yam theeyal, moong dal with green peas, fried eggplant, and crisp papads. I make substitutions due to geography but find that the balance underlying her recipes remains mostly intact. We're not always used to including all these flavors in our foods, but to do so is refreshing. I feel good after eating this way: it's tasty and satisfying, inside and out.

Radha Tilok Rice

(SWEET)

Recipe courtesy of Chef Anumitra Ghosh-Dostidar, Edible Archives, Goa
Serves 2–4

1 cup Radha Tilok rice
1:1.25 rice to water ratio

Wash the rice and drain it two or three times. In a rice cooker or a pan with a tightly fitting lid, add the rice and water in a 1:1.25 ratio. Simmer until done, about 20 minutes, and set aside, still covered. Serve hot.

Chef Anumitra says you can substitute Kala Jeera rice from Bangladesh, Gobindobhog rice from West Bengal, Kala Namak rice from Uttar Pradesh, Jeera Shala rice from across South India, or any other scented short grain rice. Long grain varieties like Basmati will not have the same balancing effect.

Yam Theeyal

SOUR YAM CURRY

(BITTER-ASTRINGENT-SOUR)

Recipe courtesy of Chef Anumitra Ghosh-Dostidar, Edible Archives, Goa

Serves 2–4

About 1 pound yams, peeled

⅓ teaspoon cayenne

½ teaspoon turmeric

Salt to taste

3 whole dried red chilies

2 tablespoons coriander seeds

3 tablespoons freshly grated coconut

4 tablespoons tamarind paste

1 tablespoon jaggery or brown sugar

15–20 fresh curry leaves

1 tablespoon coconut oil

1½ teaspoons black mustard seeds

Cut the yams into cubes about ½-inch thick. Place them in a saucepan and add enough water to cover them; add the cayenne, turmeric, and salt to taste. Bring the water to a boil and simmer until the yams are cooked, about 10 minutes. Set the yams in their water aside. In a frying pan, dry roast two of the dried red chilies, the coriander seeds, and the grated coconut over low heat until the coconut is golden. Set this mixture aside to cool.

Once the coconut and spice mixture has cooled, grind it in a mortar and pestle or spice grinder until finely ground. Add 4 tablespoons of this mixture to the yams in their water. Add the tamarind paste, jaggery or brown sugar, and half the curry leaves. Mix well. Next bring the yam mixture to a boil for 2–3 minutes. Add salt if desired. In a small pan, heat the coconut oil; when

➤

it is hot, add the mustard seeds, the remaining dried red chili, and the rest of the curry leaves, and stir together. Immediately add this mixture to the yam mixture as a tempering to bind all the flavors together.

If you have trouble finding fresh curry leaves, you can use the dried leaves available in some grocery stores. You can also substitute lemon balm or a combination of lemon basil and lime zest to approach the curry leaf's unique flavor and nutritional profile. If you get enthused, curry plants also grow well in home gardens!

Moong Dal with Peas

YELLOW DAL WITH GREEN PEAS

(SALTY-SWEET)

Recipe courtesy of Chef Anumitra Ghosh-Dostidar, Edible Archives, Goa

Serves 2

½ cup yellow moong dal

1 cup water

⅓ teaspoon turmeric

Salt to taste

¼ cup fresh or frozen green peas

1 tablespoon ghee

½ teaspoon cumin seeds

2 green chilies, split lengthwise

Wash the moong dal. In a pot, boil it with the water, removing the foam from the surface, then add the turmeric and salt. Cook until the dal is soft and beginning to look mushy but still holds its shape, about 15–20 minutes. In a separate pan, boil the peas until cooked, about 5 minutes. Drain them, then add them to the boiled dal. In a heavy-bottomed pan, add the ghee and heat over a moderate fire. Add the cumin seeds and green chilies. Once the cumin seeds begin to sizzle, add the boiled dal and peas. Continue to boil for 3–4 minutes, then cover and set aside until ready to serve. Serve hot or at room temperature.

Fried Eggplant

(SALTY-SWEET-PUNGENT)

Recipe courtesy of Chef Anumitra Ghosh-Dostidar, Edible Archives, Goa

Serves 2–4

1 large round purple eggplant

½ teaspoon turmeric

Salt to taste

1 teaspoon sugar

1 cup mustard oil

Slice the eggplant into rounds at least 1-inch thick, leaving the skins on. Mix the turmeric, salt, and sugar together in a small bowl. Coat the eggplant slices with this mixture and set aside to marinate, about 10 minutes. In a heavy-bottomed pan, heat the oil. Once the oil is hot, add the eggplant slices two at a time. Let one side cook to golden brown, then turn the slice over. The end result should be golden brown disks with some patches of caramelized black. The slices will be tender. Place on a paper towel. Serve warm.

Crisp Papads

Recipe courtesy of Chef Anumitra Ghosh-Dostidar, Edible Archives, Goa

Vegetable oil

Store-purchased papads

Heat 2 inches oil in a medium-sized frying pan. When the oil is hot, add the papads, one at a time, and fry for a few seconds. Remove with a slotted spoon to a paper towel to dry. Caution: the shortest delay can burn the papads.

The artistic balance of Chef Anu's creations—tasty and nutritious—mimics the concepts of Ayurveda in which the body is kept in equilibrium within itself, as well as with its environment. This feels extraordinarily good on a hot day in southern India. I begin to see why the British, who chose to eat heavy joints of meat and more foods distinctly not suited to the environment and drink prodigious quantities of arrack and other liquors, had a difficult digestive time of it in India. Ayurveda, with its long history attuned to place, might have helped them out.

Villagers and farmers in the region know this story at a gut level. And in fact, Chef Anu says, when "government subsidies offer hybrid rice at 2 rupees or 10 rupees per kilogram to aid those in need," the villagers "understand it's not as good for them." The proliferation of quicker-yielding hybrid varieties means the loss of hundreds of rice varieties and their accompanying nutrition profiles, textures, and flavors. Seeking out seeds to savor, Chef Anu does not see rice as a quiet bass note on the plate. For Edible Archives, rice choices open an entirely new culinary dimension. "All the communities I spoke with have their preferred combinations. It's not arbitrary."

This seems fitting to me. Many Bengalis eat rice three times a day, and there are three seasons of rice for the farmer: aman, aus, and boro—the winter, summer, and autumn crops. Who else would better know the tastiest combinations of foods that produce the best health than those growing and eating those foods in habits dating back for millennia? When I was in Tunisia working as part of the U.S. Peace Corps from 1984 to 1986, I remember that despite the delicious foods there, the people I worked with were short in stature. The men were just barely taller than my 5 feet 3 inches, the women shorter. But in the larger town nearby, the professionals I interacted with were topping 6 feet for the men, and the women were always taller than I was. It occurred to me that the mostly wheat-based heritage foods of the region—foods that had sustained people for generations—were no longer doing so. Where people had the income to purchase a variety of foods with their micronutrients included and purchase more protein more frequently, there was no stunting.

Many years later, I am working in a remote village of interior Mozambique. Under acacia trees, women cook traditional foods over open fires. They are experts at calibrating the heat of the flames, at boiling soups just the right amount, at adjusting logs to simmer liquids slowly for long periods without ever letting the fires go out. When I stagger trying to pick up a pot, soft chuckles and then help follow. I watch in amazement as corn is picked in the field next to us, shaved into the basin of a wooden vessel, and then swiftly pounded with tall poles to make cornmeal. Between good-hearted laughter and the women's beautiful kapulana fabrics, the scene is lively and loving.

It becomes dark outside and someone turns on the headlights to a truck; the light slants on cheekbones, shadowing eyes and revealing bright patterns of head scarves. The stalks of grasses, about thigh-high outside of the cleared space around the small houses, rustle softly as we spread ground cloths out with the foods: homemade bread made to eat with butter, warm soy "coffee" in metal pots with spouts, and two kinds of bean soup, including one I suggest that adds lemon. The women, who had worked all day testing recipes with focus and industry, become lighthearted and sit close together eating.

"I like this addition of a squeeze of lemon, Nina," one lady says kindly as she tastes my recipe.

"I can taste the twist," another says.

It reminded me of midwestern women drawing the outsider into the group with talk of recipes and food, bringing her warmly into the fold. When breaking bread here, everyone is welcome.

Another day, after we make biscuits that taste something like shortbread cookies, with the clever addition of soya flour to add more protein, we walk to the local market to test what the children think.

"Here, you take one side," one of the ladies says, and we carry a box of biscuits between us, the edges bumping our knees as we walk along a graveled road with bean fields on each side. Crowds come around when we reach a gathering of buildings, and as little hands reach around the torsos of older children, one touches my leg.

"I will taste one!" a voice says in Chimanhica, the village language, muffled by the back of a larger child's shirt. Judging by the smiles, the biscuits are a (high-protein) success.

Here mental and physical stunting of children reaches 40 percent, and I can spot some young ones, their eager hands thrust out, who seem less developed than their peers. Many will never develop to be fully contributing members of their communities. The mothers, caring for one and all, make beloved foods for their families, yet these foods no longer sustain them. The soils of the area are depleted. The micronutrients are gone. My work with the mothers, cooking their favorites, adjusting the protein levels by the addition of available beans, tests for what comforts and protects.

Ayurveda, one of India's traditional systems of medicine, that underpins many foods on the subcontinent, has this same goal: eat what protects health, and that balance will comfort the body and keep it in equilibrium within itself and with its environment. All over the world, humans do this. In Mozambique, the old foods, before the soils were depleted, had this balance. Even transported to Kansas and adapted to what was at hand, my mother's Bengali recipes carried hints of Ayurveda. It lurks within modern iterations in India, too. Sour yams with that slightly bitter rice. Sweet with a little heat. Pickles that do all that and more.

~~~~~~

With all the varieties on the subcontinent, it seems unlikely that rice, *Oryza sativa*, was foreign to India. Henry Yule and A. C. Burnell in their Anglo-Indian dictionary *Hobson-Jobson* consider that it is possible that southern India was the original seat of rice cultivation. Yet there is debate about this and, much like my visa paperwork, it is ongoing. Once Arab traders took arisi (Tamil) with them, westward-bound rice was called by many other names: al-ruz or arruz (Arabic), arroz (Spanish), oruza (Greek), oryza (Latin), riso (Italian), riz (French), reis (German), and rice (English). The rice of India, *Oryza indica*, cast a long shadow.

Before departing to sail the oceans and trek the deserts, rice had to first be domesticated. Many archaeologists and botanists believe that rice cultivation began somewhere along the Yangzte River between 10,000 and 8,000 BCE and spread from there toward Korea and Japan. However, archaeologists working in India point to evidence of rice cultivation in the Ganges River basin by people unconnected to the Yangzte. Pottery for rice use, and a husk-clot of domesticated rice, have been dated to 6400 BCE in Lahuradewa in Uttar Pradesh.

All this evidence of origins adds up to much more than the sum of its parts.

In Bengal and much of India, rice carries the mythology of bounty, of a baby's first feeding, of female autonomy, and of newlywed prosperity. At my son's Anuprasan baby ceremony, symbolically the first feeding of rice, he ate it up well enough. Then he reached his chubby hands out along the tray of other enticements: touching the book (knowledge and learning) and the shiny money (prosperity). But first he ate. Rice is dhaanya, the sustainer of the human race. It is pithau, paste, used to create art during the harvest season as a sign of respect for Lakshmi, goddess of prosperity, for whom food and rice in particular rank as bounty. Or it is rangoli, a pattern using colored rice, flour, sand, or flowers made by women to invite the gods into the house for prosperity and luck. Everything from naming ceremonies for children to birthdays, sister-brother celebrations, Diwali, and other rites of passage is celebrated with rice.

The diminutive grain, ranging from less than five to nine millimeters in size, has fed more people over a longer period of time across the world than any other crop. And though thousands of varieties of rice are already lost, 6,000-plus varieties are still available in India—perhaps more so than anywhere else. Yet most people even in India are familiar with and eat only a handful of those varieties. One, Basmati, is commonly found now in many countries, and its qualities of aroma and distinct grains are familiar. The Sanskrit saying—grains of rice should be like brothers, close but not stuck together—is especially visible in Basmati preparations on plates across the world.

Other rice varieties, seeds of their nonedible grass parents, are softer, shorter, mildly scented, heavily fragrant, black, red, sweet, slightly bitter, nutty, and more. The pairing of these with seasonal foods can be gastronomically transcendent.

Rice, tied so strongly to cultural identity, was presumed to be less fortifying by the British, who wanted to shape the Bengali body. "The British colonial state considered the 'rice-eating' Bengalis to be weak and emasculated," Utsa Ray says in *Culinary Culture in Colonial India: A Cosmopolitan Platter and the Middle-Class*, "compared to the 'wheat-eating' populations of northern India," and encouraged "modern" dietary changes.

To be fair, the British didn't confine themselves to promoting wheat in Bengal. As their initial government seat in India, Kolkata was the place for their first food experiments in the colony. Strangely, they identified rice eating in their subjects as something to fix.

In the push to shape the Bengali body away from what the British saw as its "effeminacy," Jayanta Sengupta says in "Nation on a Platter: The Culture and Politics of Food and Cuisine in Colonial Bengal," the term "rice eaters" became derogatory. I imagine a playground and a bully calling out, "You're nothing but a rice eater!" and think again how odd that is. But as a way to cut to the heart of a culture, criticizing rice was a direct hit. The British themselves countered the heat and humidity of the land with a diet that served as a metaphor for the racial and physical superiority of the Raj—excessive, meat-heavy, and topped off with alcohol—to no good effect medically. As history would have it, eating became something of a spectacle. It seems an odd preoccupation to me—a food fight with indigestion as the result.

However, this type of excessive eating, equated with manliness, resolve, and courage, meant that the British cast about for other crops to replace what had grown in Bengal for centuries. In fact, writes Utsa Ray, "a constant search for substitutes for rice led the colonial state to concentrate on the cultivation of potatoes and peas," pushing out land previously dedicated to rice, radishes, and eggplant. Other crops the British favored were carrots and barley, though they did little at the time to make local palates adjust to their addition in the markets.

The way that vegetables and fruits were planted in irregular rows, in damp spaces, and the way that the British had to endure "odoriferous mangoes and guavas" at breakfast made the colonizers uneasy. Since the diet and the comfort of the British in India, not food for the masses, were their chief concerns, they forged ahead with their critique of farming. By then, Ray says, scientific approaches had become conflated with cultural stereotyping.

According to Ray, the new crops were not so useful in bad times. And though it was finally found that crops such as cucumbers and pumpkins, already sown in Bengal, were the most beneficial in times of scarcity, new foods were still pursued. The British felt that their "rational" and "scientific" system of agriculture was superior to indigenous farming, and this was an idea hard to shake.

"It was a gross underestimation of what grew in the colony that led the colonial state to introduce new food-crops," Ray writes. One result, the loss of small-production rice due to the British disdain for rice eaters, heralded a reordering of existing ways and means of food production based on stereotyping of the colonized as backward and inept. It proves a cautionary tale.

The fact that rice was fetching high prices in Europe at the time seemed another incentive to the British to get larger quantities of a single variety for export. Small-batch village rice would not do. In a twist of geography, South Carolina rice became the favored rice in Europe between 1740 and 1760. Few may think of rice in connection with slavery, but it was the transfer of an entire cultural system from Africa to the Georgia sea coast and the Carolinas that made rice cultivation in the U.S. so successful. Rice seeds accompanied African slaves to the Americas, and their generational expertise in cultivating *Oryza glaberrima*, indigenous to Africa, is what made the Africans needed on rice plantations in the Carolinas. So as Carolina Gold rice became the rage in Europe, New World planters prospered; their slaves, not so much.

In the way of strange tales, rumors involving a shipwreck and a salvaged bag of Bengali rice say that Carolina Gold (an Asian *Oryza sativa* rice variety) originated in Bengal, though with all the varieties available in India, it was not the first choice of natives. With an eye to making large European profits and cutting out the Americans, the British had seed brought to Bengal to cultivate. Indian farmers did not like the results. The seed, thought to be of poor quality, was not blamed; the "backward" Bengali farmer was.

~~~~~

Despite the opinions of medical experts of the time, the British insisted on "a kind of false bravado and the exhibition of a generous contempt" for what they saw as the "luxurious and effeminate practices of the country." As Jayanta Sengupta says in "Nation on a Platter," Calcutta surgeon Adam Burt disagreed with their resulting eating habits, "warning that 'the too liberal use of wine combines with the climate to render Europeans ill-qualified for digesting the great quantity of animal food which most of them continue to devour as freely as before they left their native country.'"

I object to the idea of something that is effeminate being seen as less than. However, when applied to Bengali men and the way that the British used this as a metaphor for the racial and physical superiority of the Raj, the point is made. Regardless of what their own doctors were saying, the British in India continued to eat huge amounts of every sort of meat, including pork and beef, both roasted and curried. Loath to blame his actual diet for his poor health, Sengupta writes, Governor Philip Francis groused, "I am tormented with the bile and obliged to live on mutton chop and water. The Devil is in the climate I think." By this reasoning, the heat and humidity, not the diet, conspired to subvert British manliness, resolve, and courage. Stomach disorders, inevitably, were common.

These ideas of effeminacy and the manly Englishman carried over into treatises by eighteenth-century historians such as Robert Orme. Sengupta writes that Orme considered that the diet of the "people of Indostan" exacerbated these shortcomings, dependent as it was on rice, an "easily digestible" food, obtained with little labor, and thus "the only proper one for such an effeminate race." Again with the disdain. #eyerollhere.

As much as the men of the Raj pointed to the effeminate results of rice eating, for many British women, who came more frequently in the later years of the Raj, rice was more approachable. In David Burton's *The Raj at Table: A Culinary History of the British in India*, Emily Auckland, younger sister of Lord Auckland, the governor-general of India, writes in her diary on December 11, 1837: "The King of Oude sent his cook to accompany us for the next month, and yesterday, when our dinner was set out, his *khansamah* and *kitmutgars* arrived with a second dinner, which they put down by the side of the other, and the same at breakfast this morning. Some of the dishes are very good, though too strongly spiced and perfumed for English tastes. They make up some dishes with assafoetida! But we stick to the rice and pilaus and curries."

Cooks in British households in India continued to adapt recipes. Though many British women were fearful of native kitchens as places of filth and sly cooks, as Sengutpa says in "Nation on a Platter," some of the dishes their cooks created became favorites. One adaptation, kedgeree, from the original khichuri, came to be a common breakfast food. Since fish, its central ingredient along with rice and eggs, was caught early in the morning and might well have turned bad by evening, the timing was good. In *Mrs. Beeton's Book of Household Management* of 1861, any cold fish would do plus a teacupful of boiled rice, a bit of butter, mustard, and two soft-boiled eggs, mixed together with salt and cayenne to taste. While this doesn't sound much like my mother's khichuri—a combination of dal, rice, ghee, and a few vegetables boiled together with cinnamon, cloves, cardamom, and cumin—it's a prime example of how one recipe transmuted into another.

As David Burton says in *The Raj at Table*, khichuri, a recipe perhaps more than a thousand years old, made way for the substitution of flaked fresh fish instead of lentils and acquiesced to the subtraction of spices and the addition of hard-boiled eggs. The recipe reached Britain during the eighteenth century and rose to fame, Burton says, alongside the new stagecoach connection with

Findon, just south of Aberdeen, where there was a thriving smoked haddock cottage industry. The smoked fish could reach Edinburgh and London by coach and gave rise, during the Victorian and Edwardian eras, to kedgeree on most breakfast sideboards. It also gave rise to the idea that kedgeree was of Scottish origin because of the stagecoach route, though it arrived from far more distant lands. While there are many versions of kedgeree, a simple one follows.

Kedgeree

FISH, RICE, AND EGGS

Serves 4

1 pound smoked fish such as haddock or salmon, undyed

2 tablespoons ghee or butter

3 cardamom pods, split

1 small cinnamon stick

1 dried bay leaf

1 large onion, finely chopped

¼ teaspoon turmeric

½ teaspoon salt

2 cups Basmati or another long grain rice

3 eggs, hard-boiled, shelled, and cut into quarters

3 tablespoons cilantro or parsley, chopped

1 tomato, chopped (optional)

1 green chili, finely chopped (optional)

Additional salt and pepper to taste

1 lemon, cut into wedges

In a saucepan, add enough water to cover the fish and bring to a boil; simmer for 5 minutes. Remove the fish from the water to cool, and save the water. Flake the fish, removing any skin or bones. Set aside. Melt the ghee or butter in another pan with deep sides. Add the cardamom pods, cinnamon stick, and bay leaf, and simmer for 30 seconds. Add the chopped onion and simmer until it is soft but not brown, about 5 minutes. Add the turmeric, salt, and rice, and stir until the grains are coated. Add the fish water plus enough water to total 1 quart and bring to a boil; cover the pan, and turn the heat to low. Cook for 15–18 minutes. Once the rice mixture is done, add the fish, eggs, and cilantro or parsley and gently stir. Add the chopped tomato or green chili if desired. Adjust the salt and pepper to taste. Serve with lemon wedges.

As an optional side dish, mix 1 cup plain yogurt with 1 tablespoon chopped cilantro and serve alongside the kedgeree.

~~~~~

This staple of a simple home meal, whether transfigured by the British or served as traditional khichuri at my childhood home in Kansas as a comfort food on rainy days, is also a showcase of the teeming regional differences not only within India but within Bengal. The staple foods of each locality—rice, lentils, wheat, millet, or sometimes sorghum—tie people digestively to their soil and community. Local lore still has it that village grains are better for villagers than anything else. Thus, khichuri is sometimes made with millet instead of rice or chickpeas instead of lentils. With a little extra splurge, ghee enhances any of the styles.

As in all food cultures, what people eat and how much they eat depend on their position in social hierarchies. And during times of scarcity, those hierarchies are more evident. When the British abandoned millions to their fate during famine and even wealthier citizens were not able to avert crisis, the khichuri story goes dark. Comfort food during times of food stability, otherwise famine food in watered-down versions doled out in crisis, khichuri can also be a reminder of dire times indeed.

Chapter Four

GREEN CHILI AND OTHER IMPOSTORS

Bontius says it was a common custom of natives,
and even of certain Dutchmen, to keep a piece of chilly
continually chewed, but he found it intolerable.

—Henry Yule and A. C. Burnell, *Hobson-Jobson*, 1886

WHEN I WAS A CHILD, one of the most prized of the family possessions for me
was a large globe. It was big enough that it would have been awkward to put
my arms around it at nine years old, which is when I spent inordinate amounts
of time idly spinning it and watching the world go by. I memorized the names
of mountain ranges, great rivers, deserts spanning the width of continents,
thrilled at the earth, at danger, at foreignness.

By the time I was a teenager at Lakeside Junior High, I had become perplexed. Few of those great expanses from the globe were mentioned in class.
There was a persistently concentrated focus on Western Europe and the
United States. Sitting at my school desk in 1974, wearing Big Smith overalls
and suede hiking boots with red laces, I learned about Greek mythology, the
Roman Empire, the American Revolution, Henry VIII, and Nazi Germany. I
have vague recollections of hearing about Genghis Khan, but he seemed a car-

icature of a warrior: large and mean and extraordinarily hairy, even though as far as his impact on the world and Silk Road history goes, he reigned supreme. I learned nothing of the cultures and peoples in his path. Nor that Mongolians are not particularly hairy, at least not as hairy as my images of him are from the curriculum. I didn't understand that Khan was a title of respect. So much was left out. The world map had North America squarely in the center.

After another round with the Indian consulate for my hoped-for return trip, I am left pondering my existence. Humans have tended to group together in tribes since time immemorial. I realize that I am putting too much emphasis on getting a visa designating me as a person of Indian origin, but throughout my life in Kansas and now in Missouri this has been my identity. Why not so in India? Though I can look as if I belong, I return to India an impostor.

I consider that old family globe. If it is spun just so, countries other than the United States are at eye level, and tracing a finger along their bas-relief feels the same as tracing the boundaries of Kansas and Missouri. But we all tip into one region or another to find our place on the globe, based on allegiances that can hinge on place of birth and other surface details: language, skin color, manners, food preferences. Genghis Khan had also been an impostor on Indian ground. No one in India was like him.

Once, when my husband and I had first moved to our small town, a midwestern women's group I belong to played a game that had everyone write down on a piece of paper what type of laundry detergent they used. Concerned that writing "whatever was cheapest" might be a social snafu, I wrote down my aspirational detergent, Wisk, which was always too expensive (but darn good at stains, I still say) for me to actually buy on our young-family budget and its seventeen loads of laundry per week.

Small squares of paper crackled as the host unfolded them; a few fell off the table and were scooped back up fluttering like birds. She read everyone's answers aloud, all variations on the brand Tide, and then paused and looked straight at me.

"Weird."

I was new. I was from the city. I used odd detergent (or wanted to).

To avoid this feeling of not quite belonging, I created a persona that did not make the natives uncomfortable. How about that habit of Indians eating with their hands? I refrained from pointing out the Kansas habit of finger-licking-good fried chicken, nor did I suggest that the act of touching your food adds to the sensory experience of its texture and taste. And, no, I especially did not launch into a soliloquy on cleanliness of the human body as godly, as much cleaner than indifferently washed utensils. Behind the scenes, I migrated when I could to my mother's kitchen when I was a child, even later during visits as an adult, for installments of warm luchi, deep-fried and puffy wheat bread rolled up with a little sugar, best and really only eaten with your fingers. I requested piquant keema with tiny cubes of potatoes instead of our usual peas for accent, and, yes, I used the warm luchi to scoop it up, not a fork. No eyebrows were raised by these acts in my mother's kitchen.

Looking around, I see that almost everything in my life on the farm is foreign to it. The oft used old tractor: a foreign body, an intruding object. My kitchen stocked with cocoa and sugar, cloves and cardamom: most definitely not from my Missouri land. The people living in the surrounding county, too: foreign intrusions (unless they are hiding Otoe-Missouria blood), until they weren't.

Word is out now that green chili was foreign in India at one point. In fact, chilies hail from over 9,000 miles away in Mexico and South America, definitely not in the fold of plants native to Bengal. Before 1500, black pepper—either the hot and sweet *Piper longum* known as long pepper or the small, round, familiar-to-the-West *Piper nigrum*—was the hottest spice in the Indian culinary world. That had changed by the 1800s. In 1886, Henry Yule and A. C. Burnell's *Hobson-Jobson*, the Anglo-Indian dictionary, published this scene of discovery from the 1848 satire *Vanity Fair*: "'Try a chili with it, Miss Sharp,' said Joseph, really interested. 'A chili?' said Rebecca, gasping. 'Oh yes?'…'How fresh and green they look,' she said, and put one into her mouth. It was hotter than the curry; flesh and blood could bear it no longer."

It's a curious twist: what happened with pepper. According to Lizzie Collingham in *Curry: A Tale of Cooks and Conquerors*, along with ginger and cinnamon, black pepper in medieval Europe accounted for 93 percent of the spices annually imported into Venice between 1394 and 1405. As it was hauled out of India by the shipload, black pepper was supplanted in India itself by what the Portuguese brought to the Malabar Coast: the green chili. South Indians adapted to it surprisingly quickly, as did Ayurvedic doctors, using chili in soups and plasters instead of black pepper to treat cholera patients. Meanwhile, Europeans valued black pepper and other spices initially for medicinal uses, too: to ward off plague, stimulate appetite, and aid digestion. Eventually, pepper opened up options for cooks there trying to liven up bland fish and vegetarian dishes on the numerous fast days of the Christian calendar. And as translations of the Arabic folktale about a Garden of Delights became available in the thirteenth century, the Muslim attitude toward food as a source of pleasure fascinated Europeans with its stark contrast to Christian teachings of self-denial. Cooks in Europe never looked back.

Chili peppers, with all their heat and beauty, are eaten by more than a quarter of the people on earth every day. Few other foods have been adopted by so many people in so many places so quickly. But if you check the documented spices traded in medieval and early modern Europe, you won't see chili mentioned. The hidden cargo of chili peppers proved easy to grow and so inexpensive that merchants were not in favor of the small fiery intruders into their commerce. In many ports, they were outright unwelcome. Yet still they came.

Capsicum annuum grew robustly in most places, generating themselves in a flood of unstoppable pollination around the world. This ease of sowing reaped a cheap way to add taste and nutrients like Vitamin C to diets even in poor households. They went everywhere. Except where they didn't.

A friend once told me with an air of imparting an unsavory secret that people in poor countries used them to mask rotten meat. There's more to the story. It's obvious that nothing much can mask the taste and aroma of rotten meat, not to mention the fact that people would sicken and, if further reasons are needed, that many people in poverty would never have had the budget for meat in any case at any time. My friend's little tidbit of superiority was a reaction to the "foreign" idea of piquant foods. In fact, it was not inferior meat, inferior culture, and dead taste buds that kept chilies at bay. After consideration, it's unsurprising that it was profit that did it. State authorities and merchants making a satisfying living selling harder-to-get and more expensive spices stepped in when it appeared that the chili would make itself at home in their ports.

As any newcomer to a land can attest, the port of arrival can make a distinct difference. This was no less true as chili made its appearance. In Portugal, chilies were said to be brought via a sailor named d'Aveiro around the same time as Columbus brought his first new spice samples from the New World, Stephen Smith says in "In the Shadow of a Pepper-centric Historiography." People accepted the chili eagerly and began cultivating it. But behind the scenes, Portuguese merchants and government authorities were alarmed. I imagine groups of men standing around with furrowed brows. They did more than fret, though: they apparently took action.

The Indian and East Asian spice market that the Portuguese monopolized at the time was in decline in both Lisbon and Antwerp as shipping fleets, victorious in snatching the spice trade away from the Arabs, brought back more spices from India than were in immediate demand. Concern for profit turned fierce. A glut of tasty tidbits had caused the price of prized black pepper to plunge from 40 to 20 ducats a quintal between 1500 and 1505, according to Smith. The British Crown took documented measures against other threatening substitutes, pimiento de rabo or African cubeb pepper, for example. Almost certainly what was done about capsicum was more than just hand-wringing.

Researchers say that merchants and state authorities in Portugal made chili peppers the target of sweeping extermination, and the sailor d'Aveiro was dismissed from his post. These actions undoubtedly stamped out chili in Portugal for some time and halted the spread of capsicum into many European countries until the mid-sixteenth century. These were key years in cultural and culinary blueprinting.

There was a different reception for the diminutive chili pepper in Spain, also based on trade and commerce concerns. The Spaniards had everything to

Green chilies.

be gained economically from promoting a new pepper that would remove the massive annual national cost of importing expensive spices from other countries. Chili was, indeed, cheap and easy to sow in vegetable gardens or pots. In Spanish ports, chilies became common. Nicolás Monardes, writing in 1565, notes that hot peppers could be found in stews and soups and had a stronger taste than the common pimiento: "The sole difference is that while that of the Indies costs many ducats; the other one costs only the effort of sowing it."

The chili pepper was indeed a kind of savior for the poor, and for this it gained a reputation as the poor man's food. As late as the eighteenth century (or modern-day Missouri, for that matter, when the chili is disparaged as a way to mask rancid meat), Vincenzo Corrado's *Il Cuoco Galante* dismissed peppers as "vile and rustic."

In India, where chili has added its flavor profile to an enormous number of culinary specialties, it's odd to think that it has not always been on the subcontinent. But since the Portuguese were unlikely to sell spices, such as the sought-after black pepper, long pepper, and ginger, at expensive rates to those who were already cultivating them, the captains of commerce left the chili to emerge unmolested out of the sea captains' ships. It went everywhere. Especially in southern Indian cuisine, the heat was on.

Indian food historian K. T. Achaya writes that chili was not mentioned at all by the botanist and doctor Garcia de Orta in 1563, and not one recipe of over fifty in the 1590 *Ain-i-Akbari*, a sixteenth-century text written in Persian detailing the workings of the Mughal court of Akbar, uses anything except black pepper to impart pungency. Linguistics, often a place to ferret out foreign influences—including impostor foods from afar—shows that once chili came in, the words for it in many Indian languages were simple extensions of those for black pepper; adding on to a known word indicates foreignness.

In Bengali, the older term for black pepper is gol (round) mirch or kalo (black) longca (pepper), while chili pepper is kānhcā (raw, green) mirch or kānhcā longca. In the case of red chili, it's lal (red) longca. In Hindi, kali mirch is the term for black pepper and hari mirch for chili pepper. Tamil: milagu (black pepper) and milagai (chili pepper). In Peru today, there are likely three hundred varieties of chili, maybe fifty-plus in common use, and all with explicit names and flavor profiles used to balance specific cuisine choices.

The Portuguese, chilies in tow, came to India by sea around the Cape of Good Hope, and though this had been tried by Europeans for centuries, it took the Portuguese sailors' navigational knowledge and maybe a bit of luck to get it right. They had failed before. In 1492, Christopher Columbus set out to reach Asia only to stumble onto another world. Still, the Portuguese King João II (1455–1495), in order to wrest the enticing spice business away from Arab traders, had made reaching Asia by sea a national priority. In what must have been a relief for the royal coffers, in 1498 the Portuguese sailor Vasco da Gama rounded that elusive African continental point and reached Calicut on India's Malabar Coast, an already-thriving port where Arab, Indian, and Chinese merchants had exchanged spices, cloth, and luxury goods for centuries.

As Lizzie Collingham writes in *Curry*, the Portuguese relationship with the king of Calicut was not at first a success. The goods they brought—"cloth, a dozen coats, six hats, some coral, six basins, a bale of sugar, and two barrels each of butter, probably rancid from the long journey, and of honey"—were amusements for the wealthy court. Nevertheless, though departing under a cloud, Vasco da Gama's ship was loaded with pepper bought for 3 ducats per hundredweight. In Europe, even with falling prices, the price fetched was 22 ducats per hundredweight, a handsome profit, guaranteeing that the Portuguese would be back.

Within three years, they were. And again and again they came and left bearing full loads. In 1505, ships captained under Lopo Soares de Albergaria left India bearing 1,074,003 kilograms of pepper, 28,476 kilograms of ginger, 8,789 kilograms of cinnamon, and 206 kilograms of cardamom.

In Goa, the Portuguese went further, establishing Europe's first base in the Indian subcontinent in 1510 by seizing the region from the sultan of Bijapur and making it the capital of their Estado da Índia. Unlike other empires that came to the subcontinent, content mostly with making money and not changing culture, the Portuguese forcibly converted residents to Christianity with an Inquisition that persecuted "heretics" while running amok themselves. As Colleen Taylor Sen says in *Feasts and Fasts: A History of Food in India*, they kept vast retinues of retainers and slaves, maintained harems, chewed betel nut, drank arrack, and more.

The Portuguese port at Goa came to be a hub for their forts and factories extending from Brazil to Japan. They established trading posts not only along India's west coast but at opposite ends of the country along the Gulf of Cambay and the Coromandel Coast as well as in Bengal. To enforce their control, Lizzie Collingham notes in *Curry*, they protected their forts with a fleet of one hundred ships.

The items coming off the ships from the Americas affected foods on the coast and radiated out through the country. It is not known exactly when chilies arrived, but thirty years after Vasco da Gama's first landing in Calicut, there were at least three types of Latin American chili plants growing around the Portuguese enclave of Goa. These hot stuffs likely came from Brazil via Lisbon, and they quickly spread without check. In all, four or five species of chili entered India, but *Capsicum annuum*, its residue found in layers of sediment deep in the earth in Tehuacán, Mexico, was the most dominant.

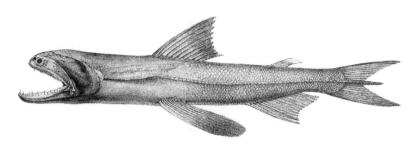

Bombay duck, lote or bummalo.

~~~~~~

All the history in the world cannot describe the taste of chilies. I visit Bela Rani Devi both for a cooking session and to get a sense of how chilies balance foods in her home region in what is now Bangladesh. The chili seed came blazing from the southwest port of Goa through the central states of India and to the northeast to settle into many bright dishes there. Everyone tells me, from my neighbor to the people I am interviewing, that East Bengali and Bangladeshi cooks have superior skills and techniques. Now I get to watch those in action.

Bela Rani Devi's daughter, Sima Bhattacharjee, and I go by Uber to her mother's house. As the car stops and starts with traffic, I do my best to find a steady horizon to watch, which always helps me avoid the plague of car sickness. It's not possible here with the many buildings and swerving traffic, and after forty-five minutes I am ready to reach the house.

It's a warm welcome there and an inviting home. The people in the entrance make it more so: family members Soumee Bhattacharya, Kakali and Sourasish Nath, and Diya and Gargi Banerjee as well as helper Priyo Bala Baral come together to talk food.

Born in Chattagram, Bangladesh, Bela Rani Devi came to this house at seventeen years old in 1960, and it is her domain. Inside, we gather in a sitting-cum-bedroom and talk for a moment. The younger family members smile and speak to me in English, the older women in Bengali. There is an effervescent quality in the air, inquisitive looks, and a warm feeling of family.

I learn that Bela Rani was homeschooled in her conservative family and began cooking at age nine. We go into the kitchen, and there I see banana leaves stacked near the stove. Taking this as a very good sign, I smile. I try out a few phrases in Bengali, relaxed enough to chuckle at how poorly I do, and because of this I do not do so very poorly after all.

We make Bombay duck, lote—*Harpadon nehereus* or bummalo from the lizardfish family—and because of the word "lizard" I peer closely at the bowl. My face is smoothed intentionally, trying to look interested and not squeamish. What can be said about this sorry fact is that I was raised in the Midwest of the U.S. and other than eating, very occasionally, trout or catfish, I am not fish-savvy. Plus, the word "lizard" is pinging around inside my head.

The fish is fleshy, wobbly in the bowl, and so tender that it falls apart easily after cooking. Bummalo makes irregular living choices along the Indian coast, and for this reason fishermen consider it strange. Though named for Bombay—now Mumbai—and caught off the waters of the state of Maharashtra, it is also caught in the Bay of Bengal and the South China Sea. These facts don't bother me in the least. Why can't a fish have its pick of waters? What niggles at my thoughts is what I know of lizardfish: they are voracious predators. Sometimes they swallow prey two-thirds their own length. And, most alarming, in addition to the regular places they have needle-sharp teeth *on their tongues.*

I sigh. It can't be helped; I will be eating this little monster of a fish. And though it may be a curious thing for a fish to be called Bombay *duck,* this doesn't faze me either. Why not? Nothing to quibble over, really. Language is often a leap of the imagination. It's just that other little thing about *its tongue* that I keep thinking about.

Many times, Bombay duck is dried and salted before it's consumed. Though its meat is not distinctive in flavor, it is extremely odoriferous after drying and is usually transported in airtight containers. None of this comes to mind or nose at Bela Rani's house, though, as I watch the preparations with the fresh version of the fish; an inviting aroma lifts from the pots on her stove and teases my nose.

The fish is washed and cut into small pieces. Bela Rani and her daughter-in-law Kakali heat mustard oil; onions and ginger and garlic are at the ready. Daughter Sima slits nine shiny green chilies and smiles shyly, chuckling politely and a little apologetically as she looks at me; I sense that she is worried that I am worried about the impending heat. The onions are sizzling and soon, moments later it seems, the dish is ready. Fresh cilantro is sprinkled across the top. I am anticipating the taste, but it's not time just yet. The small kitchen space now has three women moving within it, and I step back to see what's happening with the next dish, prawn cake.

Big and broad, bright green and glossy, banana leaves are the perfect vessel for Bela Rani's version of a griddle cake. Only it's a griddle cake like none I've had before. This one, chingri pithe, involves prawns—another king of the waterways—plus coconut and green chilies. It simmers as we talk until magic happens as the women expertly flip the cake using a banana leaf sandwich to nestle the cake onto its other side.

When I make Bombay duck in Missouri, no lote is available at our local grocery store, and so I try the recipe with inch-thick tilapia fillets, and I also try it with carp. A friend tests the recipe with steelhead trout, a sturdy salmon-like fish with a firm texture. The results? While the steelhead is not as soft and tender as Bela Rani's version, it is delicious and holds up well to the spiciness of the sauce. The carp is spot-on for the softness of its texture, though there are bones to dodge. The tilapia makes a good compromise. The dish in both houses is a hit.

Note to self: Next time reduce the chilies to a mere six serrano peppers, and skip the cayenne. Small Thai chilies—bird's eye chilies—with their seeds removed make a very tasty version. Even with adjustments, the aroma lifted in my kitchen just as I remembered. The flavor of the green chilies informed the dish without overpowering it, in a magic trick Indian food can make with the right touch. The soft smiles of the women in Bela Rani's family and their deft hands at work were much missed.

Lote Maacher Jhaal

BOMBAY DUCK

Recipe courtesy of Bela Rani Devi

Serves 3–4

1 pound lote or another soft white fish like tilapia or carp

6 tablespoons or more mustard oil (substitute a milder vegetable oil
if you prefer)

2 large onions, cut in half and thinly sliced

½ inch fresh ginger, mashed to a paste

2 cloves garlic, mashed to a paste

6 green chilies, split (serranos or small Thai chilies work well; Bela used 9)

½ teaspoon turmeric

1 tablespoon Kashmiri mirch powder or paprika or ¼ teaspoon cayenne

1 teaspoon salt or to taste

1 tablespoon cilantro, finely chopped

Cut the fish into 3-inch pieces. Set aside. Heat the oil in a deep-sided frying pan. Add the sliced onions and sauté them until light brown in color. Add the ginger paste, garlic paste, green chilies, turmeric, and Kashmiri mirch powder, paprika, or cayenne. (Kashmiri mirch is a sweeter and milder bright red chili powder grown in Kashmir. If using cayenne like I do, consider starting with ¼ teaspoon.) Mix and fry these until the spices and oil begin to pull away from the sides of the pan, about 10 minutes. Now add the fish pieces. Mix well with the spices and oil and continue to fry for 2–3 minutes on medium heat, being careful not to burn them. The fish will begin to release some of its natural juices. Add salt to taste. With a firm spatula, keep gently stirring and frying until the mixture is nearly dry. Remove from heat and garnish with the cilantro. Serve hot with steamed rice.

Chingri Pithe

SAVORY PRAWN CAKE

Recipe courtesy of Bela Rani Devi

Serves 4

1 ½ cups freshly grated coconut

1 cup uncooked prawns, shelled

1 tablespoon sugar

3 green chilies or to taste (Bela Rani Devi used 4–5), seeds removed

1 teaspoon salt

2 teaspoons turmeric

½ teaspoon black mustard seeds or to taste

½ teaspoon cayenne (optional)

½ cup water for blender, as needed

2 large banana leaves

2 tablespoons vegetable oil

Grind the grated coconut into a fine paste using a mortar and pestle or food processor. Add the prawns, sugar, green chilies, salt, turmeric, mustard seeds, and cayenne to this paste and blend well. (If using a blender, add the water as needed to process the ingredients.) The mixture should be the consistency of a thick batter. Grease the matte (not glossy) side of the banana leaves with the vegetable oil and coat a flat, heavy griddle with the oil as well. Spread the blended coconut-prawn mixture on one of the banana leaves and flatten it to about ¼-inch thick. Place the leaf on the griddle, cover with a lid wide enough to straddle it, and cook on low heat for about 25 minutes. Next move the half-done cake and banana leaf to a plate. Place the second banana leaf on top of the cake, followed by another plate. Flip the cake. Place the now-upside-down cake back on the hot griddle with the fresh banana leaf underneath it.

➤

If banana leaves are not available, a well-oiled pan will work. Flip the cake carefully, using a spatula, and cover as tightly as possible while cooking. Follow all the other instructions.

Continue to cook covered for another 15 minutes on low heat. Remove the griddle from the stove. Transfer the prawn cake carefully and gently to a serving plate—it is delicate and can fall apart easily. Serve hot with rice.

At Bela Rani's house, sitting to eat these delicacies, I notice I am smiling. The nexus of the house seems to be the large four-poster bed in the room we first came through and the table I am now facing, laden with good food. One of the younger family members is sitting for exams in June. Another talks of sports. My perpetually tight shoulders have relaxed by this time, and I nod as I am offered freshly fried luchi, then rice, and accept both. The younger set joins me, and aroma rises from the table. The little salt shaker on the heavily patterned tablecloth is not needed; the chili adds a kick but surprisingly, after seeing the nine shiny additions to the meal, not too much. Before I leave, family members gather in the front room and sing together. Soumee, a noted singer in the family, leads the way, and they sing of beauty that overcomes all darkness.

I am replete.

The curious case of eating what is sometimes too hot to handle happens with chilies over and over. At Bela Rani's house, the chilies were balanced by coconut, by sugar, by oil, and by cilantro. But this delicate touch is not always the case.

Why do humans like hot chilies so much? The science of chili heat goes something like this: the capsaicinoids inside chilies responsible for their heat are concentrated in the peppers' internal ribs and seeds. These capsaicinoids activate the pain receptors in our mouths and tongues in an age-old defense designed to stop animals from devouring the pods. But the lick of pain also releases a mild natural opiate, endorphins, in our nervous system to ease the sting in a heated mixed message.

Usually, I balk at mixed messages. And, right on cue, I get a consular email; **NOREPLY** is in bold at the top. A regular tourist visa, available to thousands of visitors each year, is an option, but I am becoming obstinate. Once, a beloved uncle sent me a family ancestry list going back a minimum of nine hundred years (if you estimate shortish forty-year life spans, longer if not) in Bengal. What is my origin if not Bengal?

When I first applied for the extended ten-year person of Indian origin visa, the voice on the other side of the line seemed confident. I included a notarized letter from my mother explaining that she and my dad were never issued birth certificates. That they no longer had their last Indian passports from sixty-plus years ago. Send my application on, the voice on the phone soothed. It could be worked out, the voice kindly said. Like the chili, I could go east.

The email that opens up today says I cannot go east. Or at least I cannot go with the particular visa for people of Indian origin. I sigh, then gear up to excavate further.

Early ship documents and trade receipts literally never mention the chili, though more expensive spices are detailed carefully. I think about being the unmentioned cargo for my parents: at the time they moved to the U.S., children were routinely listed on their mother's passport, not their father's. This is proved when, hope surging, we find my father's 1964 passport and see that under "children" there is a slash through the page. Though I was born in 1962, there is no evidence of me on his passport pages. I am not there.

~~~~~~

In India, the bhut jolokia, or ghost chili, or Naga chili after a northeastern Indian tribe that has long eaten them has no early paperwork either, but its super-hot profile gave it entry everywhere. Identified as the hottest chili in the world for a time, its heat was first measured by a military laboratory in the town of Tezpur in northeastern India at 855,000 SHU. Chilies are measured in Scoville Heat Units—SHU—named for the American chemist Wilbur Scoville, who invented the scale in 1912. Pure capsaicin measures 16 million SHU. A sweet bell pepper typically measures zero. Italian peperoncino measures about 500 SHU. Thai chilies come in at around 100,000 SHU. After the Chile Pepper Institute in New Mexico finally got enough seeds to grow bhut jolokia and measure its heat, it rang their clocks at over 1 million SHU and got everyone's attention.

Bhut jolokia is not from South America, at least not recently. Did chilies boomerang across the world, starting in India and migrating across expanses to South America only to come back again? Scientists think not: the genus *Capsicum* in general seems to have emerged from the region bordered by southern Brazil, Boliva, Paraguay, and northern Argentina. But then how to explain tribes in northeastern India that have used bhut jolokia since time immemorial as a dietary spice, as a cure for certain illnesses, as a punishment, or as a form of tear gas during war with neighboring tribes? Pre-Columbian migration of pungent chili, its seeds perhaps dispersed by birds, from its nexus in South America to India seems likely and is increasingly documented. Stone carvings of maize ears in Mysore, India, indicate that there was movement of plants and people across the Pacific prior to Europe's knowledge of the Western Hemisphere, and Mongoloians from northeastern Asia, believed to have migrated to the Western Hemisphere during the last ice age, would have discovered chili growing wild. The cultivation and use of chili were mentioned as a remedy for consumption in India's *Vamana Purana*, dated between the sixth and eighth century, well before Columbus. Could this be another case of something being foreign until it was not?

In countries that have had the chili as part of their cuisine for centuries, it's not just the heat that is important but how capsicum can enhance the flavors of other ingredients. How it can make layers of flavor balance and sync. In the case of Kashmiri mirch, the chili's ability to add a deep rich red color to every dish without much heat is beloved. In Peru or Bolivia and throughout South America, in addition to domesticated plants, wild chilies still grow. In markets, a myriad of shapes and colors of capsicum are on offer: curved red ones and green ones, tiny ones and bell-shaped ones, pea-shaped ones and heart-shaped ones, chilies with bumps and nodes, chilies sporting smooth yellow skins or purple skins or black or lime green skins in all textures, so many varieties, in fact, that there can be no doubt they were foreign everywhere else. Until they weren't.

Chapter Five

YOU SAY ALOO,
I SAY BATATA, ER, POTATO

No, no, potatoes have always been ours.
—Vegetable seller, Desapriya Park, Kolkata, 2019

WHEN NAWAB WAJID ALI SHAH was ousted from Lucknow by the ambitions of Lord Dalhousie, governor-general of British India, he had ruled just shy of nine years. Though he planned to continue on to London to plead his case with Queen Victoria, the last king of Awadh never made the trip due to a combination of a failed uprising in his home city by Begum Hazrat Mahal, who, as his second official wife, could be said to have been a warrior queen, and the outrage in England that the publicity of those events caused. The nawab, though stripped of his lands, brought the traditional hospitality and lip-smacking delicious specialties of his realm to Kolkata.

I can see food as a priority in a move. When I came over for my stay in Kolkata on economy British Airways tickets, tucked into my suitcase were packets of goodies from home—some American candy, chocolate, energy bars. Granted, when the nawab made his Kolkata journey in a steamer, the *General McLeod*, in May 1856, he had a retinue of six hundred cooks, servers, and bearers. As many as six thousand shopkeepers, tailors, moneylenders, and paanwallas from Lucknow followed their king, too. Without a retinue to call my own or a ship, I admit it's hard to see that the nawab and I traveled in any similar way at all.

Except in this one thing: though I ended up giving most of my squirreled-away food to children of friends, taste and flavor were a tangible handclasp from the home I was leaving for a long while, and I made space for them in my luggage.

Though the nawab suffered from betrayal, illness, accusations of mismanagement, greedy colonizers, eventual migration as a deposed king, and twenty-five months imprisoned at Fort William, he initiated a new culinary era in Bengal and a culinary specialty that was lasting. When Wajid Ali Shah added potatoes to his biryani, some say to stretch his newly constricted budget, others say for the novel taste of potato, an iconic dish was born. It's hard to think of potatoes as revolutionary today, but at the time the tuber made an explosive impact. It remains a point of pride across Kolkata.

"You know," a neighbor confides two days after I arrive, dropping her voice, "we have the potato in our biryani." I nod with serious eyes. Yes, this is interesting.

I didn't fully value this culinary history until much later.

As Jayanta Sengupta writes in the collection *Food in Time and Place: The American Historical Association Companion to Food History*, the potato innovation took hold as it and other tastes from the nawab's kitchen spread through the city. Men came to call at his home at Number 11 Garden Reach in Metiabruz, a Kolkata neighborhood built by Europeans along the Hooghly River, and were treated to delights never before experienced at home. The dishes combined the spices of India and the Persian use of nuts, raisins and other dried fruits, saffron, musk, asafetida, and more into a rich fusion. The simple fare—dal, bhat, chorchori—in most Bengali homes paled in comparison to dishes set before visitors at Garden Reach, in addition to other delights such as musical soirees with Lucknow kathak dancing. There were more than culinary tales to tell.

Not long after the arrival of the Awadhi king, the influence of his salons not only gave the men of Kolkata a taste of rich new cuisines to tease the palate, but his tasty foreign dishes led to second kitchens in many homes: one for the men learning about worldly entertainments and rich foods and one for the rest of the household—mainly, women likely unwilling to test the limits of their digestions.

It's hard to imagine Bengali food or most regional foods across India without potatoes today. No aloo posto, potatoes with poppy seeds? No South Indian masala dosai, rice flour crepes with potato filling? Today, for most, potatoes are standard fare in India. But the story of their tardy arrival is noted at sacred places—at the Jagannath Temple in Puri, for instance, not one potato is to be found in the food offered up to the deity six times a day, nor has it been seen for over five hundred years in the temple kitchens. The potato, as a culinary newcomer, is too foreign.

That potatoes were a harbinger of more than gastronomic delights is rather intriguing. Old homes dot the Kolkata cityscape even today with a room downstairs most typically used in its heyday by the men of the household of an evening in imitation of the nawab's convivialities. In one such room I gaze at the walls, graced with forward-for-the-time paintings of women emerging from waterways after filling water jugs, and look again. Though the women are fully clothed, naturally, in cotton saris, these are not typical paintings of women in early Bengal. An early wet T-shirt display made rather more elegant by restraint.

The New World tuber, now embedded in India, was a slow starter at first. Other food crops such as tomatoes, okra, chili peppers, pineapple, papayas, and cashew nuts that came to India in the sixteenth century as a direct result of the Columbian exchange, so named for the extensive movement of food crops, ideas, diseases, and populations following the voyage to the Americas by Christopher Columbus in 1492, assimilated more quickly. Though mainstays today, the papaya and cashew followed the example of the potato and took more time to spread.

In fact, although the Portuguese had brought potatoes to India's western coast in the sixteenth century, it wasn't until the nineteenth century after a

British colonial push that they became known much in places like Bengal. Utsa Ray in *Culinary Culture in Colonial India* writes that the Brits pushed certain crops to bring what they deemed "modern food" to the subject population as a symbol of progress and to re-create a sense of belonging for the colonizers.

The potato, not limited by a slender stalk like wheat or rice, can grow to indefinite weight underground without falling over. Charles Mann says in "How the Potato Changed the World" that a Lebanese farmer dug up a potato in 2008 that weighed nearly twenty-five pounds. It was bigger than his head. Tubers led, many say, to the end of famine in northern Europe by underpinning the ability of peasants to withstand the requisitions of their grain crops by armies passing through. Potatoes, capable of yielding abundantly everywhere, even outside their native Andes, gave European peasants enough calories to avoid starvation and may well have instigated worldwide population surges.

Potatoes overrode resistance to and alarm about their novelty with the help of publications such as John Forster's 1664 *England's Happiness Increased: A Sure and Easie Remedy against All Succeeding Dear Years by a Plantation of the Roots Called Potatoes*. Adam Smith in his 1776 treatise, *An Inquiry into the Nature and Causes of the Wealth of Nations*, claimed that should all laborers be fed a diet of potatoes, public happiness would increase. And there was the juicy kernel: as an embodiment of happiness, the potato was a tool to justify the supposed moral right of the British to rule India. Underlying the lofty affirmation of happiness, however, the colonizers banked on the fact that potatoes could cheaply feed laborers.

Tubers, it turns out, led the charge to empire, according to historian William McNeill in "How the Potato Changed the World's History": "By feeding rapidly growing populations, [potatoes] permitted a handful of European nations to assert dominion over most of the world between 1750 and 1950." In other words, the potato fueled the rise of the West.

While today it is the fifth most important crop worldwide, after wheat, corn, rice, and sugar cane, the potato was startling and a bit scary in the eighteenth century—it was poisonous, it was an aphrodisiac, it was pig food, it was famine food, among other claims. Sir Francis Drake, in 1580, is said, falsely, to have introduced potatoes into England along with his other booty when he returned from his famous circumnavigation of the earth. In 1853, a sculpture was erected in Offenburg, Germany, portraying the English explorer gazing toward the horizon with his right hand resting on the hilt of his sword, his left hand gripping a potato plant. The plaque at the base of his feet read, "Sir Francis Drake, / disseminator of the potato in Europe / in the Year of Our Lord 1586. / Millions of people / who cultivate the earth / bless his immortal memory."

This questionable claim—no tuber would have survived his two-year journey home intact enough to spawn—was pulled down with the statue by the Nazis in early 1939. But the aims of colonialism, as well as Enlightenment theories on happiness, held the imagination. The East India Company began to heavily promote the potato among Indian peasants.

It became an obsession. Seed potatoes were given away in Bengal, and in Bombay the potato was exempted from transit taxes. The East India Company handed out 100 rupees to reward peasants who grew potatoes. It held contests for the best potato with a 40-rupee and silver medal prize.

Already in Europe, the potato had finally accomplished what grains had not: it had created for the first time a continent that could feed itself. Hunger was familiar between the seventeenth and eighteenth centuries in Europe with country dwellers experiencing upward of forty nationwide famines and perhaps numerous more local ones. England, historian Fernand Braudel says, had seventeen devastating famines between 1523 and 1623. Potatoes changed all that for Europe, at least until the blight of 1845–49 arrived, as small farmers could avert starvation with their potato fields even when their grain crops were requisitioned. Political and economic leaders alike understood that potatoes could fuel their aspirations, which may have, um, added urgency to the happiness assertions of Enlightenment thinkers.

I slice wedges out of a thin-skinned Yukon Gold potato for bati chorchori in my Missouri kitchen. The knife splays gold-toned starchy flesh into sections that rock a little on the cutting board. A moist sliver of potato flies off the chopping block and lands on the counter. Hello there, food, I murmur until I catch myself, then retrieve the small deviant. I am practicing making this simple dish—wedges of potatoes, chopped tomatoes, onions, green chilies, mustard oil, salt, and nigella seeds—because for the first time I am being filmed while cooking. The U.S. consulate's American Center in Kolkata has put together a program, *Adda Bites*, featuring a discussion about historic food trails between Ranjini Guha, University of Calcutta assistant professor and food blogger, and me on Facebook Live. "Adda," the Bengali term for convivial conversation, is warm and inviting in tone. We are attempting this via technology, spread out across the world due to the pandemic. They tell us after it's scheduled that we will also cook on camera.

"If I turn this way, can you see the ingredients?" I ask, peering into the digital screen that holds the faces of technical people in Kolkata and Ranjini in her home kitchen. The potatoes are oblivious to my maneuvers, their shape familiar and steadfast; I decide they will not trip me up.

I research the potato for the talk and learn that the simple tuber affected how the entire world handles agriculture to this day. Though the International Potato Center in Peru identifies nearly five thousand varieties of potato—each Andean village often planted ten or more favorites based on elevation and taste and texture preferences—the handful of varieties taken to Europe by the Spaniards during the Columbian exchange ended up creating what we know today as monoculture farming. Since the potato is cultivated not from seeds like many plants but from pieces of tuber, the resulting plants are clones.

Not knowing this, potato advocates like the Frenchman Antoine-Augustin Parmentier, who survived the Seven Years' War in relatively good health due to eating potatoes while he was held five times in Prussian prisons, encouraged huge fields of exact replicas. He did more: Parmentier so loved potatoes that he set up publicity stunts, including one, Charles Mann says in *Smithsonian* magazine, that Thomas Jefferson attended as a guest. Jefferson was so delighted by one of Parmentier's potato recipes that he introduced French fries to America.

All this potato enthusiasm completely changed the fates of millions of French fry–eating teenagers in the U.S. and, arguably, had an even deeper effect on world agriculture. In 1840, when chemist Justus von Liebig published his findings that plants depend on nitrogen for growth and health and suggested guano as an excellent source of it, all European and American potato-growing eyes turned to the Chincha Islands off the coast of Peru.

The three tiny Chincha Islands were home to millions of nesting seabirds and few predators, and guano was feet deep everywhere—nearly two hundred feet deep. Elsewhere, frequent rains washed out the all-important nitrogen but not on the rainless Chinchas. The Smithsonian Museum archives has photos of men mining guano while standing on huge mountains of dried excrement. Other photos show thousands of pelicans, guanay cormorants, and boobies minding their own business.

Once farmers tried out the substance and their yields doubled and tripled, the private business of seabirds became very public. The pressure was on. Peru exported 13 million tons of guano over the next forty years, but it wasn't enough, or it was too expensive, or there were other complaints that led to whispers of war and threats of legal action. In fact, the U.S. passed the 1856 Guano Islands Act on official letterhead of the Thirty-Fourth Congress of the United States of America. It was a land grab of any island that had seabird guano on it, as long as there were no other claims or inhabitants, to ensure that U.S. farmers got first rights to guano, Paul Johnston notes in "The Smithsonian and the 19th-Century Guano Trade: This Poop Is Crap." The U.S. Navy got involved, too, in testing guano from other places to see what land should be grabbed. Two hundred guano islands were claimed in the nineteenth and early twentieth centuries.

The Guano Question was fraught: before intensive fertilization, European living standards were roughly equivalent to those in Cameroon today, Charles Mann says. Potatoes in partnership with seabirds burst billions out of poverty. For the first time, agriculture formed an addiction to high-intensity fertilizer that it hasn't shaken since.

The agricultural revolution started by the potato, along with its guano sidekick, was susceptible to disease—a water mold called *Phytophthora infestans*, a blight resulting in mass migrations out of Ireland and ghastly human suffering, and the Colorado potato beetle, originally from south-central Mexico, both spelled trouble. The brilliant orange beetle, following in the wake of the Columbian exchange of foodstuffs and animals, ended up encountering those vast monocultures of potato planted for the happiness of all. In fact, in the 1860s, it burst everyone's bubble in a big way around the Missouri River, not far from where I live today.

When they were confronted by a buffet of fields of genetically similar plants, Charles Mann writes, the beetles spread in such numbers that by the time they reached, via railroad cars and steamships, the U.S. Atlantic coast, they carpeted beaches and made train tracks slippery and impassable. Desperate farmers tried everything; one farmer threw emerald green paint over infested plants. The Paris green color was made from arsenic and copper and surprised everyone by working. Farmers diluted it with flour and dusted it on their potatoes or mixed it with water and sprayed it.

Then the chemists stepped in and agriculture took another significant turn, this time to modern pesticide use. By the 1880s, a French researcher discovered that they could dispense with diluted paint and that spraying a solution of copper sulfate and lime would kill *P. infestans*. Both the beetle and the blight were done for. Until the beetles began showing signs of immunity and then growers had to use ever-greater quantities of the newest variant, calcium arsenate, then DDT, and each time the beetles adapted. By the mid-1980s, a new pesticide was good for about one planting. In 2009, the potato blight wiped out most of the tomatoes and potatoes on the East Coast of the U.S. This was one foreigner that would not be assimilated.

Disease is far from my mind as I inhale the aroma of a plate of Kolkata biryani. I realize as I gaze contemplatively, my eyes trained on the potato peeking out from under my rice, that Wajid Ali Shah's addition of potato to classic biryani is still of note. Across India, whenever the topic of biryani comes up, I am told that Kolkata's version includes the tuber. This happened in Delhi, in Kochi, in Darjeeling, and in Bodh Gaya anytime I mentioned that I was living in Kolkata. Waiters would impart this as an aside once they heard my American accent; Uber drivers, too, explained it.

Cooking rice with meat, popularly associated with Mughlai food, is a historic synthesis of delicately flavored Persian pilau and the pungent, spicy rice dishes of Hindustan. Lizzie Collingham writes in *Curry: A Tale of Cooks and Conquerors* that the Persian technique of marinating meat in yogurt married the onions, garlic, almonds, and spices of India to make the notably thick meat marinade of biryani. After the marinated meat is briefly fried, as with pilau, partially cooked rice is heaped over it, saffron soaked in milk is poured over the rice, and the whole dish is covered tightly and cooked slowly, Collingham notes. Kolkata's version with potatoes and eggs hones it further: it is multidimensional in flavor, and it's tasty enough that you'll need restraint.

On a quest to talk with cooks about this dish and to taste it, I soon intentionally open conversations asking about biryani. I do this at markets, in a movie hall I visit, in a bookstore. Other than a startled look or two, most people are happy to talk about food in Bengal. I hear about the Royal Indian Hotel restaurant near the Nakhoda Masjid and its branch near College Street in Kolkata that is run by descendants of a chef for Wajid Ali Shah. I hear there are a thousand restaurants in the city that serve it. I hear chefs offer special Lucknow versions on their rooftops for invited guests. My mouth waters thinking about it. I hear about a traditional Bengali restaurant, Kewpies, in south-central Kolkata that I must visit. My ears perk up. The owner, Rakhi Purnima DasGupta, is the daughter of Minakshie DasGupta, the author of *Bangla Ranna*, the book that arrived at my Missouri farm and opened up possibilities about my grandmother's elusive green mango chutney recipe for me.

Deeply intrigued, I go in search of the perfect dish of slow-cooked rice, potatoes, and more. In Rakhi's cozy sitting room, upstairs from Kewpies, we talk about food in Bengal. Near my home in Missouri, Kewpies is the name of the high school mascot, little mentioned in my world otherwise. The Kewpie doll was created by Rose O'Neill, born in 1874 in the Missouri Ozarks, who rose to great heights illustrating for magazines such as *Ladies' Home Journal*, *Good Housekeeping*, and more, where she was the only female illustrator. Her sweet little cherub, the Kewpie, a child's pronunciation of "cupid," though meek on the surface, was shown carrying banners in the magazines of the day in support of the National American Woman Suffrage Association (Give Mother the Vote!) in 1914 and 1915, among other feats of derring-do. Rakhi tells me that Kewpie was her mother's nickname.

Kewpies in Kolkata was a pioneer in offering authentic and traditionally served Bengali food, before all the newer establishments heralded that specific food lineage, and it has a gamut of Bengali favorites: daab chingri (prawns cooked in tender coconut shell), ilish bhape (slow-cooked hilsa fish), doi begun or potol (eggplant or Bengal's favorite squash in a savory yogurt sauce), the regional aromatic rice Gobindobhog with choices of dals and chutneys, and much more. Bengali food, Rakhi says, is a delicate cuisine. One to savor.

"It's slow food. It's not something you mix," Rakhi says. Each sauce, each gravy, for lack of just the right word, is separately spiced, separately tasted on the tongue.

She pulls out a few old recipe books from her mother's collection. One, the *Anglo Indian Cookery Book* by Mrs. Dora Limond, reveals "Bengali sweets and other useful items." Another is loose in its binding and so fragile that its pages have brown edges and holes. "It's one of the first Bengali cookbooks written in English, and I don't even know who wrote it." Though the publishing date and author's name have been eaten away, the title appears to be *Indian Cookery and Confectionary*. Rakhi peers more closely. "Here's kheer with oranges, achar of mangoes, things we still do. But this one is so unlike Bengal."

I lean forward. "Hilsa roasted with meat." The traditional hilsa fish of Bengal is not typically combined with meat in current times. "It's sort of a British quasi Bengali dish," Rakhi says. "Oh, you have to see this one." We both bend closer.

The pages have instructions on how to treat your servants, advising you that they will all steal from you, which elicits a gruff laugh from Rakhi as the racist implication is clear. "It tells you how to pronounce pullao." One heading, "Ordinary and Approved Recipes from Every Department of Cookery," tries for authority; another explains which rice variety is consumed at breakfast, tiffin, and dinner.

The potato was assimilated easily into Bengal, Rakhi says. "Why? Two things: it was cheap, and the land was fertile. The potato was filling, and as my mother would say when, say, three more guests would drop by—she would tell the cook, add two more potatoes. Potatoes have always been a stretcher."

Rakhi brings out her book-in-progress, *Eating Kolkata*, and I gulp at the massive collection. A life's work. She graciously shares her recipe for chicken biryani. I flip through the pages and see that she is particular with spices, allowing enough for aroma and flavor but careful not to overwhelm any dish.

The length of the biryani recipe is intimidating, but it unfolds simply enough if your ingredients are handy. It needs a bit of time. The rosewater and the screw pine essence give Rakhi's recipe panache, a mark of a chef who cares about the rich history of her recipe. But I find when I don't have those ingredients in Missouri that the dish is still delicious, though less multidimensional. I have made this without having the blade of mace on hand. I have substituted butter for ghee. Still delightful, I promise.

I took a cooking class with Rakhi before I left Kolkata, joining a discriminating Japanese chef, and the array of pots and concoctions she laid out—tiny deep cinnamon-red clay pots filled with various spices, white onions, black cloves, a plush pile of fresh vegetables—was like a painting. The assortment was a palette of color and flavor, and Rakhi's smile lit up the room.

Calcutta-Style Chicken Biryani

Recipe courtesy of Chef Rakhi Purnima DasGupta, Kewpies, Kolkata

Serves 4–5

2 cups Basmati rice

3–3 ½ pounds whole chicken, cut into 8–10 pieces

1 teaspoon saffron strands

½ cup warm milk

1 teaspoon screw pine essence

2 tablespoons rosewater

2–3 tablespoons ghee

4 medium potatoes, peeled, halved, and fried in ghee until
    browned in spots and about half-done

4 eggs, hard-boiled and shelled

6 ½ cups water

1 teaspoon salt

Peanut oil for frying onions

2 medium onions, finely sliced

MARINADE

1 tablespoon ginger, mashed to a paste

1 tablespoon garlic, mashed to a paste

1 teaspoon cayenne

½ teaspoon Kashmiri mirch powder or paprika

½ teaspoon turmeric

1 teaspoon garam masala

Juice of 1 lime

2 tablespoons peanut oil or other vegetable oil

½ cup plain yogurt, whisked

¼ cup heavy cream

1 teaspoon salt

1 teaspoon sugar

3 green cardamom pods

2 bay leaves

4 whole cloves

1 teaspoon black cumin seeds

1 blade mace

1 teaspoon salt

Wash and soak the rice for 20 minutes in cold water. Drain. Set the rice aside to dry. In a large bowl, mix all the ingredients for the marinade together, then add the chicken pieces. Rub the marinade into the chicken and marinate for 30–60 minutes or longer. While the chicken is marinating, soak the saffron in the milk for 3–5 minutes. Mix in the screw pine essence and rosewater. Melt the ghee. Set aside. In a separate pan, fry the sliced onions, drain, crumble, and set aside. In a large deep pot with a tight-fitting lid, simmer the chicken with its marinade for 25–30 minutes or until tender. In the last 10 minutes of cooking time, add the potatoes and eggs, ½ cup of the water, and the 1 teaspoon salt. Gently mix. Once the chicken is cooked through, remove from heat and set aside.

Meanwhile, as the chicken mixture is cooking, in a large pot bring 6 cups of the water to a boil. Tie the whole spices and the salt in a muslin bag and put this into the pot; reduce the heat and simmer for 5–7 minutes. Add the drained rice and boil for about 8–10 minutes or until the rice is three-quarters cooked. Drain the rice well. Remove the spice bag. Next, after the chicken-egg-potato mixture is cooked, place the rice on top of it in the pot. Sprinkle the saffron-milk mixture over the rice. Then pour the melted ghee over the rice. Cover the pot with a tight-fitting lid and cook over low heat for 10–15 minutes or until all the liquid has been absorbed and the rice is cooked through (check by fluffing with a fork). Remove from heat and leave it to rest for 5–10 minutes with the lid on before serving. Mix in the fried onions and serve with raita (see the recipe on page 179) and salad on the side.

Chapter Six

THE ART OF REPLACING

A meal for the Bengali is a ritual in itself even if it is only
boiled rice and lentils (dal bhat), with of course a little fish.
Bengalis, like the French, spend not only a great deal of time
thinking about food but also on its preparation and eating.

—Minakshie DasGupta, *Bangla Ranna*, 1982

THIS IS WHAT HAPPENS in the world. A new thing becomes a blush on the
cheek, an overheated brow, an aroma in the passing wind molding itself
around what has always been. Sometimes this is a form of forgetting. Then
there is history that stands firm. Farah "Flower" Silliman upholds her Jewish
community's history and sees clearly where the wider world of Kolkata meets
it over the table, potatoes included. To showcase Jewish-Bengali food, Flower
has specific dishes in mind.

"I would do a Shabbat meal. On Shabbat we had a hybrid called aloo
makallah. Aloo means 'potato' in Hindi and makallah means 'fried' in Arabic.
So it's fried potatoes, but they're fried very, very slowly so the outside is hard
and crusty and brown and the inside is soft. Even the Jews of Bombay never
knew about it until they ate it here and took it there."

The dish, now popular in many parts of the world, because "anybody who knows about it, anybody who's had it, wants to eat it again," was slow-cooked small whole potatoes eaten with plaited Jewish challah bread and Indian pullao during Flower's well-populated Shabbat meals. For a second course, the kitchen would send out yellow rice and a chicken stew with either beets or okra in it and sometimes mahashe, an Arabic word that means "stuffed," much like a Turkish dolma.

"We stuff tomatoes, eggplants, vine leaves—lettuce leaves here because we can't get vine leaves—beet root leaves, and cabbage with chicken and rice and bake them." The stuffed vegetables are spiced with ginger, garlic, salt, and tamarind, though lemon can be used. The dishes all have a distinctive sour note. It seems a hybridity itself, albeit an old one, that the sourness central to Flower's Baghdadi Jewish dishes is obtained from lemons or tamarinds, the citrus a plant of India, the tamarind a transplant from Africa many centuries ago. There are other hybrid clues. Flower uses ginger, which wasn't available in Iraq in early times; they used mint.

"So that's what I would make. I would make aloo makallah, Jewish roast chicken, and I would make hilbeh, which is very Yemenite. It's a sauce, eaten all over the Middle East."

Flower tells me that the potatoes were fried so crisp that if you tried to eat them with a fork and knife, they jumped off the plate—hence they are sometimes called jumping potatoes. The trick is choosing the right potatoes. She specifically says that the potatoes for her recipe are best three or four months old and never frozen—"Ask for potatoes used for chips or French fries"—but I am at a loss to find these in Missouri. I buy new potatoes, sensing that if I can't get the stored potatoes she preferred, fresh might be best. Even without the proper aging, the potatoes were delightful and hard to resist. If you are a meat eater, Flower suggests you serve this with roast chicken and her special hilbeh chutney.

Aloo Makallah

SLOW-FRIED POTATOES

Recipe courtesy of Flower Silliman

Serves 5–6

1 tablespoon salt

1 tablespoon turmeric

20 potatoes the size of very large eggs, peeled

4–6 cups vegetable oil, enough to cover the potatoes

Heat a large pan of water. Add the salt and turmeric to the water once it is boiling. Add the potatoes and cook only until the water comes back to a boil. Drain and cool. Heat the oil in a large wok or heavy pan. When hot, add the drained potatoes so that the oil covers them and continue cooking, rarely stirring, until the potatoes form a thin yellow crust. Turn off the heat and leave the potatoes in the oil. When cold, use a skewer to prick three to four holes in each potato. One hour before serving, put the wok or pan with the oil and potatoes on low heat and allow them to come to a boil, stirring gently. Turn up the heat to high for the last 20 minutes as the potatoes brown. When brown and crisp, drain and serve hot with hilbeh. The potatoes should be crisp, not soggy. The oil can be reused.

Hilbeh

FENUGREEK-CILANTRO CHUTNEY

Recipe courtesy of Flower Silliman

Makes approximately 1 cup

Flower's hilbeh chutney, made from ground fenugreek seeds, cilantro, and chilies, is mixed with lemon juice, ginger, and garlic. "If you eat it in Egypt or in Yemen, will be a grayish green color; it will not have chilies, and it will not have ginger because those two things were not available there," Flower says. "When we came here, we brought the original with us, we added chilies, we added ginger, and we added cilantro. It makes it a bright green color. Far more tasty."

2 tablespoons fenugreek seeds

1 cup fresh cilantro

1 tablespoon ground ginger

1 tablespoon garlic, mashed to a paste

4–6 green chilies

3–4 tablespoons lemon juice

½–1 teaspoon salt

Soak the fenugreek seeds overnight in water. In a blender, grind together the cilantro, ginger, garlic paste, chilies, lemon juice, and salt, adding water to make a smooth paste. When well blended, add the soaked seeds without their water and continue grinding until smooth. Taste the mixture and adjust the spices. The sauce thickens as it stands, so you may need to whisk in more water or lemon juice if you eat it later. The end result should be a thick sauce.

Entering Flower's living room, near La Martiniere school, is like being drawn into a deep cavern: cool and dim with interesting textures. The walls are dappled with art and the floors are the wonderfully smooth traditional red oxide cement found in older homes in Bengal and elsewhere in India. The latticed front windows allow stippled sunlight about twenty feet inside to touch the patterned carpets and low chairs. Everything has a comfortable air.

Flower and her daughter, the author Jael Silliman, seem an extension of their home of high ceilings and warm shadows, and I'm drawn in by their talk of exotic Friday feasts, sailing ships, sea journeys, spices, and fezzes—tales as deep and rich as the city surrounding their home.

Their building, constructed spaciously as residency apartments for pre-independence British burra saabs—big bosses—of Calcutta sits among several newer, sharper-lined edifices on the lane, many of which now expand to fill almost all the land behind their walls. But the Sillimans' building, fading and chipping on the outside, still has open space around the back after you enter the gates. Inside the building's age-darkened front doors, a staircase that clings to the wall has varying degrees of angle to its steps. The elevator is the old kind with levers and a sliding door that clicks shut. The ride is smooth as silk.

When I set out to find how the heritage foods of Bengal evolved over time, the essential question became, Whose heritage? Kolkata, long a confluence of people from many lands, has a history of communities—Mughals, Armenians, Portuguese, Dutch, Jews, Hindu Bengalis, Muslim Bengalis, East Bengalis, Chinese, Britishers, Anglo-Indians, and more—that left their trace in the tastes of the city.

In the Sillimans' home, I found the flavors of Jewish Asia that were birthed in colonial port cities such as Rangoon and Shanghai as well as Calcutta, the eighteenth-century hub of the British Empire. Flower's family, descendants of the Baghdadi Jewish community, came to India from Basra in the late nineteenth century; her husband's family arrived earlier, in the 1790s, from Aleppo, Syria, with trading networks, both ancient and medieval, already in place. Like other traders of the day, such as the Armenians, Greeks, and Portuguese drawn to the contact zone of colonial power and local culture, they were poised to become integral to the capitalist days of the Raj.

The community flourished around three synagogues—Neveh Shalome, Maghen David, and Beth-El—the Jewish Girls' School, the Elias Meyer School, and a cemetery in Narkeldanga built in the 1830s. Flower, born in 1930, enjoyed the cultural rituals and foods revolving around these Jewish community spaces growing up. They made, apart from traditional matzo for holy days, their own kosher wines and a lovely vinegar from its residue.

"They don't make it anymore." Flower says this matter-of-factly. "Nobody here to buy the wines or make the wines." Her voice drops low at the thought of never having the special vinegar again. "It was almost a malt. Like a balsamic." Over her lifetime, Flower has borne witness to the Jewish community's heyday of about 5,000 strong in the city after World War II, when Jewish refugees fled from Burma and other nations, to a "norm" of about 3,000 for many years, to just a handful today.

In the eighteenth, nineteenth, and twentieth centuries, the Baghdadi Jewish (a liturgical lineage term much like the term "Roman Catholic") diaspora stretched from Baghdad to Shanghai to London, in one sense spanning a trail similar to the potato. Jael Silliman writes in *Jewish Portraits, Indian Frames: Women's Narratives from a Diaspora of Hope* that theirs was a migration not of loss, as the story is told of much of Jewish history, but of a flourishing interconnected world. Many of the early traders, like Flower's grandfather, took spices to the West and brought goods from the Middle East to Calcutta and further ports; other families dealt in indigo and opium (laudanum in its oral tincture), both in demand by the Raj.

Though there were not many Calcutta stops at first, Flower's grandfather, based in Basra, came to Bombay, then went on to Colombo, Rangoon, Singapore, Jakarta, Surabaya (near Bali), and back, exporting to the Far East the flat-topped and cylindrical fezzes worn by Muslim men worldwide at the time and bringing dried pepper, nutmeg, and more back to the Middle East. "I like connecting these dots. Thinking of how these people did it," Flower says. "No computers. No telephones. No telegraphs. Nothing."

The cities her grandfather lived in for periods of time mirror the commerce route itself. "We have my grandfather's prayer book and in his handwriting inside he writes where all his children were born." Flower's father: Singapore; her aunt: Penang. It was unusual for the time, Flower says, that the family traveled together on their forays into the world of colonialism and commerce. Flower's grandmother, from a family that looked after the burial site of Ezekiel the Prophet in Iraq for 2,000 years or more, came to India in the 1870s at sixteen. She went along on her husband's journeys, which, after her family's stationary life, must have been either exhilarating or completely disorienting.

International flavors originating in these wanderings infuse the Jewish palate: olives and oil from Spain and Portugal; sweet-and-sour stews from the Germans; cucumbers, herrings, butter cakes, and grain rolls called bolas from the Dutch; fish stewed and stuffed from Poland; blintzes from Russia and Romania; buckwheat groats called kasha and puddings called kugels, fruit compotes and preserves, and borscht thin or thick, according to M. F. K. Fisher in *The Art of Eating*. Even with this rich base, the art of substitution out of necessity marks Jewish cuisine throughout the world. The lack of leaven, for instance, in Passover dishes resulted in challenges well met by fine cooks with almond cakes and puddings, matzo and its meal made into dumplings, puddings, and much more. The exciting element in the foods of Jewish Calcutta, Jael Silliman writes, is that very art of replacing.

"Cooking in the Middle East is mostly rice, meats of various kinds—chicken, lamb, and beef," Flower says, "fish not so much because they didn't have too many rivers, and they used very little spice because they had to import their spices from the Far East."

In Flower's kitchen, any issue with spices has been resolved, and bubbling pots with lids set slightly ajar release aromas that prove it. A brisk stir of a ladle sends out hints into the air evocative of past travels. A cookbook Flower wrote, *Three Cups of Flower*, has chapter headings for vegetarian and nonvegetarian

Indian cooking, Far Eastern cooking, Middle Eastern cooking, and Jewish cooking, among others. When I spoke with her, she had just completed an interview for a television program on the curries of India. Her "living foods" segment highlighted Jewish-Bengali food and her deft touch with spice and taste.

Together we make chitanee, a tasty chicken-based sour and slightly hot dish that Flower calls a cross between a curry and sweet-sour chicken, and bamia khatta, a chicken and okra stew, to taste the hybridity of Jewish foods in Bengal. She tells me that bamia khatta is derived from the Iraqi version, probably koubeh, dumplings, with bamia, okra. The Indian version used more ginger and garlic than the original.

Flower sits upon a high stool in her kitchen. Her eyesight has dimmed in recent years, which makes it hard for her to cook, but with Parven Nessa, her cook, at the ready, we walk through the steps.

Chitanee

HOT-SOUR CHICKEN STEW

Recipe courtesy of Flower Silliman

Serves 4–6

1 whole chicken

½ cup vegetable oil

6–8 medium onions, finely chopped

1 tablespoon ground ginger

1 tablespoon ground garlic

6–8 dried red chilies

¼ cup water

2 teaspoons ground coriander

2 teaspoons ground cumin seeds

2 tablespoons pureed tomato

2 tablespoons tamarind paste (or use 8 tablespoons fresh lemon juice)

½ teaspoon salt

1 teaspoon sugar

Cut the chicken into 8 pieces (in this dish, the neck, wings, and giblets may be used, if desired), and remove the skin. Set aside. Heat the oil in a large pot. Add the onions and fry them very slowly until they are soft and light brown, not crispy. Add the ground ginger and garlic and the chilies. Add the water to the ground coriander and cumin seeds and then add this mixture to the onions in the pot to make a gravy. Add the chicken, pureed tomato, tamarind paste, salt, and sugar. Add a very little extra water if needed to keep the mixture from sticking. Cook, covered, until the chicken is tender, about 20–25 minutes. During the last few minutes, uncover the pot to dry up most of the liquid. Serve with rice.

On the way to visit Flower, I stop at the corner chicken seller. He has me point to the live bird I want, and within moments he has grabbed it by its neck, flipped it on its side, and whacked its head off. The meat, when he's done with the rest—removing the feathers, dunking the headless carcass in water to clean it—quivers on the paper he wraps it in. As he hands the package to me, I note the sympathy in his eyes. He had not expected me to watch. He knew the consequences.

Bamia Khatta

CHICKEN AND OKRA STEW

Recipe courtesy of Flower Silliman

Serves 4–6

3 ⅓ pounds whole chicken, cut apart at the joints

2 tablespoons vegetable oil

2 medium onions, chopped

1 tablespoon ginger, mashed to a paste

2 cloves garlic, mashed to a paste

½ teaspoon turmeric

1 pound fresh or frozen okra

2 cups chopped tomatoes

4 tablespoons lemon juice or 1 tablespoon tamarind paste

1 teaspoon salt

1 tablespoon sugar

1 ½ cups water

½ cup chopped mint

Use all the chicken including the back and wings. Heat the oil in a large pot and add the chicken pieces, onions, ginger, garlic, and turmeric. Add enough water to just cover the chicken, and cook slowly until the chicken is soft and the water is almost dried up. Add the okra, tomatoes, lemon juice or tamarind paste, salt, sugar, and water, and continue cooking until the vegetables are done. Add the mint. Season to taste and serve with rice or pullao.

Flower says you can substitute 3 ½ pounds sliced beets or 1 pound cubed white pumpkin for the okra.

After creating the dishes, with all their fresh immediacy, we sit at Flower's table in the kitchen. I hoist myself up on the stool on one side and my feet don't meet the floor, making me realize again that Flower is a tall woman. We eat companionably, my toe occasionally catching the stool's leg, and the utensil sounds softly attest to scoops tasted. Aromas have been rising in the room all afternoon, and now the flavors that emerge fit: piquant, savory, and tangy. The sauces use ginger, chilies, and tamarind, ingredients spanning the world—India, Mexico—and ideas—Jewish, Bengali—that span cultures. All this in the pots and the conversations in Flower's kitchen.

Flower's cookbook reflects these dishes and more: Far Eastern salads made from papaya, peanut satay curries, Bengali sweets such as rasamalai and gulab jamun, honey cake for Rosh Hashanah, the Israeli version of the North African spiced tomato and egg shakh shoukha, 298 recipes in all that document her family story in the tastes of cultures they were open to, in code. The foods showcase the Jewish tradition of artful substitutions with Kolkata at its vortex.

Despite the difficulty with communication in early times, Jewish cultural connections superseded Indian ones in Kolkata. The community's web of relationships made it possible to depend on each other for religious, financial, and social support even over great distances, Jael Silliman writes. Travel for Flower's mother meant a visit to another Jewish home in the port her husband was heading to; other traveling Jewish families stayed with her in her home in Kolkata. Looking at a plate of food at a typical Friday Shabbat meal at the Sillimans reveals a story of this intimate cultural exchange. Flavors, alike across the world yet infused with locally available ingredients, are its hallmark.

My own mother did a version of this where I was raised in Pittsburg, Kansas, making mustard fish and other typical dishes out of locally available fish, not hilsa from the waters of Bengal. But, for me, unlike the interconnected world of Jewish Asia, leaving India with my parents in 1963 seemed like crossing an unbridgeable gulf.

Visits every five or seven years, though, were a different matter. Then India came alive for me in the delight of my grandmother's table, in the sidewalks full of people who looked like me, in the soft wap-wap of ceiling fans, creaking rickshaws, and the wonder of elephants lumbering down avenues with political signs and loudspeakers blaring from their backs. This must have been what Flower's mother felt as she traveled with her husband to Jewish communities throughout the East. For me, my trips to India in 1966, 1969, and 1978 were the demarcations of my young life. Before India. After India. Between.

~~~~~

The between part rises again with another **NOREPLY** email regarding my visa for a person of Indian origin. After a generation of being tethered to the Midwest, I handle clear demarcations with ease. City of birth: Bangkok. Nationality: U.S.A. Parents: Indian. Borders define my life. I feel sure that my trail of crumbs is irrevocable, unalterable. But still there are delays.

Though I search for my mother's passport, dusty boxes tucked into drawers turn up nothing else. Her passport, my mother says, listed my brother and me as babies traveling with her, all of us traveling to a new world written down on one page. But the ephemera of India has been allowed to drift away, and I am not Indian enough without it. She writes another letter explaining the situation, and I send it with a tiny spark of hope. The next **NOREPLY** email comes and it's not good news.

~~~~~

I consider the mobile history of the Jews of India. How Flower's grandmother, who could have reasonably expected to stay in her home country of Iraq for life, experienced many ports in her day. Yet she never left the warm encircling community of the Baghdadi Jewish diaspora. History or a keen sense of who and what she was had made her adept at knitting tradition over vast spaces.

Before the Jewish community put down its roots in Kolkata, India's southwest coast drew the earliest families. Jewish settlers of Spanish, Dutch, and other European descent built the Paradesi Synagogue in 1568 in Cochin, modern Kochi, along the Malabar Coast, scene of the biennale art festival. Even and perhaps especially there, trade developed early.

In fact, trade between King Solomon's kingdom and the Malabar Coast was ongoing long before the Paradesi was built, beginning in 992 to 952 BCE. According to the synagogue plaques in modern Kochi, nearly a thousand years before the destruction of the Second Temple in the year 70, when the Jewish community was dispersed across the globe from Palestine, teak, ivory, spices, sandalwood, and peacocks were exported by the Jewish people of the Malabar Coast.

Inside the Paradesi, a painted time line of history depicts this as an idyllic scene of ships in a quiet harbor. The raja of Cranganore received the community and went so far as to allow a Jewish kingdom complete with its leader crowned the prince of Anjuvanam at Cranganore in the year 72. There was trouble coming, however, in the form of the Moors and the Portuguese, who eradicated Cranganore in 1524. A painted plaque shows Joseph Azar, the last Jewish prince, swimming to Cochin with his wife on his shoulders. Azar put the community under the protection of the maharaja of Cochin, who consented to the construction of the Cochin synagogue, the Paradesi, next to his palace.

This is pauseworthy: everywhere the Jewish community was struggling to find its place, but in India its members were allowed to thrive under the maharajas of Cochin. In modern-day Kochi, I look to find what could be seen of that history on the ground.

~~~~~

I start at the sun-washed courtyard downstairs from the All Spices Market. The market, a cooperative of female growers at the top of a rickety staircase, has spices in packets and barrels. Iron bars protect the window looking out on a whitewashed colonial Portuguese building. Below, I gaze out at a courtyard stretching from the front of the building on Kochi's Bazaar Road to the sea, which is hidden behind gates but can be heard gently drumming the shoreline. The tops of palms sway a bit in the breeze over the back wall. Two long buildings with great patches of mottled yellow paint on their walls flank the

*Drying ginger
in Kochi.*

*Spice worker
carrying sack of ginger,
Kochi, 2019.*

courtyard full of ginger drying in the sun. Their rooflines are pleasingly sloped but blackened, the traditional Portuguese red tiles only partially discernible. I shade my eyes against the glare, drinking in the color and the heat. It has been thus for centuries: ginger, pepper, and more, cultivated and dried, sacked up and stored, sent to sea.

Just a few streets away, the Paradesi Synagogue sits at the end of a cobbled lane. The inner sanctum, visible through an arched doorway, is behind a room with painted scenes of history. I poke my head through the opening to get a feeling for the space: airy with a grouping of gorgeous crystal chandeliers hanging over a brass-railed pulpit. Warm yellow walls flank benches running the length of the room with high broad windows, and the floors are covered in hand-painted blue willow–patterned tiles brought from Canton in the eighteenth century. The overall effect is open, inviting, and quiet. Outside, the synagogue has sun-washed white walls and a clock with a chalky green face in a tower added in 1760, more than two hundred years after the synagogue was built. The bell, hanging in the synagogue tower's cupola, silent the day I am there, is jaunty with its own red-tiled mini-roof. A blue door with a lively green metal awning reaches into the stone street.

Down the lane and just around the corner from the Paradesi, the India Pepper and Spice Trade Association's structure is testimony to long commerce with the outside world. The building, nearly covered now by newer shops for T-shirts and advertisements for saris, feels diminished and anticlimactic compared to the notions in my head. Next I walk to the Saint Francis Church, with its tall Portuguese colonial façade, another few blocks away. Vasco da Gama was first buried here in 1524 prior to being moved to Lisbon. The trees brush the old façade with a pleasing rustle but no other sounds emerge. All these structures, within blocks of each other, remain mute—quiet in their testimony to the sweep of history.

The last maharaja of Cochin, whose ancestor had given the Jewish community refuge, relinquished his throne in 1949. Now both the tradition of the kings of the Malabar Coast and the Jews there are footnotes, something for visitors to marvel over. Though the gatherings of the faithful in Kochi are tiny in comparison to the Shabbat gatherings of the Jewish community in its heyday in Kolkata or other parts of India, the small remaining settlement, including the Cranganore Jews transplanted early to Cochin, is one of the oldest Jewish settlements in the world.

In Kolkata, too, the dwindling faithful remaining in a metro area of over 15 million carry on. A year after India's independence, Jews there as well as in Kochi and throughout India saw an exodus to Israel. Thereafter, sons and daughters left for other climes and later brought their aging parents to join them. As ever, however, the Maghen David Synagogue on busy Bradbourne Road in central Kolkata is lined by mostly Hindu vendors and guarded by Muslim watchmen outside in a Kolkata-style embrace of multiple histories. Kochi's synagogue is a busy place, too, primarily tourists stopping in to see living history. They come to admire the cool blue tiles underfoot, the colorful chandeliers, to read the story hung in paintings of the Jews in India on the walls in an outer room.

~~~~~

The diminishing presence of Jewish Bengal does not come to mind the day I am inside Flower Silliman's bright kitchen. Sauces in pots bubble and Flower squints against the afternoon sun filtering through the kitchen window.

In addition to the sour note that seems favored in the Jewish-Bengali foods that Flower teaches me, we nibble on her special fruitcake. Steeped in rum, wrapped but not refrigerated for nearly a year, it is perfect with tea. It's a dark molasses-tasting fruitcake, without actual molasses, with rich bits of dried fruit and nuts. I'm told about the Jewish bakery in the city, Nahoum's in New Market, that makes famous fruitcakes for Christmas, and I determine to try one. In fact, after I try one with friends, I buy two.

It's delicious. Jewish bakers, Christian holiday, Muslim watchmen, Hindu and Muslim enthusiastic eaters. It's a perfect Kolkata stew.

Flower Silliman's Special Fruitcake

Makes 1 10-inch-diameter fruitcake

1 ½ cups butter (Flower says no substitutions—use only butter)

1 ¼ cups brown sugar

6 large eggs

5 ½ cups mixed dried fruit in any combination

1 cup candied citrus peel (recipe to follow)

½ cup glacé cherries

1 cup ground almonds

2 ¾ cups all-purpose flour

¾ teaspoon nutmeg

¼ teaspoon ground cloves

1 teaspoon allspice

1 cup slivered almonds

Zest of 1 ½ lemons

½ cup brandy or rum

Preheat the oven to 300° F / 150° C. Butter and lightly flour a 10-inch cake pan, or line the base of the pan with buttered parchment paper and butter the sides. Beat the butter and brown sugar together until smooth and light, then add the eggs one at a time, beating well after each. Set aside. In a separate large bowl, mix the dried fruit, citrus peel, and cherries. In a medium-sized bowl, combine the ground almonds, flour, spices, slivered almonds, and lemon zest and mix this into the dried fruit, using your hands to distribute it evenly. Add the butter, sugar, and egg mixture, and work until well mixed. Transfer the mixture to the prepared cake pan. Bake for 3 hours and 15 minutes. Cover the cake with aluminum foil for the last hour to keep it from browning excessively. Remove from oven and cool thoroughly. When cool, make holes on the top of the cake with a skewer and pour the brandy or rum over it. Pack it in foil and let it mature at least 1 month—hint: it tastes best after 2 or 3 months. You may put a layer of marzipan on top or eat it as is. Keeps 6 months to 1 year wrapped well in foil, no refrigeration needed.

After we get home to Missouri, my husband remembers Flower's fruitcake fondly. So much so that we gather the prodigious amounts of dried fruit needed to give it a go. We take an extra step and candy our own citrus peel, which I highly recommend if you have a little time and patience. Homemade peel tastes exquisite and is good to eat alone as candy in case you are not a fruitcake fan. I started with Georgina Hartley's excellent recipe online at From the Larder and adapted it slightly due to my love of grapefruit. For best results, don't take shortcuts. Making your own candied peel sounds drawn out, but it is easy.

Though it goes against my instincts not to refrigerate or freeze the finished cake, we leave it alone for one month, wrapped tightly, even though we are barely able to resist slicing it. I remember the Kolkata heat and know that if this cake can survive that without deep cold storage, our air-conditioned home is a piece of cake, so to speak. In fact, as we slice through our August cake in September, the crumb is a little pebbly with molasses flavor, and it's super with morning coffee. It's even better in October and better again in November; you get my point, patience is rewarded with this recipe. Fruitcake fans, take note: this one's a keeper.

Candied Citrus Peel

Adapted from Georgina Hartley, From the Larder
Makes about 2 cups

3 organic oranges
3 organic lemons
2 organic grapefruit
9 ¾ cups cold water
6 ¾ cups sugar

Day 1: Wash off any wax from the fruit skin. Cut the oranges, lemons, and grapefruit into quarters, then with a sharp knife remove the skin from the pith and the flesh. Cut the peel lengthwise again. Then cut it widthwise into short thin strips. Put the peel into a saucepan with the cold water and bring to a boil. Turn the heat to low and simmer for 1 hour. Remove from heat and pour the contents of the saucepan through a sieve into a bowl. Return about 4 ¾ cups of the cooking water to the saucepan with 4 ½ cups of the sugar. You can top up the water if needed from the tap. Bring the water and sugar to a boil and simmer for 10 minutes until the sugar has dissolved. Pour the sugar syrup over the peel in its bowl. Cover and leave it to soak for 24 hours.

Day 2: Strain the syrup into a large saucepan and return the peel to the bowl. Add the remaining 2 ¼ cups sugar to the saucepan. Bring to a boil, then turn the heat down to simmer for a couple of minutes, making sure the sugar has completely dissolved. Pour the syrup back over the peel. Cover and leave for another 24 hours.

Day 3: Pour the peel and syrup into a large saucepan. Bring to a boil, then turn the heat down to simmer for 30 minutes. Pour everything back into the bowl. Cover and leave to soak for the final 4 days.

Day 7: Drain the peel, place on a wire rack, and leave in a dry sterile place until it is no longer sticky, perhaps as long as 7 days to completely dry. Store in a clean glass jar for about 2 months.

Chapter Seven

PEA SOUP

They sowed the duller vegetables first, and a pleasant feeling of
righteous fatigue stole over them as they addressed themselves to the peas.

—E. M. Forster, *Where Angels Fear to Tread*, 1905

I LOOK OVER THE spreading rooftops from my fourth-floor balcony in Kolkata and see a pea soup of haze. The parts per million of carbon dioxide in the city, pushing 50 metric tons, caresses the tops of the buildings, envelops the rooftop rose gardens, the top-floor one-room refuges, the people walking their exercise circuit on the flat roofs of their buildings. Some distance away, above the height of the 42, a modern residential building sixty-five stories tall located at 42B Jawaharlal Nehru Road, a strip of bright clear sun peeks through the ceiling of gray: the real weather, obscured.

On ground level, as I walk to the corner vegetable sellers or to the butcher with the live chickens in their cages, it is an ordinary day, and despite the levels of carbon dioxide in the air people are not wearing masks or coughing a noticeable amount. I walk along, watching for broken pavement, as the laden air moves over the tops of my toes in their sandals, between my fingertips, past my palms to my elbows, along my collarbones, eventually pushing against my long tunic and creating a playful flip as I walk. None of the air seems particularly ill omened. Daily, something as small as a part per million is little noticed or commented on. Yet there is no evading the exchange of this air, our inhale, our exhale, all of us a part per million.

I remember Tom Spanbauer's lovely writing about the Kansas sky and feel it now although, here in Kolkata, a less expansive feeling rises. "There was sky everywhere: outside the windows, under the beds, between the ceiling and the floor there was sky....When you took a breath you were breathing sky. Sky was in your lungs. My mother hung up wash across the sky. I swung in my swing through the sky. There was no escaping it."

As I write this book, concern for carbon dioxide levels in the air worldwide is taking a back seat to the COVID-19 virus as it spreads through every country. The air that concerns us all now also carries a new and virulent augury. Though it has always been so, we all are linked across that sky of Spanbauer's in a newly worrisome way. "My life is in your hands; yours in mine," Insight Dialogue founder Gregory Kramer says in an email letter to a meditation class. "We are related in life and death, at every moment; that's always how it's been."

The truth of our reciprocity is sinking in. Masks are now being touted across the globe. Online, I get a photo from a friend of the sky above Eden Gardens in Kolkata, across from the historic Metropolitan Building. The busy thoroughfare of Chowringhee Road is quiet, like the roads in my town at the beginning of the pandemic, and only a few trundling buses, taxis, or Ubers are in the street. Above, the hovering gray is breaking to blue. I am struck dumb by this evidence of a higher, cleaner plane. Nature is resetting itself. The humans are retreating.

In 2019, before the outbreak, it was the carbon dioxide levels that seemed obscene. Daily carbon dioxide levels clocked in higher than the levels during the deadly 2018 forest fires in California that burned 259,823 acres. Residents in the state sicken, wear masks, and flee due to the ominous air. The sudden, obvious shift in air quality woke everyone up. In Kolkata, over the past years of gradual worsening, only a few raise questions.

There is a story of a frog in gradually warming water that does not try to jump out until it's too late. As I fly in from a brief week away from Kolkata, my spirits drop as I watch the plane sink through clouds fluffy white on top and charcoal gray on the bottom.

That high, hidden sun, imprinted on my brain, makes me think about clarity. What don't we see while we're in the middle of muddy unfolding events? In food history, as in most of life, the portents and foreshadows are clearer in hindsight.

Take the pea. Or, more specifically, pea soup. More than just the linguistic origin for a phrase for murky air—"pea soup" was coined during World War II for the greenish tint and thickness of the sooty sulfur dioxide–laden air over London—the pea tells a walloping story of nation, agriculture, colonization, and race. It is hard to imagine such forces coming to a head over the taste of the diminutive pea.

Yet it is so. The foods of power have always altered diets. Think of the Spaniards arriving in South America in 1492, McDonald's muscling its way to the Spanish Steps in Rome in 1996, the Jell-O salads in neon green and pink of my husband's midwestern family. Powerful forces are revealed when you see that so many Furstenaus have come to love the jiggly texture.

But colonization adds a twist to the sharing of food: more than diet is affected. During the British Raj, confidence in India's regal history and lived knowledge became suspect. In order to appease colonial demands for "modern" and "reason-based" agriculture, local farming took a turn.

There is a strange feeling that something is amiss when I think about garden peas in India. Gondogol is the Bengali word for some mix-up or trouble you can't quite put your finger on. Say the word aloud (gon-do-gol) and feel your eyes go wide.

~~~~~

The delicious breads stuffed with peas, koraishutir kochuri, matar paneer (a curry of peas and cheese), my mother's keema with peas, and the British mushy-pea fixation prove the pea holds the comforts and taste cravings of distinct cultures in its tiny orb. The medieval British pease porridge rhyme, first published by John Newbery in 1781, is a pea anthem with a clapping, singing version:

> Pease (clap hands to thighs) porridge (clap your own hands together) hot,
> Pease (clap hands to thighs) porridge (clap your hands together) cold,
> Pease (clap hands to thighs) porridge (clap your own hands together)
> in the (clap right hands with the person you are rhyming with) pot
> (clap your own hands),
> Nine (clap left hands with the person you are rhyming with) days
> (clap your own hands) old (clap both partner's hands).

But enthusiasm aside, peas are by no means British. Though today 35,000 hectares of garden peas are grown in the United Kingdom each year, producing 160,000 tons of frozen peas, and its citizens eat an average of 9,000 peas each per year, peas are, in fact, thought to have originated wild in Ethiopia. Peas were present at the beginnings of agriculture in the Fertile Crescent along with wheat and barley, with archaeological remains dating back to 8000 BCE. Peas are the earliest of domesticated plants. At one point, the Romans noshed on thirty-seven varieties.

Though early types of the pea are not mentioned in England until after the Norman conquest, the first sweet-tasting garden pea is of English descent, specially bred by Thomas Edward Knight of Downton in the eighteenth century, says the British pea website Yes Peas! Ken Albala says in *Beans: A History* that garden peas were specifically bred in Europe in the sixteenth and seventeenth centuries. Whether bred in the U.K. or Europe, a pea craze erupted almost everywhere.

Growing up in Kansas, not having the nursery rhyme to aid my interest, I was not among the pea-crazed, and I pushed peas around on my dinner plate in hopes of avoiding eating them. In keema, a tasty ground meat delight that my mother serves with fragrant white rice, the bright green color of the sprinkling of peas gave them entry to my palate, but peas alone were forever suspect.

This is not unusual. Like other legumes, the pea is not often the star of the plate. Yet peas have played a large role in the daily lives of people and still do, judging by those 9,000 peas eaten each year by everyone in the U.K. Peas and their family of legumes appear as the stalwart supporting cast of early diets in providing nutrition. Like the film *Twenty Feet from Stardom* about backup singers onstage with stars, the pea has broad range and stamina. It appears a linguistic accident that we distinguish peas from other legumes such as beans, and it isn't surprising that we get the plurality off as well. As Kimberly Flint-Hamilton writes, "Peases (from the Latin *Pisum*, and an older related form in Sanskrit) denotes many individuals and pease originally meant one single pea."

Peas—small spherical seeds produced by the genus *Pisum sativum*, related to all plants in the Fabaceae family that produce pods with seeds inside them such as lentils, chickpeas, beans, and peanuts—were overlooked by early classical writers such as Pliny and Theophrastus because they were thought to be common, not the stuff of gastronomic delight. Much later, in what might be seen as a bid for attention, the steady-gene expression of the pea is why we understand human genes today; this trait led the Augustinian monk Gregor Mendel, the father of genetics, to his discovery of the laws of inheritance, more appreciated after the early twentieth century. Before that recognition, in times of scarcity, the Fabaceae family did its work of sustaining humanity almost everywhere on the planet without fanfare. For this, it is often tied to the idea of the "common man" and poverty, despite the fact, as I've said a time or two, that we are all full of beans.

The one place the legume wasn't associated with lack is India. In the ancient world, most peas were dried like other beans for storage—toor dal (split pigeon pea), chana dal (yellow gram), and more in India can long attest to this. In the *Ain-i-Akbari*, these types of peas are in the list of spring harvest produce in several regions, along with wheat, vetches, pulses, barley, linseed, safflower, millet, mustard, fenugreek, and rice. Though the tiny orb frequently appears in archaeological excavations alongside wheat and barley in the oldest settlements of the Near East and Greece, peas took a little time getting to India, researchers say. In ancient agriculture, the *humile* variant made its way through the Levant, eastern Turkey, Syria, and northern Iraq; a related shorter *elatius* subspecies overlaps this territory and spread into the Balkans as well. But all cultivated peas today reached Western Europe by 4000 BCE, cruised south into Egypt, north through the Caucasus and Eastern Europe, and then eventually east to reach India around 2000 BCE.

Their goodness is measured—in addition to tasty dal served almost everywhere in India—in healthy soil that legumes replenish with nitrogen and in the protein and fiber they provide for humans and animals. Peas do their soil magic thus: deep in their roots, a symbiotic relationship is established with the bacterium *Rhizobium radicola*, which stimulates the growth of nitrogen-capturing root nodules. The nitrogen is then converted into a form that the plant can use. When the plant dies and decays, the usable nitrogen in the root nodules is released into the soil.

You might think all this pea talk is skirting something. What is the gondogol? Where is there mischief? There are two sides to the pea story of usefulness to fields and health. The same features of legumes that make them a world crop may well have resulted in the evolution of toxins concentrated in seeds and pods, likely as a defense against foraging animals. Thorough cooking, since high temperatures can neutralize certain toxins, makes them safe to eat. Under certain conditions, though, eating large amounts of legumes with little or no variety in diet can result in a nervous paralysis of the lower limbs called lathyrism, named after the grass pea or chickling pea, *Lathyrus sativus*. Western Europe had outbreaks of lathyrism as recently as World War II, and there are still occasional outbreaks in regions of China, Ethiopia, Bangladesh, and India, where portions of grass peas are sometimes substituted for paychecks in lower economic levels or when there is food scarcity.

But there was another issue with pea history in India, and it involves a longing for home, dominance, and power. The garden pea, that bright green happy orb, was a newcomer to India's fields until the last century, and it elbowed its way in.

The world's pea past reveals how things can go wrong even in the hands of mostly good-minded people. As Utsa Ray says in *Culinary Culture in Colonial India*, there are "little histories that fracture the narrative of the grand history of the empire." In an effort to re-create a sense of belonging for the British in the Indian colony, peas and other foods from England were deemed essential to cultivate.

This longing for a taste of home led the British to create a new and darker supremacist story: the colonized subject was backward and inept. Farmers needed to be educated. The ways of the garden pea, still relatively new in Europe but already much loved, were pushed. Never mind that the plethora of vegetables and grains tended successfully in Bengal for centuries put Britain's small history and fields to shame. Plots of land normally given over to eggplant and squash suddenly were in peas. It was a gross underestimation of what grew in the colony that led the colonial state to introduce new food crops, Ray says. Regardless, the farmers of Bengal were given incentives to raise the new crops of herbaceous annuals.

I think about the peas in my life and realize that the best of them were always in my grandmother Rani's recipes. Her generation was the recipient of many foods popularized by the British Raj—a delicious mixing of two cultures, one palatable to the British and one exotically foreign for Indians. Chops, cutlets, and even my childhood comfort food of keema with peas, all tasty, all what I thought were Bengali in origin as I grew up in Kansas—all incorporated the foods of conquest.

At breakfast in Ranchi at my grandparents' house in 1969, I peel back the thin foil wrapper of a segment of Western-style soft cheese. Along the wedge, imprints of the foil are visible. Bits of escaped whitish lumps still cling to the wrapper, and I nibble them off happily as my legs swing under the dining table. There are very thin white toasts with pots of butter and guava jelly on the table and some green chili omelets. The door to the back garden stands open and reveals the mango-laden trees and the goldfish pond. I munch, switching between that view and my grandfather at the head of the table mixing rice with fresh yogurt, formed just the evening before in the bowl on my grandmother Rani's windowsill.

My mother's keema with peas in Pittsburg, Kansas, came out of a rich history I had no knowledge of. There are so many other tales—tomatoes in salads and the ones in sauces, potatoes, papayas, guavas for that jelly on Rani's table, and more—that tell us of a circuitous historical journey from South America to Mexico to Europe and back to North America with an additional loop through India. Jayanta Sengupta writes in the collection *Food in Time and Place: The American Historical Association Companion to Food History* that the Portuguese introduced to India not only potatoes, tomatoes, and chilies but also kidney beans, maize, tapioca, papayas, pineapples, guavas, custard apples, cashews, peanuts, sunflower seeds, tobacco, and turkey from the New World, okra and coffee from Africa, and soybeans and litchis from China. In fact, as Ken Albala says in *Food: A Cultural Culinary History*, the simple act of eating contains a multitude of stories. Not only what we eat and cook but our ideas of what tastes good to us change over time. Recipes and the way these foods are put together are no accident.

Flavor preferences shift dramatically over time for all kinds of reasons—socioeconomic, religious, even political. Then, too, we humans are fickle—we like novelty and want to set ourselves apart. Five hundred years ago in Europe, sugar and cinnamon would have been liberally sprinkled on every dish. But once slave traders provided the needed workers, in all too horrific ways, the price of sugar dropped and so did its popularity. Once sugar was commonly available, the wealthy relegated it mainly to dessert. The poor still loved it sprinkled over almost all their meals.

Food in my childhood was a combination of cleaving to what belonged on most Kansas plates and a seeming reaction to my father's childhood under the Raj. My father was nineteen when India gained independence, and his young life was spent knowing that manliness for the Western man meant wheat breads and meat. Now I see his notion of mealtimes in Kansas emerging in this context. Though his mother was orthodox Hindu, what is called vegan in the West, he raised his own family to eat meat and plenty of wheat at almost every meal.

Food and belonging are in lockstep. The British preoccupation with peas, as well as potatoes and barley, led to replacing indigenous crops with their favored ones, all for a sense of belonging for the colonizers. As potatoes, tomatoes, okra, chili peppers, pineapples, papayas, and cashews, introduced earlier by the Portuguese in the sixteenth and seventeenth centuries, became more common in the diet of Indians in the nineteenth century under the British, the colonizers began to push the way of the pea. The pea maneuvering revealed that this new crop did not store well in the Bengali climate and was not useful in times of scarcity. In fact, because fresh peas deteriorate quickly in warm temperatures—with much of their sugar turning to starch—they need to be distributed quickly and kept as cold as possible. But as Sengupta writes, despite the fact that "not much was done to figure out a way to make the local palate accustomed to these new crops," at the time the push was on.

～～～

Not well known in the West, the famine of 1866 in Orissa and Bengal wiped out more than a million Indians. A weak monsoon appeared that year as an omen, but indifferent colonial administrators, who likened the drought to nature's way of responding to overpopulation, believed that no relief was the best relief. This mimics the British response to the Irish famine twenty years earlier when ships full of food sat in Irish harbors, only to set sail for England though achingly needed by the Irish.

Early nationalist Dadabhai Naoroji found that India also had enough food to feed the starving in 1866, but colonial officials chose to export 200 million pounds of rice to Britain at the height of need in Bengal. And those pea fields did not fare well enough to make up for the lack. Naoroji discovered mass exportation during other famine years: 1869, 1874, and the Madras famine of 1876 to 1878 when 5 to 6 million died. By 1901, Romesh Chunder Dutt, another leading nationalist, counted ten mass famines and 15 million dead in India under British rule since the 1860s. In the famine of 1943, four years before independence, known in Bengal as Panchasher Akal, the British recorded 100,000 dead, though now historians estimate that the number was more accurately 2 to 3 million.

Hoarding and an appalling indifference were the culprits. But there were other contributions. A cyclone flattened the winter rice crop in 1942, but what started with natural disaster, Sharanya Deepak says in "A 'Forgotten Holocaust' Is Missing from Indian Food Stories," escalated into crisis under British policy. If you read histories of these times, it becomes apparent that the hero of many Western war stories, Winston Churchill, then prime minister, was no help—and worse. While Churchill intensely opposed the barbarism of the Nazis, he crushed India's freedom movement and had a profound contempt for the lives of its citizens. Streets were lined with corpses in Kolkata, but available food was shipped out to build stockpiles for postwar Britain and Europe. There was no rescue for the millions dying. When officials wrote of the catastrophic toll, Churchill, Madhusree Mukerjee says in *Churchill's Secret War: The British Empire and the Ravaging of India during World War II*, asked, "Why hasn't Gandhi died yet?"

Survivors of the famine suspect it was a way to keep Bengal within the control of the empire. In fact, abetting Churchill's open scorn of Indian citizens, the British government created the denial policy, in which more than 40,000 tons of rice were taken from rural Bengal to "deny food to a Japanese army advancing towards India" in 1942, after Burma fell in World War II. Administrators also removed or burned 65,000 boats belonging to citizens mostly in East Bengal that were used to fish, which affected the food supply of more than 3 million people. Boats were lifelines to homesteads built above flood levels and linked to the fields below them, and this policy broke the infrastructure of villages.

With no rice or fish, the mainstays of diet notwithstanding the new British-preferred crops, people walked miles to middle-class homes in Kolkata to ask for fain, the starchy water left over from boiling rice. Even as some harvest was recovered in 1943, Churchill declined to allow ships to stop with food supplies in India during the height of the famine, and Bengalis had to buy food in an escalating free market that hit the poor hard. Despite some rationing and price controls, in Bengal families who could began to hoard food, a phenomenon we all witnessed again with perhaps different consequences at the beginning of the COVID-19 pandemic in the U.S. and elsewhere. Wealthy and middle-class Kolkata residents and British imperials bought what they needed. The rest, millions, died.

In Fulton, Missouri, near my home farm, America's National Churchill Museum is housed in the beautiful seventeenth-century Christopher Wren–designed Church of St. Mary the Virgin, Aldermanbury, painstakingly moved from London to Fulton to commemorate Churchill's 1946 Iron Curtain speech given on the Westminster College campus there. I stand in the church, a serene affair, and juxtapose this quite lovely tribute with the known facts that as the people of Bengal starved, Churchill directed the British to ship food out of the country. Not one Western tribute acknowledges the millions of lives taken to feed the West, the slow deaths of children as well as adults. On the museum's website Churchill is quoted as saying, "Leave the past to history especially as I propose to write that history myself." This reveals something of his wit, among other things.

~~~~~

On my flight to Kolkata from the U.S. at the beginning of my Fulbright, I marveled at the meal choices on Air India. I could request an Asian vegetarian Hindu meal with no meat, fish, or eggs; a Hindu meal with lamb or chicken but no beef or pork; a Muslim halal meal that could contain lamb, chicken, fish, eggs, fruit, and dairy but no pork; a Jewish kosher meal prepared in a certified kosher kitchen with seventy-two hours' notice; a Jain vegetarian meal without roots or tubers such as onions, garlic, ginger, peanuts, turmeric, radishes, turnips, potatoes, and beets and no dairy; a vegan meal with all types of fruits and vegetables but no dairy, meat, fish, fowl, eggs, or animal fat; and a vegetarian meal. Then there were medical dietary options: a bland meal, a diabetic meal, a gluten-free meal, a fruit platter, a lacto-ovo meal, and a low-calorie meal.

Of course, on the flight I was asked if I wanted veg or non veg with no other distinctions. Still, had I planned ahead and requested it online beforehand, my personal worldview would have been distinctly revealed via my meal choice. Food as personal identity is pointed in India.

Food as personal message, a means of communication like clothes can be, has long been part of history. As the Romans moved into their imperial period, the simple frugal diets of the rich and poor alike were centered on wheat and barley, cheese, olive oil, vegetables, and a little meat now and then, according to food historian Ken Albala. But as expansion happened and the Romans came into contact with older, wealthier cultures used to luxuries like the Greeks, they connected with ancient trade routes and found spices such as pepper and cinnamon from India and even, a little later on, citron, ginger, and cloves. Food became an unmistakable marker of social status, and only the wealthiest could afford the lavish feasts and wild juxtapositions of flavors that came into vogue.

Not only what was served but how, in what quantity, and to whom was critical. *De Re Coquinaria* or *On the Subject of Cooking*, by Apicius, later the most famous cookbook of Roman times, reveals the rare ingredients and ingenious cooking tricks employed to titillate guests at the all-important Roman formal dinner party. Not only did flavors abound—sweet, sour, savory, spicy all competing in one dish—but the foods served showcased the world on one plate—flamingo, the fish sauce garum from Spain, dormice, ostrich, apricots, and more.

But then, Albala points out, an alternative aesthetic emerged that rejected fancy and expensive foods in favor of honest simple foods. In Satire 11, the Roman poet Juvenal tells his friend to come by his farm and get things you cannot get in the market—"from my farm at Tibur there shall come a little kid, the fattest and tenderest of the flock ... with more milk in him than blood....

And huge eggs, still warm in their twisted hay, and grapes...fresh upon the vines"—continuing with delicious lists of the freshest foods the guest would have at a humble farm, dining with good friends. Juvenal creates an aesthetic out of poking fun at ostentatious combinations and the habit of posturing with food.

This was, of course, another way to posture with food. In Missouri, people shop at the farmers market in town purposely to show support for a clean food system, an organic one, and one that has a direct tie between consumer and farmer. The costs, my students tell me, compared to the groceries in town, are higher, and for many this is an elitist message, though well intentioned. Only those who can afford it are food heroes.

Just as easily, food can reveal cultural values. Think for a moment about the table arrangements when a host sits at the head with the guests arranged in order of closeness to the host or by importance. Compare that to a picnic or an American barbecue. Both this form of posturing with food and the cultural values that food reveals were honed under the Raj. Meals under the British had a sense of public spectacle.

Food is also a major catalyst, as many including Albala have pointed out. From the accidental "discovery" of the New World due, in part, to a quest for food, the population surges in China tied to the sweet potato's calorie-laden arrival in 1593, and the many migrations throughout history from prehistoric times to the Irish potato famine, food moves and changes world culture.

Before ideas of advancing a particular civilization formed in the minds of the British colonizers in India, it was the taste for spices, for lands to grow tea, for textiles and sugar that spurred a national acquisitive spirit. In fact, the English had done this before. After losing the American Revolution, though, and all that meant for England's ambitions, the Brits focused on India, a rich storehouse for them. In India, they became absorbed in making themselves more comfortable and found food crops one sure avenue for doing so.

In search of the green pea story on the modern Bengali plate, I meet Sharmistha Banerjee in her office at the University of Calcutta across from the National Library, where she is a professor of business management. So much seems possible in Sharmistha's presence. She has held two Fulbright fellowships in the U.S., worked with female street vendors in Kolkata on a United States International Education Foundation grant, and spearheaded the Global Links project on social entrepreneurs with Rollins College in Florida as well as another Indo-U.S. 21st Century Knowledge Initiative project with Claflin University in South Carolina. Her infectious smile radiates energy. In between students and faculty dropping in, she and I get down to business: her mother's peas. A few weeks later, we cook.

Sharmistha's parents, Ria and Dipen Banerjee, are warm hosts and have many goodies already laid out on the table when I arrive at their flat in the Benubon Apartments complex of the city. Clean-lined chairs and settees furnish the room. Low-voiced conversation and a congenial air fill the apartment.

The goal is to make wheat breads stuffed with mashed peas, though that description does not do koraishutir kochuri justice. The flaky layers of unleavened bread are light with a slight crispiness, and the mashed pea filling is satisfying, robust, and comforting all at once. This bread of the Banerjee home hearth seems a sublime marriage of cultures. Ria, born and raised in Buxar in the state of Bihar and educated at Banaras Hindu University, learned how to make it from her aunt in 1959. Nearly sixty years later, the steps are ingrained.

As we enjoy savories and cordial conversation, I hear soft sounds from the kitchen. Utensils clink, feet patter. I have the urge to pop up and round the corner into Ria's galley-style kitchen, fearing she would premake the breads out of politeness. But Ria, completely unmussed while she works in her blue cardigan unbuttoned over a black print sari, is a natural teacher. She steps back, smiles calmly, and folds her palms together after pointing out a pot of peas already blended with green chilies into a smooth paste. The paste has been fried with cumin seeds, ginger, sugar, and salt and waits ready to use.

On one side, a bowl of fresh chartreuse green unseasoned peas is there for comparison. I lean closer over the tidy counter—the color is obviously darker in the bowl of prepared peas. The aroma is subtle and delicious. All the other components of the breads are laid out neatly as well—the bread dough in a ball in a bowl, small rounds of dough pinched off in a line on the counter ready to roll, a wooden belan, the Indian-style rolling pin, a pan with oil in its base heating on the stove.

I am reminded of bread making in my mother's kitchen as Ria has me mix flour and oil in a large bowl using my fingers. A ball of soft, pliable dough is ready to use, but she knows that bread is made by feel and lets me give it a try. I pinch off a bit of dough, roll it into a ball, and flatten it into an awkward disk. The warmth of my palms helps, but still my dough is a little tougher than it should be. Ria's disks are uniform and tender; mine are thicker in places, not quite round as I roll them out, but I gamely continue.

Ria presses a tablespoon of the spiced pea mixture into a dough disk, folds the sides over the top of the filling, and pinches the dough to seal it closed. My packets of dough-encased peas look a little like pot stickers or the Tibetan momos common in Kolkata, but then Ria uses her palms to gently pat them into a round shape, flattening them slightly. We both look down, examining a filled kochuri to check that it is closed up before rolling it out to a larger five-inch round. Ria's have a slight green tinge in the middle and I hope for that, not a hole with green ooze. Under Ria's helpful gaze, my kochuri remarkably do not ooze. As we fry each in hot oil, I remember how I fried luchi, another unleavened but unstuffed Indian bread, with my mother. I used the large round sieved spoon to twirl the frying disks to encourage puffing; I flipped them carefully. This I do again, under Ria's kind and patient eye, and then we feast.

The anticipation of the group coming to the table tells the story more than words can: this flavor is sought after in home kitchens all over Bengal. Conversation softens, plates are picked up, there is a gleam in more than a few eyes. The pea, harbinger of change, somehow tastes just right in traditional kochuri.

Just as the pea and its nursery rhyme suggest, the British have this feeling about the orb as well, and a (relatively) new classic was born.

Back in Missouri, I make koraishutir kochuri and learn the hard way—three tries—that kneading a full eight minutes really helps the texture of the dough. Put your weight into it, folks. Ria's dough was soft, pliable, and tender—and this takes a little elbow grease. I also found that using less of the pea mixture—you'll want to put more in than you should, too—made sealing the breads much easier. My guest the day I tried making these delicate treats loved the pea stuffing enough to take pinches of it out of its bowl and found it tasty on its own.

Koraishutir Kochuri

PUFFED BREAD WITH GREEN PEA FILLING

Recipe courtesy of Ria Banerjee

Serves 6–8

1 ¼ cups fresh or frozen green peas

1 green chili

8 tablespoons vegetable oil, plus more for frying

⅛ teaspoon cumin seeds

½ teaspoon salt

2 teaspoons sugar

2 teaspoons ginger, mashed to a paste

2 pounds all-purpose flour

Before you begin, keep 2 cups of water handy. Next blend the peas and green chili into a smooth paste with a hand masher or blender. If you use a blender, add 1–2 tablespoons water. Set aside. Heat 4 tablespoons of the oil in a medium-sized pan. Add the pea paste, cumin seeds, salt, sugar, and ginger paste. Stir and fry, being careful not to scorch the mixture, until it becomes very thick and the color darkens, about 15 minutes, or until the mixture pulls away from the sides of the pan. Set aside.

Mix the flour and the remaining 4 tablespoons of oil in a large bowl using your fingers. Add enough water—begin by adding ½ cup at a time—to make a firm dough that is smooth when rolled between your palms. Knead the dough on a clean hard surface sprinkled with a little flour until it is soft, about 6–8 minutes. Pinch off the dough into balls, roll them between your palms, then flatten them with your fingers into disks 3 inches in diameter and about ¼-inch thick. Press a tablespoon of the pea mixture into the dough disk, taking care to put the mixture in the center. Beginners, try a smaller dollop of pea mixture first. The important thing is to seal the kochuri properly so it will puff

➤

up while frying. Fold the sides over the top of the filling and pinch the dough to seal it closed. Using your palms, flatten it slightly, checking to make sure the seams are closed. The uncooked filled kochuri will resemble a flat-topped round soft puck about ½-inch thick. Using a rolling pin, gently roll each filled kochuri to a round about 4 inches in diameter.

Heat 1–2 inches oil in a small wok or deep-sided pan. When the oil is hot, fry each kochuri, tapping and spinning it slightly in the oil with the back of a slotted spoon to encourage it to puff up into a round. Turn it over and fry until cooked through, about 20 seconds. Remove the kochuri with a slotted spoon and place it in a bowl lined with paper towels. Serve warm.

This bread is flaky and light as long as it puffs up in the hot oil. If it does not, remember that practice is the key and don't be discouraged. Sealing the mixture inside the dough without creating holes can be tricky and is something to celebrate once you have mastered it.

Chapter Eight

TRIFLE-ING WITH EMPIRE

The conflict lies in balancing the knowledge that
food can neither be divorced from its cultural context nor
forcibly contained within a geographical area.

—Vidya Balachander, "On Knafeh and a Vision
of the World without Borders," 2020

IN THE HONKING CENTER of the city, surrounded by sturdy porticoes, Suchitra
Mukherjee, a cousin I rarely saw in my life up to this point due to geography,
waits while her elegant sari falls perfectly to the floor. Just steps away, everyone has someplace to go: bus engines snort, a flyway overhead gives the city
a bustling feel, and pedestrian-choked sidewalks flank the block. But the Calcutta Club seems a world away from this determined activity. As we proceed to
tea at one of the dark wooden tables, the paisley silk cascading from Suchitra's
shoulder dances and flows with her vigorous walk.

I can see the open lawn beyond the veranda doors as we enter the casual
dining area. A rectangle of green space has little required of it in the middle of
a city with a population of 14.8 million people; breathing space is its own gift.

The flowers bordering the grass, swaying a little as they sieve the air, are well tended. As we move to our seats, I note dark wooden beams high overhead and absorb the soothing atmosphere marred only occasionally with sharp clicks as a member with hard-soled shoes taps by. Amid the soft tinkle of silverware and the murmur of guests talking, as the waiters in white jackets and dark pants bring out hot tea or ginger-lime drinks, a breeze sifts through.

Outside, this current of air has brushed over the flyway and people and cars and carts and buses and trees hidden by concrete edges of buildings—and now, strangely, it evokes my Missouri farm. I can see myself standing there in this same airflow, connected until, like the light touch of butterfly wings, the vision is suddenly gone. Still, the moving air lifts the day away, revealing a scene not much changed from the era of the Raj and, for the observant, it unveils a trail of crumbs.

The Calcutta Club, established in 1907, notably allowed Indian members, unlike the 1827-era Bengal Club not far away. For those eighty years behind closed doors at the Bengal Club, enticingly foreign foods were being made. When I read in Colleen Taylor Sen's *Feasts and Fasts: A History of Food in India* that the Bengal Club was known for its omelets, now popular all over India made with minced onions and chilies, I sit up. My mother produced those omelets when I asked for "Indian" omelets growing up. She made them thin in a piping hot pan with only a single egg. She would add a sprinkling of minced onions and even more finely chopped green chilies and salt, and suddenly a childhood Saturday morning or late Sunday brunch was replete with flavor. Such a small step, a bit intimidating before you try it, to add the green chili infiltrator from South America. I begin to make a list of foods I ate in Pittsburg, Kansas, by way of Thailand (where my parents first moved after leaving India), Chicago (where my parents first moved after coming to the U.S.), Bengal (my family's cultural homeland), and the Bengal Club during the era of the Raj. Turns out, the green chili omelet, the cutlets, and the chops were food trails right back to the days of the Portuguese traders and, later, the British.

Sipra's Omelet with Green Chili

Recipe courtesy of Sipra Mukerjee and my memory

Serves 1

1 teaspoon finely diced onion

¼ green chili, minced

1 teaspoon water

1 egg

⅛ teaspoon salt or to taste

1 tablespoon vegetable oil

Combine the onion and green chili and set aside. Beat the water, egg, and salt in a small bowl until incorporated and slightly frothy. Set aside. Heat the oil in a small frying pan to medium-high. When hot, add the onion-chili mixture and stir-fry for 1 minute. Add the egg mixture. Fry on one side, pushing the edges of the egg toward the center and tipping the pan so the raw egg fills in, until the omelet bubbles up and is slightly brown. Cover the pan with a lid briefly, if needed, to cook through. Slide the omelet onto a plate, folding it in half as you do. Serve hot.

Tasty omelets drew a crowd for breakfast at the Bengal Club, but the Calcutta Club was formed when Lord Minto, the British viceroy of India at the time, invited Rajen Mookerjee to dine at the Bengal Club, and its anti-Indian code was revealed. No membership, and certainly no dining with Mr. Mookerjee, was allowed, and thus the white-stone, porticoed Calcutta Club was born—for men only. This small step for nonwhite man became a giant leap for humankind when female members were allowed in 2007.

I ask to meet the club's chef to seek recipes of the Raj era, many unchanged since 1907, in search of what I thought might be India's early fusion foods. My cousin, retired from the British Council and adept at languages and teaching, inquires about recipes from Kasturi Raha, a board member walking by our table. "Oh, yes, happy to help," Kasturi says and waves as she goes forward to meet her group.

That promising start led, eventually, to a meeting with the club's chief officer, the added happy introduction to food writer Salmoli Mukerji, a quick nip into the kitchen to see the inner workings of the club, and more promises of recipes. Kasturi reassured me again. "No problem at all."

Months into emails that start to feel like a negotiation, the club's chief officer retires. This means new inquiries with a new chief. A definite setback, but I receive an email from the club's chef, Peter Gomez, and recipes seem tantalizingly close. A week or two go by, then Chef Gomez comes through with details for the club's Fish Véronique, shepherd's pie, and tipsy pudding. I am especially tickled by the last, something about the name, well, tickles me, and I envision portly men with cigars chuckling over dessert. Though typed, the chef's recipes feel like a handwritten dash of ingredients. Thrill snakes through me until I see the lack of measurements and cooking details. Then I hear that Chef Gomez, too, has retired from the club, and all hope of getting exact measurements is lost.

I note that the recipes he sent are British, albeit with a touch of the Continental in the Véronique title. Then I see that bekti, a much-loved fish in

Bengal, has infiltrated the kitchen's crispy fish fillets. I am put in touch with the incoming chef through an email connection with the newly appointed chief officer. I get a gracious invitation to attend an international dinner, complete with delicious Bengali fare, to taste foods in person, 8,180 miles away in Kolkata (I have now left India and am peck-

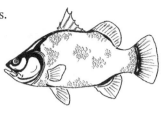

Bekti.

ing away at a keyboard in Missouri). Not overly worried yet, I banked on my return trip to India to inquire in person. Then health issues in the family postpone my trip, COVID-19 hits, and all travel halts for the duration. I decide to make the recipes with midwestern substitutions and my own measurements, although with a melancholy tip of the hat to the Calcutta Club.

Though the recipe calls for about a quarter pound of bekti fish, *Lates calcarifer* or Asian sea bass, I substitute what I can find in my Missouri home: black sea bass. And I buy more than called for—two fillets or about half a pound. Bekti is also known as barramundi, a word appropriated from an Australian Aboriginal language in Queensland meaning "large scaled fish." This was the name promoted by marketers in the West from the 1980s onward—you can see why when you say it aloud and feel the syllables roll off your tongue, barramundi—and it is also known as pla kapong in Thai. The fish can reach close to an eye-popping six feet and up to about sixty pounds, but that's unusual. Most are two or three feet long in Indian markets, large enough to make an impression, though larger ones, too, lay magnificently across the tables there.

Walking through Lake Market in Kolkata, I see that the fish tables are full and there are no cloudy eyes or wan-colored skin in sight. A monger grabs several fish by the tails, shifts them just as I near the tables, and settles back behind a heavy and intimidating bonti knife secured at table height. The bodies gleam silver to shadow to silver as he moves them, the resilient texture of the skin obvious. These are not your grocery store fish in the Midwest.

I think of the poet Pablo Neruda's "Ode to a Large Tuna in the Market": "this torpedo," he says, "from the depths that swam like a missile, and now lies dead surrounded by the earth's green froth of lettuces and bunches of carrots." While in Lake Market the fish area is all fish, all the time, I can see connections. These fish lived through the river's truth, echoing Neruda's "ocean's truth," and survived "unfathomable torrents, and flexed their fins like wings." Now the bekti in the market, still slippery and sleek as in life, is the "only shape left with purpose or direction in this jumbled ruin of nature."

In life, bekti males migrate during monsoon season, from freshwater river abodes downstream to salty estuaries and tidal flats. In areas without fresh water, they can adapt to purely salt conditions year round. Either way, they go about their business, swishing their long shiny bodies enticingly to meet females. The females lay millions of eggs in brackish water but do not guard them, leaving the fry and fingerlings to the gods to protect. An intrigue: bekti maturing as male become female after a spawning season or two. This act of being sequentially hermaphrodite is rare anywhere but does help with the survival of the species—twice useful, those bekti males.

Here's my version of the Calcutta Club's classic Fish Véronique.

Fish Véronique

Recipe courtesy of Chef Peter Gomez, Calcutta Club, Kolkata, with adaptations

Serves 2

½ pound black sea bass fillets (1-inch-thick tilapia fillets also work well)

1 cup milk

1 teaspoon salt

½ teaspoon black pepper

½ teaspoon ground mustard seeds

Juice of 1 lime

½ cup all-purpose flour

Salt and black pepper to taste

1 egg, beaten

Enough oil to fry the fish

Parsley, snipped, for garnish

Lemon slices or fresh grapes for garnish

2 tablespoons raisins, braised (optional)

Soak the fish fillets in the milk, salt, black pepper, ground mustard seeds, and lime juice (this may curdle the milk but not to worry) for 2 hours. Remove the fillets from the marinade and dust them in the flour; add more salt and black pepper to taste. Next dip each fillet in the beaten egg, and fry it in a skillet in about 3 tablespoons oil. Garnish with snipped parsley, lemon slices, fresh grapes, or braised raisins—Chef Gomez's note says, "We use braised raisins in the Club." To braise raisins, heat 4 tablespoons water in a pan on medium heat; add the raisins, cover, and cook until plump, about 4 minutes.

Finding new forms to fit in the world, to survive, is a neat trick. People, too, though not usually to such an extreme as male bekhti, absorb what is around them to create their lives. Tethered to the Midwest of the U.S. for half a century and counting, I am something other than I would have been had my family stayed in Bengal. I absorbed my environment, what I needed to fit into it, and formed.

Foods, also, leave a trail. Take the food trail of pullao. Lizzie Collingham writes in *Curry: A Tale of Cooks and Conquerors* that at first it was Persian pilau that spread throughout the Muslim world, taking on the forms of biryani as conquerors trekked southeast across India, couscous in North Africa as they went westward, and eventually, with the addition of seafood and saffron, paella in Spain. With the addition of butter, it became risotto in Italy. All dishes made in a single pan with rice or, in the case of North Africa, with wheat, with oil, vegetables, and sometimes meat or fish, layered and seasoned and sealed to cook.

But as I look at the recipe for tipsy pudding sent by Chef Gomez, I am hard-pressed to see the shift, that telling slide into a new form that reveals movements of cultures, peoples, and thoughts on taste. The shift in this recipe appears to be its location. The population of the Calcutta Club did the shifting to the new "exotic" creation, taste buds absorbing flavors new to their city.

Chef Gomez says to take milk, egg yolk, custard powder, and cream to make a sauce and layer it between layers of sponge cake and "jam liquid." In order to get into the right frame of mind, I pour myself a cup of strong black tea, add a dollop of milk, and proceed to come up with what this might mean.

The jam liquid he mentioned could be many things, so too the sponge cake. So, eyes bright, taste buds at the ready, I begin to experiment. Given that some sources say the sponge for tipsy pudding should be dry and a few days old to better soak up the juice or alcohol poured over it, and others use ladyfingers, the long slim configurations used to make tiramisu, as a shortcut, I succumb to a few tangents. Here's what Chef Gomez sent me—abbreviations, punctuation, measurements, and capitals, all are his:

TIPSY PUDDING

Milk - ½ cup - 75 ml

egg yolk - 1

Custard pwd - 15 gm

Cream - 30 ml

Sponge cake to cover base of serving cup, twice

Layer the serving cup with Sponge cake

Wet with jam liquid

add dice assorted fruits - 50 gms

layer with custard sauce

layer with another slice of sponge cake, cover with Custard.

Finish with cream and Jam sauce piping.

The recipe does not mention sherry or rum or wine. Not so tipsy after all, Chef Gomez. It's possible, though, that alcohol might be lurking with furtive shyness in his "Jam sauce" or in a sponge cake presoaked with rum, brandy, or some other liquor. I tap my chin and consider. I decide that the ability to replicate is the better part of valor. And rum, sitting conveniently in my cupboard, is always a good idea.

What astonishes me is that an English trifle was served in royal style by waiters in white jackets in a club for people sitting in the Calcutta heat. This recipe is for the refrigeration confident. In the early club days, as in the early days of trifle in Britain, the chances that cream had withstood the conditions were worrisome, and no doubt this is why it became essential to pour it over everything before it spoiled.

I made a version with ladyfingers and appreciated the convenience. Then I buckled down and made a tipsy with a Victoria sponge, slightly dry with the trademark air pockets so it soaked up the rum and custard well, and decided that was the version for me. Here's the recipe, only by wish resembling the Calcutta Club's original.

Tipsy Pudding

Recipe adapted a great deal from Chef Peter Gomez, Calcutta Club, Kolkata
Serves 4–6

1 cup milk

1 ½ cups heavy cream

5 eggs

½ cup sugar

2 tablespoons cornstarch

3 ½ tablespoons rum or, if you prefer, sherry or brandy

2 cups mixed berries such as strawberries, raspberries, blackberries,
   and blueberries

¼ cup sliced almonds

Zest of ½ lemon

Store-bought sponge (or see the recipe to follow if you want to
   make your own), angel food, or pound cake or ladyfingers

First, make the custard by heating the milk and ½ cup of the heavy cream in a saucepan over medium heat and bringing them almost to a boil. Remove the pan from the heat. In two bowls, separate the egg yolks from the egg whites, reserving the egg whites. Beat the egg yolks and sugar with an electric mixer for about 5 minutes until pale and thick. Add the cornstarch. Beat on medium-low speed until well combined. Slowly pour the hot milk mixture into the egg mixture, stirring as you go. Pour this combined mixture back into the saucepan and cook over low heat, stirring constantly, for about 5 minutes or until the mixture thickens. Stir in 1 teaspoon of the rum, sherry, or brandy. Remove from heat. Place plastic wrap directly on the custard and refrigerate until chilled, about 30 minutes.

Slice the strawberries and set aside with the rest of the fruit.

Toast the sliced almonds by heating a flat pan and gently stirring the almonds on the surface until the aroma begins to lift and the nuts just begin to brown. Quickly remove from heat and place in a small bowl. Add the lemon zest to the almonds. Set aside.

Next beat the remaining 1 cup of heavy cream in the bowl of an electric mixer for a few minutes. Add ½ tablespoon of the rum, sherry, or brandy and continue to beat until the cream forms stiff peaks. Separately, beat the egg whites until they reach a soft peak. Gently fold the beaten egg whites into the whipped cream. The egg whites are uncooked; be sure to use good-quality eggs and refrigeration.

Place a layer of the cake—cut into cubes—or the ladyfingers on the bottom of a glass bowl. Sprinkle these with 1 ½ tablespoons of the remaining liquor and top with a layer of berries, a layer of custard, and a layer of the almond mixture. Repeat the layering, being sure to sprinkle the remaining liquor over the cake or ladyfingers, once or twice, depending on how deep your bowl is—this makes one gorgeous medium-sized bowlful. Top with the mixture of whipped cream and egg whites. Garnish with toasted almonds and a few whole berries. Serve immediately or chill before serving.

Victoria Sponge

Makes one 8-inch cake

If you decide to make your own sponge cake, try this Victoria sponge.

1 cup self-rising flour (or use all-purpose flour and add 2 more teaspoons
baking powder)
1 teaspoon baking powder
2 large eggs, at room temperature
½ cup sugar
4 tablespoons butter, softened

Preheat the oven to 350° F / 180° C. Lightly grease a pan 8 inches square with 2-inch sides or an 8-inch round if you don't mind some cake pieces with rounded edges, and line the bottom of the pan with lightly greased parchment paper. In a bowl, sift together the flour and baking powder. Set aside. In a mixing bowl, beat the eggs, then add the sugar and beat with an electric mixer on high until light and pale yellow, about 3 minutes. Add the flour mixture gradually, beating as you go. Add the softened butter and continue to beat until soft and well combined, 2–3 minutes. The batter will be very thick and creamy. With a rubber spatula so you get all the good stuff, scoop the batter into the baking pan and lightly smooth the surface with a knife to make it level.

Bake 20–22 minutes or until the cake is golden brown on the surface. Do not open the door of the oven while baking. Once the cake has risen and is golden, you can check for doneness by opening the door and gently pressing the center of the cake—it should spring back easily. Remove the cake from the oven and place on a cooling rack for 5 minutes. After the cake begins to shrink away from the sides of the pan, carefully invert it, remove the pan, and let it cool completely. Cut into cubes for layering into trifle. If you like, spread ½ cup fruit jam of your choice over the cake before cutting it into cubes.

In Britain, trifle recipes outlasted a long history of hedgehog puddings, fruit creams, tansies, syllabubs, flummeries, junkets, and probably more soft creamy desserts with fanciful names. Its popularity and status as a comfort food in Britain were no doubt why it made its way to the club scene in Kolkata. That was the whole point after all: comfort for those posted in the colonies. Tipsy pudding and other choices on the menu had an added benefit: they were an enticing taste of foreignness for Indians.

By the eighteenth century, trifles made from thick custard, fruit, sponge cake, fruit juice, and whipped cream arranged in layers in transparent glass bowls were popular on banquet tables in England. Rita Jacobs, in "English Trifle: Serious Dessert," writes that trifle confections were mentioned as early as 1598 by the translator John Florio, who referred to "a kinde of clouted creame called a foole or trifle in English." They beat out flummeries certainly and even overtook syllabubs in a long, slow three hundred–year win.

The tipsy part of the story emerged by the middle of the eighteenth century, just in time to make it to the Calcutta Club menu, when trifles expanded to include almond-flavored biscuits or macaroons soaked in sweet wine, covered with custard, and topped with whipped cream. Trifles, rising as they did from making use of leftover stale cakes, could be said to have a rags-to-riches story after they began appearing in the great dining rooms of clubs halfway across the world. Tales of sponges soaked with sherry, brandy, and rum were hard to resist. I'm not sure which version was Queen Victoria's favorite, but Isabella Beeton in her 1861 *Mrs. Beeton's Book of Household Management* includes a recipe for Victoria "sandwiches," also called a Victoria sponge. With or without the jam spread she includes, the recipe works as the base cake for a trifle appropriate for the Calcutta Club's tipsy pudding created, after all, during Victoria's era in India.

Fair warning: though the concept and taste of these Victoria sandwiches are sound for your trifle, the name is off. Joyce White in her blog, *A Taste of History*, says the historic recipe is not actually a sponge cake but a cream cake made when sugar is creamed or mixed vigorously with butter until light and

VICTORIA SANDWICHES.

1491. INGREDIENTS.—4 eggs; their weight in pounded sugar, butter, and flour; ¼ saltspoonful of salt, a layer of any kind of jam or marmalade.

Mode.—Beat the butter to a cream; dredge in the flour and pounded sugar; stir these ingredients well together, and add the eggs, which should be previously thoroughly whisked. When the mixture has been well beaten for about 10 minutes, butter a Yorkshire-pudding tin, pour in the batter, and bake it in a moderate oven for 20 minutes. Let it cool, spread one half of the cake with a layer of nice preserve, place over it the other half of the cake, press the pieces slightly together, and then cut it into long finger-pieces; pile them in cross-bars on a glass dish, and serve.

Time.—20 minutes. *Average cost,* 1s. 3d.

Sufficient for 5 or 6 persons. *Seasonable* at any time.

Excerpt from Mrs. Beeton's Book of Household Management.

fluffy. A sponge, to cake terminologists, is made by first whisking eggs and sugar together to incorporate tiny bubbles into the batter. It's lengthy, this whisking, but the end result is a light aerated crumb.

I bow to those early versions and the elusive one from the Calcutta Club. May the foole makers take no offense.

Before the trifles hit the shores of India, early British traders ate and lived much like the local populations, as did the early Portuguese traders before them. The agents of the British East India Company often spoke the language, dressed like locals, established Indian mistresses or married high-born Indian women, and many times took pains to understand local history and culture by studying Indian classics.

This changed with time. Ideas about the effeminacy of Bengali rice eating rose, and company men began to look with displeasure and a sense of superiority upon the food of the natives, though when they first arrived the highly spiced food of India would not have seemed unusual, according to David Burton in *The Raj at Table: A Culinary History of the British in India*. Spice prices had finally come within reach of many in England as the Arab traders were circumvented by the Portuguese. The Indian dumpokhed chicken, stewed in butter and stuffed with spices, almonds, and raisins, was similar to an English chicken pie of the same period. Forks were still relatively uncommon in England, and the English scooped food into their mouths with pieces of bread—just as the Indians did. Even the Indian custom of eating spices after a meal to aid digestion, Burton says, has its counterpart in voidee, the English custom of offering departing guests assorted spices and wine at the end of a banquet.

Colleen Taylor Sen writes in *Feasts and Fasts* that the British in India ate prodigiously and drank wine, beer, rum, punch—made with the requisite five ingredients of local arrack, rosewater, citron juice, sugar, and spices—as well as arrack straight up. The habit of the burra khanna dinners served during the time of the East India Company with crowds of servants—one invariably pulling a rope attached to a large overhead fan to cool the diners and disperse the flies—hookahs burbling behind the dining chairs, men wearing airy white linen, and huge saddles of mutton, hams, turkeys, and curries strung across the table was de rigueur. Stomach disorders became rampant but were blamed on the climate, not on the heavy eating habits. Eating became a kind of spectacle, a way to show status through body size and excessive amounts of food. European physicians were aghast at the overconsumption, but it did not stop.

The food pendulum swung away from local fare after the British government took the reins from the East India Company. Lord Wellesley, the new governor-general appointed in 1798, showed open contempt for Indians, and the social atmosphere changed accordingly. By the early nineteenth century, Sen tells us, French cuisine and imported bottled peas—or, as E. M. Forster says in *A Passage to India*, "bullety bottled peas...the food of exiles, cooked by servants who did not understand it"—tins of sardines, and other canned fish were all the rage at British dinner parties, in addition to the usual quantities of bland joints of meat, legs of lamb, mutton, and boiled chicken. The rice and curries of the past were relegated to lunch, if at all. With the introduction of steamships, more British women came to the subcontinent who had little understanding of India and less interest in learning about it and who created islands of England in the settlements. These new sahibs and memsahibs aimed to demonstrate the superiority of the British race and uphold its prestige. Lizzie Collingham writes in *Curry* that men began to don black evening dress at table, even in the stifling heat, to show that "British officials were not in India to run the country for a money-grubbing trading company but to bring to its backward and impoverished people the benefits of civilization." And David Burton in *The Raj at Table* notes that the arrival of missionaries in the early nineteenth century turned opinion even more firmly against the "barbarous" and "pagan" Indians.

Meanwhile, in middle-class households all over Kolkata, a kitchen resistance was rising. One of the largest transformations in Bengali history was in gastronomy after the British arrived. I nod to myself as I read in Utsa Ray's *Culinary Culture in Colonial India* that Bengali cuisine never aspired to the public character of French haute cuisine. Recipes were private, belonging to the people of Bengal: a history of a home-kitchen resistance in code—in recipes—to colonial dictates elsewhere. This makes sense to me when I think that this beautiful tradition is relatively unknown in places like the U.S., Britain, *anywhere* else outside India. Bengali food emerging out of colonial times was emphatically regional, kept close. While some cultures have robustly declared their place on the stage of world cuisines (think France), claiming certain tastes or techniques as their own, other cultures (think Bengal) have been quieter, burbling along unsung in the background yet deliciously complex all the same.

Despite the growing disdain of Indian culture by British men and their wives, as Colleen Taylor Sen notes, the two cultures had lasting effects on each other's foodways. Dishes of curry, kedgeree, and mulligatawny soup made with peppers, lentils, and coconut milk or cream continued to be served at breakfast or lunch until the twentieth century, but they were no longer served at dinner. Indian customs were not for formal meals any longer.

This informality carried over to early Indian restaurants in the West.

~~~~~

I talk with Mohammed Ali, also known as Aerosol Ali, a muralist, perform-ing artist, and founder of Soul City Arts in the U.K., whose father opened an Indian restaurant in Britain in the 1950s. Mohammed's exhibition, *Knights of the Raj*, at the Brooklyn Museum of Food and Drink in 2018 revealed the origins of Indian street food in the U.S. and Britain as products of Bangla-deshi cooks creating foods that fit the palate of their customers. In England, curry house tradition continues to change—chain restaurants with bright and quirky street-food vibes trend over the early British Indian restaurants with their Mughal-inspired dark interiors and photos of the Taj Mahal on the walls. Menus at Mohammed Ali's father's restaurant from the 1950s and 1960s reveal a shift in flavor preferences as well, showing much milder versions of today's offerings.

"These British curries have their own distinct narrative that came from a certain place," Mohammed says. "Chicken tikka masala is very sweet with almonds and coconut cream on top, and it's bright red." This sauce version of tandoori chicken, he says, fit the palate of its customers. "It's crazy, but it tastes good."

The first Indian restaurants in Britain were established as early as 1809, according to Colleen Taylor Sen, but the boom happened in the 1980s after large-scale immigration allowed more South Asians to enter. Restaurants like Mohammed Ali's father's served the tastes of these mostly working-class immigrants and others with tandoori and tikka and the like. In the U.S., where Indian immigrants were relatively affluent, their tastes were quite distinct. Yet restaurants in the U.S., too, have not offered food genuinely reflecting the vast regional diversity of India.

In Brooklyn, the *Knights of the Raj* exhibition, which included a flavorsome three-course tasting menu of the savory-sour-sweet potato snack of aloo chaat, prawn and pumpkin curry, and the steamed or baked yogurt dessert of misti doi, pointedly revealed the life behind the scenes of the men who brought curry culture to New York. That life—with its crowded shared apartments, years of sending money back home to family, and little integration into the wider community—was a grim reminder that though these men changed the palate of an entire nation in Britain and altered the streets of New York, their own dreams of a better life did not always materialize.

The flavors were not what many in Bengal would consider their own. One theory is that as many people left the newly forming country of Bangladesh, formerly East Bengal, for better opportunities, they became cooks aboard ships who then stayed behind in foreign ports of call. Once they came ashore, the men transferred their cooking skills to street stalls and eventually restaurants.

"The biggest lie of the century," Mohammed Ali says, "is that these are Indian restaurants." Bangladeshis really didn't celebrate their own regional dishes, he says. "I don't think they had that confidence. Remember Bangladesh was just becoming a country in 1971. They thought, 'We have to give fancy names like tikka masala and vindaloo' for their customers." But at home they ate more delicate dishes.

This fits my understanding, too. Everywhere in Bengal, people told me how the cooks of Bangladesh create delightful and subtly flavorful dishes. In Bela Rani Devi's kitchen, I witnessed firsthand the fine calibrations of flavor she learned during her childhood in East Bengal before partition. The heavily spiced, oil-laden foods I think of in early British or American Indian take-out restaurants seem to belong to another cuisine entirely.

"We thought, 'The British don't want this. This is too simple; they want tomatoes chopped up, onion garnishing, decoration, and food coloring and all that kind of thing.'" Mohammed Ali remembers one longtime customer of his family's restaurant coming into the kitchen to say hello to the chef, spying a large wedding-sized pot burbling for the staff, and asking for a taste. It was a rich, very simple bhuna kind of meat dish. The customer "has just one spoonful of that meat bhuna and goes silent for about thirty seconds. Then he says, 'Why are you not selling this food?'" To this day, it was a moment Mohammed Ali never forgets.

"He just entered our world, basically."

To get additional perspective on the British impact on dining in colonial India, I visit an academic based in Kolkata to discuss Bengali foodways. Of all the people I meet in India, he most closely embodies the disdain that I imagine many Brits felt toward the local population during the Raj. To my amazement, he catalogs in Bengali my poor language skills to the next visitor in line to meet with him—"Can you believe it? Listen to her speak"—and the echo in the high-ceiled room made it seem like he said this more than once. Then, as the next visitor squirmed a little, I realized that he *did* say it more than once. Like many, the man did not realize that my poor pronunciation did not equate with poor understanding. From my end, I couldn't believe his less-than-adequate command of education and manners. Unfortunately, his legacy from the British came from their later, superior period. I am, yet again, too foreign.

For the comfort of the British colonizers, in addition to food, language was also Anglicized for foreign tongues. So Bombay, Madras, Calcutta, and other city names, now back to their pre-British-era names of Mumbai, Chennai, and Kolkata, were used and disseminated worldwide. Why Calcutta was easier to pronounce than Kolkata I'm not sure, but I grew up saying it in the Americanized version: *Cal*-cutta. When I try to get it right, it leads to all sorts of pronunciation awkwardness that ends up making everyone uncomfortable. But in Bengal, when locals are speaking English, they seem to be fine saying it my way. When they are speaking Bengali, there is an emphasis switch on the syllables, the tempo speeds up, and all in all there is an enviable flow.

The Portuguese Estado da India had engaged in trade for much of the sixteenth century, and the Dutch had as well. In 1600, after Elizabeth I granted her royal charter to the East India Company, everyone continued to butcher place-names in India at will, and the flavors of the subcontinent were again extracted, this time directly by the British. With spices, fabrics, and more in mind, the company, its sights set on the lands between the Cape of Good Hope and the Strait of Magellan, proceeded to head straight into opposition and

*Portrait by Dip Chand, likely of William Fullerton of Rosemount,
an East India Company official, the second surgeon in Calcutta in 1751,
and the mayor in 1757. The portrait was commissioned by the company
between 1760 and 1764. Victoria and Albert Museum, London, http://
collections.vam.ac.uk/item/O16731/painting-dip-chand.*

defeat with Dutch spice ships outside of Java and the Moluccas. It was a hard loss—among other things, ten company men were beheaded in the Moluccas in 1623—and the British pivoted to concentrate on India, where they felt the vast land mass would cloak their trading posts from attack.

Though the company's first ship landed at Surat near Bombay in 1608, it did not get trading concessions from Emperor Jahangir until after skirmishes with the Portuguese. The first company factory or trading post, established at Surat in 1612 to handle indigo dye from Agra and cotton cloth from Gujarat, did not fulfill its ambitions. The East India Company harassed Portuguese ships to get access to the Malabar Coast and its black pepper and got it at Goa through the Treaty of Madrid in 1630. By 1647, twenty-eight more company factories were in operation throughout India.

Next, a wedding tribute shifted history. In 1665, when the Portuguese gave Bombay to the English as part of the marriage settlement of Charles II and the Portuguese princess Catherine of Braganza, the gift solidified the company's influence. In a final coup, in 1696, the Mughal emperor allowed the company to establish a new settlement in Bengal, Fort William, later known as Calcutta and later still as Kolkata.

At first, Colleen Taylor Sen writes, when the Mughal emperors were still able to enforce their authority, foreign activities were limited to trade. Pepper, ginger, opium, and more were dried and bagged and sent on their way around the Cape of Good Hope, and some goods such as opium went into China. Fortunes were made, minds were lost. But political instability from the mid-eighteenth century onward led the British traders to seek political power. And after the 1757 Battle of Plassey, when the British along with Indian allies defeated the forces of the Mughal viceroy, the British collected the Mughals' taxes in return for an annual tribute to maintain order. Almost directly, they installed puppet rulers in Bengal, Bihar, and Orissa and extended their control over Malabar and much of the west coast. Power shifts continued from there.

In the late eighteenth century, the government of Britain created a civil service to run India. It appointed governors in Madras and Bombay and a governor-general in Calcutta, which remained the capital of British India until 1905. In the second half of the nineteenth century, the British annexed the Punjab, Nepal, and Burma. By the time of Indian independence in 1947, Queen Victoria was empress of much of India and its princely states.

But food and dietary concerns, or at least rumors about these, turned the tide in those last hundred years in British India.

What the British call the 1857 Indian Mutiny and Indians call the First War of Independence ignited over the false rumor that the British were using the grease of pigs and cows on army gun cartridges. Observant Muslim and Hindu soldiers felt they risked defilement if they used them, because with their hands full of guns they had to tear open new tallow-greased cartridges with their teeth in order to load them. The U.S. phrase "bite the bullet," meaning to do something unpleasant to reach a desired result, had rather dire consequences. Since in Britain tallow was made of beef and pork fat, the rumor gained traction. In truth, the company was getting ready to introduce a new model rifle, the Enfield, and though it caught the tallow mistake and never issued a single greased cartridge to any Indian troops, it was too late to curb the rumor. This added fuel to the suspicion all over India that the British wanted to break long-held Indian beliefs and traditions.

The thought of this was enough to ignite slaughter. After years of rising tensions, in 1857, the Indian regiments in Meerut routed British commanders and local British residents. Though their aim of restoring the Mughal emperor Bahadur Shah II to power in Delhi failed, the reprisals by the British were savage, ending the reign of the Mughals for good and afterward causing the dissolution of the British East India Company and the transfer of all its rights to the Crown.

Another food-related issue caused an uproar just a few months earlier, according to Mike Dash in *Smithsonian* magazine. In what may be the most nonsensical example of the old game of telephone, rumors about chapatis, the common unleavened wheat bread eaten in most Indian households, sprang up. And they were ominous.

"There is a most mysterious affair going on through the whole of India at present," Dr. Gilbert Hadow wrote in a letter to his sister in Britain in March 1857. "No one seems to know the meaning of it.... It is not known where it originated, by whom or for what purpose, whether it is supposed to be connected to any religious ceremony or whether it has to do with some secret society. The Indian papers are full of surmises as to what it means. It is called 'the chupatty movement.'"

What this rumor speculated about was the distribution of many thousands of wheat breads, passed from hand to hand and from village to village throughout the interior of the subcontinent. A few chapatis were delivered to the chowkidar, the village watchman, who would make fresh ones and carry them to the next village. The chapati movement was real, but no one knew for sure what they were for. Opinion was divided on whether the bread spread originated in the east near Kolkata, from the north in the province of Awadh, or from Indore in the center of India. The stories were plentiful, the facts on the ground thin; even the runners and watchmen who carried chapatis from village to village didn't seem to know the reason for the distribution.

The speed of the breads moving through the countryside spooked the British, given that chapatis were traveling much more swiftly than the fastest British mail at the time—connecting villages at the rate of almost two hundred miles a day, according to a worried George Harvey, an official in Agra in February 1857. Mark Thornhill, magistrate of Mathura, a little town near Agra, intercepted a small pile of chapatis one morning to try to get to the bottom of the culinary chain letter. Suggestions that the breads hid seditious letters forwarded from village to village led to an examination. No messages were found, though crumbs were likely flung all over Thornhill's shirt.

The British, by now much removed from and often disdainful of the local population, understood the culture they presided over less and less, had fewer and fewer officers who spoke Indian languages fluently, and guessed more and more wildly about the portent of the menacing chapatis. It was felt that those that received them took the breads as some sort of sign and that the situation was much more widespread than the British had realized. Some British officials, seemingly calm, linked the spread of the chapatis to an effort to prevent an outbreak of cholera in central India, whose citizens associated the disease with the movement of the company's armies since, as Mike Dash says in *Smithsonian*, "there was widespread belief that the British were in fact responsible for the disease." Others speculated that the chapati movement had spells behind it and that villagers felt the breads would protect their crops against hail. The British did not know what to think, and anxiety increased in British homes.

With the advantage of time, it is generally believed that the chapati movement had nothing at all to do with the 1857 uprising. After the First War of Independence bloodbath, it was hard for the British to believe that such an uprising could have been set in motion without plotting for months or years in advance, and so an effort was made to link the events—there must have been secret messages, there must have been hugger-mugger. Modern historians, however, concede that the uprising was spontaneous, that regiment after regiment mutinied against British rule at will. The most recent study, by Kim Wagner in *The Great Fear of 1857: Rumours, Conspiracies and the Making of the Indian Uprising*, shows the chapati movement in early 1857 to be a bizarre coincidence that built on the ever-present superstitious impulse that still encourages the transmission of chain letters to this day.

Mike Dash writes, "Although the original specific meaning of the chapatis had been lost early in the distribution, the dire consequences of breaking the chain of transmission remained, and thus ensured their successful circulation over an immense area…the significance attributed to them was a symptom of the pervasive distrust and general consternation amongst the Indian population during the early months of 1857."

Chapter Nine

CHAPATI LOVE

Good bread is the great need in poor homes, and oftentimes the
best appreciated luxury in the homes of the very rich.

—*A Book for a Cook*, Pillsbury Company, 1905

WOMEN WORK TO GET breads ready for dinner in kitchens all over the subcontinent. They tuck their saris into their waists and push into the dough, causing bangles to lightly chime and anticipation to climb. Bread and love. Even in rice-rich Bengal, the slap of the rolling pin and the circles of roti made with the basic ingredients of wheat flour and water can transport you with tender texture and aroma. No wonder these were the breads that were suspect in the chapati movement. Such power in their simple sustenance.

Wheat breads in Bengal reveal a sweep of foods coming from the northwesternmost reaches of the subcontinent, along with new customs. According to K. T. Achaya in *A Historical Dictionary of Indian Food*, four types of wheat—einkorn, emmer, durum, and common or bread wheat—showed up as early as 9500 to 7500 BCE in excavations at Mehrgarh in present-day Pakistan. By 7000 BCE, though rice was on the scene as well as millet, these seem to have been domesticated later—by 4500 BCE. While the Harappans (2500–1700 BCE) ate wheat, the Aryans (1500 BCE) from Central Asia initially favored barley, making few references to wheat in early texts like the *Rigveda*.

Colleen Taylor Sen in "Tracing India's Food Journey" writes that while some people dispute the idea of a migration of Indo-Aryans, there were new people in India who, in addition to being seminomadic and practicing some settled cereal cultivation, raised cows and sheep. They came with ideas, naturally, about what was good to eat, and throughout their civilization from around 3000 to 1500 BCE in the Indus Valley, which stretches more than a million square kilometers, there are few references to wheat or rice. Barley, very minimally consumed today, and lentils were staples.

This is also the time when chickens may have first crossed the proverbial road to the stockpot. These Indus Valley denizens around 2000 BCE appear to have domesticated the chicken, which led, many years later, to a wish in the seventeenth century by Henry IV that peasants could enjoy a chicken in the pot every Sunday, as well as the 1928 Republican slogan in the U.S. of "a chicken in every pot and a car in every backyard to boot." Those Harappans helped so much with catchy phrases.

In modern India, grains provide about 70 percent of the calories eaten, though that is declining with urbanization. Although wheat in India's northwest is one of the oldest of the cereal crops, it wasn't introduced into modern Bengali agriculture until 1930 or 1931, and it was recognized as an important food crop only around 1942 or 1943. Relative to its long arc of history on the subcontinent, wheat is a newcomer to Bengal.

The tale of bread crossing the subcontinent in the infamous chapati movement, scaring officials willy-nilly, points to the importance given to common bread. The chapati—roti in Bengal—is among the simplest of breads in India, unleavened, wheat-based, and commonly made in home kitchens. The rumors that abounded about their movement from village to village in British India use the word "gritty" at times when a British source is involved. The stone-ground wheat flour described this way reflects on how basic Indian foodstuffs were seen as lowly and unsophisticated by British officers of the East India Company.

Consider other Indian bread varieties that were not chosen for this movement across the subcontinent. So many breads were possible: breads made from wheat flour and also rice, buckwheat, millet, corn, or a combination of several whole grain flours, breads made in a variety of shapes and sizes, fragile breads or firm ones, paper thin or fat, seasoned or stuffed, unleavened or leavened, bound with water, milk, buttermilk, or yogurt and incorporating oil, butter, ghee, or other options. But it was chapati that was hustled across the continent, and it was chapati that, rumor had it, signified resistance before the 1857 uprising.

Why chapati? Perhaps its very status as a simple, nutritious, and everyday bread made it the natural suspect. Accessible breads like this coincide with most religions in most countries and become symbols. In Christianity, bread becomes the staff of life, and the Bible references bread no fewer than 250 times. Catholics take communion by symbolically eating bread, "the body of Christ," and say "amen" (or "I believe it!") in response. Mahatma Gandhi tied bread to spirituality and hunger as well as sustenance when he said, "There are people in the world so hungry, that God cannot appear to them except in the form of bread." Bread carries its message daily, a swift, filling armada of meaning, whether intended or not. Amen.

At home when I was growing up, this message was clear: when I ran through the kitchen and heard the slap of the rolling pin against the countertop as my mother shaped roti into perfect rounds, I would skid to a stop, raise my eyes from whatever had my pre-teen attention, and help. My mother would pinch off a one-inch piece of dough and press and smooth it between her palms, roll it out, and delicately place it on the lightly flour-dusted counter. As I watched, the thin disk of dough would contract, just a little, as it awaited the flat, hot iron tawa or griddle. A wire rack straddled another burner, where the partially cooked roti would land next in order to be puffed, layers separating, made light before they exhaled back together.

I think of the cook we shared with other families during the months I am in Kolkata, Sandhya Singh: her deft touch with the belan, the Indian rolling pin, the roti she would always ask if my husband wanted with his lunch, the gentle way she would smile each time he nodded yes enthusiastically. Filling food. Simple. Tasty good care.

~~~~~~~

When the Portuguese first came to India, they missed the crust and crumb of a good loaf. It was more than taste, though. According to Lizzie Collingham in *Curry: A Tale of Cooks and Conquerors*, wheat bread was of enormous religious significance to sixteenth-century Europeans. Portuguese settlements were largely Catholic, and bread was the only food allowed to be used to celebrate Mass. Yeast, essential to a good white wheat loaf, was not available, so Goan cooks used an alcoholic toddy made from the sap of a palm tree to ferment the dough. The results created a repertoire of crusty white rolls, croissant-like burbuleat, and pão de ló, a sweet milk bread, to add to India's fascinating list of unleavened breads. Over time, Goan cooks replaced the European ingredients in Portuguese recipes especially when making cakes—coconut milk instead of cow's milk, a simple syrup made from date palm sugar instead of the refined sugars used in Europe, ghee instead of fresh butter, rice flour instead of wheat. But the breads remained.

Street vendors in Kolkata offer lots of tasty snacks, including paratha-wrapped wonders called khati rolls. I first heard of these rolls from someone not wholly approving of them—they were fast food, they were not healthful with all that oil, they kept the younger generation from knowing good home-cooked food. I postponed my planned trip to check them out. Yet when did I stop at a street stall one day, a little nervous, and picked the first roll—chicken and egg—that I saw on the handwritten sign, I was floored by its explosion of flavor. A fresh hot khati roll is nothing if not a sublime blend of tangs and textures. Nizam's, a Mughlai eatery behind New Market in Kolkata, started the tradition in colonial-era Calcutta in the early 1900s with juicy roasted kebab fillings wrapped in tender parathas—griddled unleavened bread—for an easy takeaway for the bureaucrats commuting to the adjacent business district of Dalhousie Square. The term "kathi" or "kati"—stick—comes from the bamboo skewers Nizam's began using sometime midcentury instead of heavy iron bars to grill the meat.

Some say that slowly cooked, juicy, charred-by-a-grill-in-a-smoky-kitchen meat is key, unless you opt for a vegetarian roll, which has other attractions. True, grilling aroma is irresistible. But for me, the carrier, the paratha, far from being a nondescript wrapping, is essential to the whole package. The day I taste a khati roll, I stand on a sidewalk in the city and sink my teeth into the flaky, slightly crispy bread. The bread's tender texture is closely followed by the kick of creamy-spicy sauces, crunchy vegetables, and richly marinated chicken. Traffic noises completely fade from my thoughts. I immediately begin plotting: how can I try another before my grant time is up? The vendor, like so many I come across in India, senses that I am new to the game, and while continuing to cook other orders, amid sizzling sounds and smoke, he glances at me to see my reaction. Our eyes meet over the top of my paratha wrapped in wax paper and a pleased look comes over his face. Another convert made, he turns away to crack an egg over the next paratha on the griddle.

At home in Missouri, trying to come up with a similar roll, I consider my options. In Kolkata, other eateries now have rolls they are known for. Kusum Rolls on Park Street, founded in 1971, uses cheese in its fillings. Hot Kathi Roll, a few blocks away still on Park, deep-fries its parathas for a more indulgent meal. I use less oil than I remember seeing on Park Street to give my insides a break, but not without a certain sadness. The recipe looks lengthy, but it unfolds fairly easily and is very, very tasty in both the chicken-egg and vegan versions.

Kolkata Khati Rolls

PARATHAS WITH SPICY FILLING

Makes 5 rolls

PARATHAS

1 ½ cups all-purpose flour

¼ teaspoon salt

2 tablespoons vegetable oil

Cold water as required to knead the dough

CHICKEN OR TOFU FILLING

1 ½ pounds boneless chicken, cut into ½-inch pieces, or 1 pound firm tofu cubes

1 inch fresh ginger, mashed to a paste, to make 1 ½ teaspoons

4 cloves garlic, mashed to a paste

1 ½ teaspoons ground cumin seeds

1 ½ teaspoons ground coriander

½ teaspoon garam masala

1 teaspoon cayenne

½ teaspoon turmeric

1 tablespoon lemon juice

3 tablespoons plain yogurt

2 tablespoons mustard oil (substitute a milder vegetable oil
    if you prefer) for frying

Salt to taste

TOPPINGS

½ cup cucumber, cut in half lengthwise, seeds removed, thinly sliced

1 small onion, cut lengthwise and thinly sliced

½ cup cilantro, finely chopped

5 green chilies, seeds removed, finely chopped

⅓ cup grated carrot

5 teaspoons mustard oil or other vegetable oil

5 eggs

In a large bowl, sift the flour and salt. Add the oil and mix with your fingers to uniformly distribute it. Add the cold water in small amounts and knead until a soft and smooth dough forms, about 5–7 minutes. It should not stick to your fingers at the final stage. If it does, you have added too much water; add a little more flour to correct this. Cover with plastic wrap or a clean towel and allow the dough to rest for 15 minutes.

Meanwhile, mix the chicken pieces or tofu cubes with the ginger, garlic, cumin, coriander, garam masala, cayenne, turmeric, lemon juice, and yogurt in a shallow bowl. Marinate for 15 minutes or longer.

Once the chicken or tofu has marinated, add the 2 tablespoons oil to a pan over medium heat. Add the chicken or tofu mixture, and sauté for 15 minutes until there is no moisture left. This is important—if the mixture is too wet, the khati rolls will be soggy. Add salt to taste. Set the cooked mixture aside. You can make this up to 7 days ahead of time and refrigerate until needed, reheating before use.

Mix all the ingredients for the toppings—cucumber, onion, cilantro, chilies, and carrot—in a bowl and set aside.

Next divide the dough into 5 equal parts and roll the portions into balls. The dough is likely to have become a little stiff—to soften it, roll and squeeze each ball between your palms until it feels soft, about 2 minutes. Now, using a rolling pin, roll each ball into a flat disk about 7–8 inches in diameter. Roll all the balls into disks—the parathas—and set aside on a lightly floured surface to prevent sticking.

Heat a large flat pan—an iron griddle is ideal—over medium heat, add 1 teaspoon of the oil, and once hot gently place a paratha disk on the pan and

➤

let it begin to cook. If you are doing the chicken-egg version, once the paratha starts to bubble up (about 30 seconds), crack a whole egg on top of it. Spread the egg over the paratha with a fork or the edge of a spatula, breaking the yolk, and cook for 1 minute, then gently flip it. Cook until the egg clings to the paratha. Though most of the egg should cling to one side of the paratha, it is okay if some of it creeps to the other side. Once the paratha begins to have light brown spots, lift the egg-paratha off the heat and set aside. Repeat until all the parathas have their egg lining. If you are making the vegan version of this recipe, skip the egg step but fry the parathas as above in hot oil, flipping each after it begins to bubble, and cook through.

To assemble the chicken version, take one egg-lined paratha, egg side up, and add 5–6 sautéed chicken pieces and several dollops of toppings. Add plain yogurt or raita (recipe to follow), tomato-chili sauce (recipe to follow), or store-bought hot sauce according to your taste. Roll the paratha up and wrap it with wax paper to keep it secure. Serve warm on a plate, or for a portable version, grab a napkin and off you go.

For the vegan version, take a plain paratha and add several cubes of sautéed spicy tofu, toppings, and tomato-chili sauce or store-bought hot sauce as you prefer, and roll it up.

Be careful not to overstuff the parathas or they will not hold together.

Raita

Makes 1 cup

1 cup plain yogurt
½ teaspoon ground cumin seeds
¼ teaspoon salt
½ cup cucumber, peeled, seeded, and chopped

For a fancier version, you can add one or more of the following: ¼ teaspoon minced green chilies, ¼ cup minced cilantro, ¼ cup finely chopped onions, and ¼ cup chopped walnuts. Mix all ingredients in a small bowl and you are ready to serve!

Tomato-Chili Sauce

Makes about 2 cups

2 pounds ripe tomatoes, cut in half
2 cloves garlic, finely chopped
2 fresh red chilies, minced, or to taste
½ teaspoon paprika
¼ cup sugar
Salt to taste
¼ cup white vinegar
1 teaspoon cornstarch
2 teaspoons water

Blend the tomatoes and garlic in a food processor or blender until smooth. Pour the mixture into a medium-sized saucepan and add the red chilies, paprika, sugar, salt, and vinegar. Cook over low heat, about 10–15 minutes, or until the mixture darkens, stirring occasionally. Strain the sauce into a large bowl to remove the tomato seeds. Return the mixture to the saucepan. Stir the cornstarch and water in a small bowl until smooth. Add this mixture to the saucepan and stir continuously until the sauce becomes thick—this can take 40 minutes or more. Take the pan off the heat and let cool. Pour into a sterilized jar and store in the refrigerator.

For a quick version of this recipe, add the minced chilies and vinegar to taste to store-bought ketchup.

Parathas would have pleased those interested in replacing rice in the colonies. Unleavened wheat was just what the British thought would strengthen Bengalis. After tasting a khati roll, I admit to admiration.

Other thoughts on bread creep in for consideration: the fact that wheat is the only crop grown exclusively for human consumption; the fact that wheat can be a hard grain for humans to digest; and the fact that, unlike in the rest of the world, in the U.S. most bread and whole wheat flour available in stores is made from hard red wheat berries with high protein content. This makes flour great for baking with leavening agents to lift it but not so good for unleavened chapatis. I've learned when making bread that you want gluten in the dough. This way, while baking, the walls of little air pockets formed by yeast expand but don't burst open. If you're making cookies or a piecrust, you want to keep the gluten content of the dough and batter low. Otherwise, your results will be tough and gummy.

Other grains also contain protein, but wheat along with barley, rye, and spelt contains varieties of protein that aren't broken down by human digestive enzymes. In wheat, the difficult-to-digest protein is gliadin, in rye it's secalin, and in barley it's hordein. These proteins don't always faze our guts. But if our immune system misreads the situation, according to the Harvard Medical School, and thinks the proteins are intruders, it unleashes a furious inflammatory response. In people with celiac disease, this goes further to damage tissue—the small intestine, with its millions of slender projections called villi that produce digestive enzymes and soak up nutrients, can be attacked from within the body's own immune system and become stubby, even flat. The villi produce fewer digestive enzymes and absorb fewer nutrients. Many people with a sensitivity to wheat may not have this war of the villi worlds inside them but feel bloated after eating, unless this has gone on so long that they no longer notice. Still, an internal system constantly fighting inflammation is troubling. Eating less wheat is likely good for a lot of people, but in India, with its delicious breads and long history with wheat, that's challenging.

My first try with parathas is a stellar example of not using the right flour. I use a high-quality white flour known for its protein, my friend for years of baking cakes, but I find it hard to use when making unleavened Indian breads. In India, the most common wheat berry for flour is durum wheat; with its light golden color, it makes a soft yellowish-tan dough, ideal for breads that do not use any type of leavening.

While I am in India, I do my best to limit the wheat I eat, but not when faced with chapatis at lunch. And sometimes dinner. Paratha, luchi, bhatura—a large puffy fried bread—koraishutir kochuri, and so many more are hard to resist. Okay, I completely failed to skip bread in India.

Most of the time, I am not thinking about enzymes, only about taste. If you pass a kitchen in many homes in India around dinnertime, you can hear the light slap of chapati dough being placed on the counter, see fingers gingerly lifting disks of dough to place them on the heat of the flame, watch layers separate with air and then deplete as the breads are placed on a platter. Unleavened flat bread has long been daily fare for millions in India, and paired with dal it makes up sustenance. Identity and bread. The staff of life. Staple grains. Ancient story.

Chapter Ten

A NEW HYBRID CUISINE

...although a well-considered curry, or mulligatani—
capital things in their way—are still very frequently given at breakfast
or luncheon, they no longer occupy a position in the dinner menu.

—Arthur Robert Kenney-Herbert, *Culinary Jottings for Madras*, 1878

AFTER MY THWARTED AND serial search for the Calcutta Club's tipsy pudding recipe, I take my search for foods influenced by the British outside the club scene of Kolkata. To find the Anglo-Indian taste of India, I learn from friends that I need to visit Bomti Iyengar, art gallery owner and culinary tour leader in Kolkata.

Bomti showcases the many faces of food in Kolkata for visitors over tasty meals in his home. I arrive in his glorious high-ceilinged space three stories above a busy Kolkata thoroughfare in the weathered Metropolitan Building, a colonial structure dating to 1905. The building sits masterfully across from Kolkata's Eden Gardens, and inside I initially feel as if a warren of small offices and mysterious portals will lead me into dim spaces. But before I reach Bomti's door, a long corridor with dark green shutters promises something enticing.

Stepping into Bomti's place is like stepping into an art gallery settled into

Metropolitan Building, Kolkata.

a comfortable sigh. The colors, textures, and settees are Old World elegant yet relaxing, and the food is sumptuous. Before the meal, I peer out the front balcony, and traffic sounds of the Esplanade rise to meet me. It's what a bird might see—this grand design of Kolkata—hidden to most at street level. Coming into focus from Bomti's balcony: the Victoria Memorial amid its lush greenway, Eden Gardens, the Tipu Sultan Masjid, and, though mostly hidden from my vantage point, the red buildings of New Market. The expansive view makes everything else, even blaring horns and trundling bus engines, fade. The building's exterior, complete with domes, pediments, balconies, and a clock tower, is enticing from the street, but from within, without leaning out and craning my neck up, I witness only how these embellishments support pigeons. The birds, chortling on the way to their perches, seem content to go about their business as moving parts of the façade regardless of the vista.

We eat chicken jhalfrezi, fish molee, yellow rice, rasam (pepper water), and kofta (meatball curry). Yes. All of that. For lunch. But first I watch Bomti's cook, Sankar Patra, who hails from West Midnapore, prepare bekti in fish molee. It seems so simple, so effortless, that of course it comes from much practice. The end taste of Sankar's fish molee is piquant, creamy on the tongue, with a hint of citrus and a touch of spice. Fish, important in the Anglo-Indian diet, as it is for most Bengalis, is made into a molee or stew with coconut milk.

A year later in my Missouri kitchen, I see photographs of the Esplanade area from Kolkata online: the pandemic has lessened traffic to the extent that the skies are no longer hazy, and blue prevails. This astonishing sight adds to the allure of Bomti's veranda, I have no doubt. I think of his lovely rooms and art-covered walls as I make his molee with the tilapia available in Missouri and savor the dish's unique creamy flavor, not hard to replicate even 8,100 miles away in the American Midwest.

Fish Molee

COCONUT FISH STEW

Recipe courtesy of Bomti Iyengar, art dealer and culinary tour leader, Kolkata

Serves 4–6

Salt to sprinkle on each fillet

¼ teaspoon turmeric to sprinkle on each fillet

1 pound bekti fillets or another sturdy mild fish like tilapia or black sea bass

3 or more tablespoons vegetable oil

1 teaspoon cayenne

¾ cup water

⅓ cup onion, mashed to a paste

½ inch cinnamon stick, broken into pieces

3 whole cloves

3 cardamom pods

⅓ cup garlic, mashed to a paste

1 cup coconut milk

1 lime, cut in half, seeds removed

Sprinkle salt and turmeric on each fish fillet and set aside for a few minutes. Heat the oil in a wok or deep-sided pan and fry the fish until cooked through and lightly browned. Set aside. In a small bowl, add the cayenne to the water. Set aside. Add more oil to the wok or pan if needed to bring it to about 3 tablespoons. Heat. Add the onion paste and fry for 2–3 minutes. Add the whole spices, and after 20 seconds or so add the mashed garlic. Continue to stir and fry for 2–3 minutes. Then add the cayenne-water mix. Stir until well mixed and bubbling, about 3 minutes. Add the fish and gently stir. Add the coconut milk. While this is heating, squeeze the lime juice into the sauce to your taste.

Chicken Jhalfrezi

Recipe courtesy of Bomti Iyengar, art dealer and cuisine tour leader, Kolkata
Serves 4–6

According to Patricia Brown in Anglo-Indian Food and Customs, the jhalfrezi on our menu stems from the Chittagong Hills and is a long-standing Anglo-Indian favorite. The story is that the local cooks employed by the memsahibs of the British Raj were bored with the bland food of the English and gradually spiced up the leftover cold beef, chicken, or pork roast to their taste. It became a staple in Anglo-Indian households.

8 chicken thighs, skinned and halved, or other chicken pieces

MARINADE
½ teaspoon turmeric
½ inch fresh ginger, mashed to a paste
2 cloves garlic, mashed to a paste
1 teaspoon ground coriander
1 teaspoon ground cumin seeds
1 teaspoon cayenne
1 teaspoon garam masala
1 teaspoon salt or to taste
2 tablespoons plain yogurt

3 tablespoons ghee (you can substitute butter or vegetable oil)
3 medium onions, cut in half, then sliced very fine into half-moon shapes
½ teaspoon cumin seeds
1 large green pepper, diced
½ cup hot water
1 bunch cilantro, finely chopped   ➤

Mix all the dry marinade ingredients with the yogurt. Rub the chicken pieces with the marinade and set aside in a bowl for 4 hours. Add the ghee to a heavy-bottomed pan, and over medium heat sauté the onions until they are golden brown. Lift the onions out and set aside. Add the cumin seeds to the pan and fry until they sputter, about 20 seconds. Add the marinated chicken to the pan and sauté until nicely browned, about 10–15 minutes, turning as needed. Lower the heat and stir in the diced green pepper and any remaining marinade from the chicken bowl. Continue to fry the chicken on low heat for another 10 minutes, adding as much of the hot water as needed for consistency. Test for sufficient salt. Stir in the chopped cilantro. Cover the pan and allow the jhalfrezi to simmer until the chicken is tender, about 10 more minutes. Stir in the fried onions. Serve warm with Indian bread or rice. Excellent with raita (see the recipe on page 179) and vegetables.

Though it came to mean more, at first the term "Anglo-Indian" referred to British colonials residing in India. Eventually, the term also meant the offspring of mixed-culture families. In 1982, when I was studying for a semester in Reading, England—where I met the man later to be my husband—an intimidating-to-me professor singled me out one day during class. She had just made a sweeping statement about food customs in India, and I had screwed up my courage enough to say something like, "Er, not always."

"Anglo-Indian?"

She had me in her laser focus, and at the time I had no idea what this term meant. My family for generations into antiquity hailed from Bengal. I understood, though, that she intended to convey that if my food heritage was refined in the way I said, I could not be in anything but a family that followed British customs or had a British parent. The power of her will froze my tongue. I felt my face heat. Though someone distracted her at that point, I felt for the first time the residual power of colonialism and the attitudes it might foster even in the educated. That moment, with that unlikely professor, aroused ideas about identity that continue to stay with me.

After the various Western empires—Portuguese, Dutch, French, English—dropped anchor off the shores of the Indian subcontinent and spent years in trade and later in colonization, there emerged the likely first Eurasians—first, in Goa, Portuguese men who, along with acceding to forced conversions in the Indian Inquisition, married noble Indian women and, later, those born to British fathers and Indian mothers. Families emerged throughout the subcontinent with not only British and Portuguese surnames but French and Dutch ones as well, all with the requisite one Indian parent.

Patricia Brown writes that after Indian independence, the term "Anglo-Indian" came to mean a distinctive subculture whose members are Christians of one denomination or another, speak English, mostly wear European clothes, have substantially European dietary habits though they are addicted to the fairly lavish use of Indian spices, are occupationally engaged in a restricted number of trades and professions, and are by and large endogamous. Being endogamous, the practice of marrying within a specific social or ethnic group and rejecting others as unsuitable for marriage or other close personal relationships, is not so uncommon in India and could be expected to enhance community growth. Not so for the Anglo-Indians, who over time have dwindled.

About 500,000 Anglo-Indians remain worldwide, Patricia Brown says in *Anglo-Indian Food and Customs*. Most left India after independence, using their British passports acquired during the Raj, for ports in England or for Australia or Canada. In "What Does Anglo-Indian Mean?" journalist and historian Anthony Khatchaturian says the minuscule community remaining in India of about one lakh—100,000—within the country's 1.3 billion people may be close to unique, having been around only for a few hundred years, dying out within the next hundred, yet leaving a lasting mark on India.

Khatchaturian defines the community by its legal history. India's 1911 census counted Anglo-Indians as a separate category of citizen for the first time as someone with a European father and an Indian mother. The Constitution of India improved that category to allow descendants of those unions to identify themselves clearly as persons whose father or another progenitor in the male line is or was of European descent but who lived and is or was born within the territory of India.

During the colonial years, Khatchaturian says, many Anglo-Indians served in roles that the British didn't have the numbers to fill but still didn't trust Indians with—officials in the police, railways, post and telegraph offices, customs and excise bureaus—and gave these stable, de facto guaranteed government jobs with their perks of living quarters, community hubs complete with churches, free medical coverage, and more to Anglo-Indians. Many were teachers, too, making use of their native English-language skills. The best-paid positions were in the railroads. Wherever you find a railway junction city—Kolkata, Asansol, Dhanbad, Jamshedpur, Nagpur, and more—Khatchaturian says, there would have been a hub of Anglo-Indians.

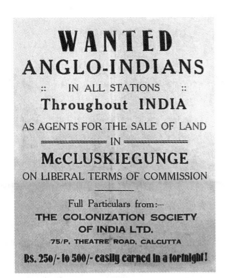

(left) "Wanted / Anglo Indians" advertisement; (right) Frank Anthony stamp, India Post, 2003. Wikimedia, https://commons.wikimedia.org/w/index. php?curid=74404271.

This buffer layer of citizenry was encouraged. Early on, the East India Company paid 15 silver rupees per child born of an Indian mother and an Anglo father, according to Malcolm Hourigan, a descendant of the community, in "Holding On: Anglo Indian Settlement in McCluskiegunj." Even so, loyalty to their Anglo roots and their English-language skills were the critical qualifications for the British hiring officials. Though convenient, Anglo-Indians were never equal in British eyes.

When Indian independence from British rule came, change came to the British community living in India. Frank Anthony, who was the Anglo-Indian representative in the Parliament of India as well as the president of the All India Anglo-Indian Association, lobbied for a home for the remaining dispersed community. Enter Ernest Timothy McCluskie, a British official who founded the Colonisation Society of India, through which he bought 10,000 acres of land about 45 miles from Ranchi on the Chota Nagpur Plateau, perfect for farming. The plateau, previously owned by the raja of Ratu in what is now Jharkhand, has the Dugadugi River running through it, picturesque hills, and a climate that cools off in the evenings of summer, no small thing in India. Even so, as independence came, the British went home and McCluskie's idea of the place as a refuge for the British in India failed. This left an opportunity for the Anglo-Indians.

The erstwhile office wallahs, railway men, teachers, and other Anglo-Indians, however, did not actually farm well, and there were no outside jobs. The land needed to be cleared, food needed to be raised. The original houses were built of bamboo that needed replacing, and there were wild animals in the jungles of the area.

"Anthony had made a fundamental miscalculation," Khatchaturian says, "which might have sealed the fate of the community forever—he knew that Anglo-Indians made very good employees, but they weren't very good at business, so although they were ready to, once again, work hard and establish themselves, there was nobody to work for."

The Merediths, Jennings, D'Rozarios, Barretts, Hourigans, Perkinses, D'Costas, Mendieses, and others were on their own. By 2015, only six or seven of the original three hundred and fifty families were left in the homeland they had called, in the past, Chota England, Little England. Many Anglo-Indians looked outside India, and Britain had many midlevel government posts open after two generations' worth of war. Anglo-Indians who didn't leave migrated to large cities, where they rented apartments in areas such as Elliot Road, Ripon Lane, Wellesley Street, Park Circus, and Bow Barracks in Kolkata. Khatchaturian mentions that members of the community often rented because in their pre-independence lives their living accommodations were provided by virtue of their government work, and often they had not saved for their own properties. Many went back to jobs they knew well—teaching, for example, where their English-language skills were sought after for a time. Soon, though, their own students with degrees backing their language prowess gradually supplanted the cadre of Anglo-Indian teachers.

Descendants of McCluskiegunj today return at times searching for their roots, making short films, and taking photos of a vanishing era. Photos surface online of the bamboo house days, prior to the rose gardens and red-tiled roofs of British-style bungalows, with dead leopards sprawled in front of serious men with guns. The old dreams of a homeland have faded for most, yet the establishment of a school, the Don Bosco Academy, has rekindled hopes of livelihood: teachers and hostels for students are needed. The government of Jharkhand has designated the area as an official tourist destination. McCluskiegunj may not yet be in its last days. The foods most certainly have carried on.

Chapter Eleven

TRUTH IN TEA...
PLUS, CHILI CHICKEN

Come, oh come ye tea-thirsty restless ones— /
The kettle boils, bubbles / And sings, / Musically.

—Rabindranath Tagore

IN THE LAND OF noble Himalayan vistas, steep slopes, and delectable teas, indoor heat is not de rigueur, even in January in Darjeeling. Unprepared, I layer: wool socks, leggings underneath hiking pants, a cashmere button-up sweater my mother gave me one Christmas thirty years ago, a T-shirt, and a somewhat dressy tunic I had brought for an interview. I wore this every day. For three days. But there are worse things than a roly-poly silhouette (you'd have to ask those who saw me if this is strictly true).

In India, tea is a braided story: Assamese wild bushes—British tea planta-tions—Chinese advisers—and, for me, my grandmother's veranda in Ranchi at 4:00 p.m. I was on a quest to find the source of all the pleasant hours I had spent sipping a cup at Rani Villa and, later, in Kansas and Missouri over the years. Darjeeling was but a short flight and a longer drive up steep slopes away from Kolkata.

I go by plane from Kolkata to Siliguri and see, on the drive up the sides of mountains, tea bushes literally lining much of the route. The farther up the slopes we go, the more I wish for warm layers. I shrug this off, fascinated by my mission.

I am seeking truth in tea. Tea is courtesy of the British; no, it is the Chinese; wait, no, it was already in India before all the hoopla and tea cozies. It seems a good idea to seek beautiful vistas and proximity to ancient homages to God to help sort this out. Beauty and grace I find in abundance. Plus, there is a tiny steam-powered train. And cheese toast.

Before I tiptoe through the tea bushes, ride the toy train to visit ancient monasteries, explore an old church, and eat cheesy toast at Keventers in Darjeeling while gazing at high clouds, I consider a reading of tea leaves to get to the root of things. It turns out that other information is at hand.

According to Sara Sohail in the *Madras Courier*, "Although the world came to know of tea first from the Chinese, it is a fact" that the Assamese tribes of India such as the Singphos "were used to drinking tea prepared in their native ways. This tea flowered wild in Upper Assam and was popular there; the locals believed it had memory-boosting powers." The local tribes and their tea-drinking habits, knowledge of medicinal uses for tea, and indigenous preparations—sometimes dried for storage over years, sometimes fermented prior to boiling and drinking—sparked the idea of establishing tea as a colonial business in India.

Tea plant.

The British, importing tea from China and looking for ways to circumvent the costs of doing so, and their Scottish agent Robert Bruce "discovered" tea plants growing wild in the Upper Assam jungles in the early 1820s with help from Singpho chief Beesa Gam. Well aware of the plants, he no doubt led them straight to their "discovery," according to Sohail in the *Courier* as well as Pradip Baruah in *Science and Culture*. The British thought the Assamese "near savages," Sohail says (and, yes, we may all inhale sharply at this bit of colonial-era snark), and imported tea experts from China to meld the "wild" Indian tea with the cultivated Chinese variety. The Chinese, passionate for 5,000 years about drinking what they called t'e in the Fukien dialect and ch'a in Cantonese, for both medicinal purposes and enjoyment, documented it in 780 BCE when Lu Yu wrote *Ch'a Ching* or *The Classic of Tea*. Then, too, poets got involved. Baruah quotes a mystic poet from the Tang dynasty:

The first cup moistens my lips and throat
The second shatters my loneliness
The third causes the wrongs of life
   to fade gently from my recollection.
The fourth purifies my soul
The fifth lifts me
   to the realms of the unwinking gods.

Chinese tea experts applied their knowledge to Assam tea plants. They taught locals techniques for cultivating both black and green tea. By 1840, tea produced for British export in Assam was acknowledged to be superior, and by the 1850s tea estates were beginning to be established in Darjeeling.

More than 150 years later, in 2014, Silver Tips Imperial tea from the organic Makaibari Tea Estate in Kurseong sold for $1,850 per kilogram or $45 a pot at the Ritz-Carlton in Tokyo, according to the *Times of India*. It was the most expensive tea sold in India at the time.

I sip Silver Tips Imperial at the Makaibari tea factory, strictly for research purposes, of course, during a tasting session. The notes and undertones are delicate. For me, judging the qualities of tea is as intricate as tasting wines, and the process of doing so is very similar: put your nose near the infused leaves, inhale deeply, make a slurping noise to oxygenate the sip, indulge in contemplation while gazing into the distance or by closing your eyes, as you are inclined. And again. I know, I know, you're thinking that is heavy lifting in four layers of clothing, but I fight the good fight and have two cups.

My definitive thought? Teas in Darjeeling are a matter of taste. The finest teas in the world are grown here: delicate and aromatic and really lovely when produced in biodynamic soils in sync with natural cycles. The process of plucking and drying the leaves, thus determining if the end result will be green, white, or black tea, is synchronized with events such as the full moon at Makaibari. The tea factory and estate, sold in 2014 to the Luxmi Group, were established in 1859 by the family of Swaraj Kumar Banerjee, who pioneered biodynamic organic practices for tea and tropical agriculture in 1988 before it was popular to think of such things. Though practices may change with the new ownership, during Raja Banerjee's stewardship the estate was run as a multilayered living organism.

Banerjee mapped the course of the tea estate using the principles of Rudolf Steiner's agricultural course lectures of 1924. Steiner, who was one of the first public figures to warn that widespread use of chemical fertilizers would lead to the decline of soil, plant, and animal health with the subsequent devitalization of food, used natural fermentation to heal poor soils and plants. The result at Makaibari is tea with exceptional taste and flavor. Steiner's ideas, which complement those of India's cow culture, value the cow's continuous rumination and four compartmentalized stomachs as a path to bring the energy of the sun and the minerals of the earth back to the soil and harvest.

"The whole community is organized as a rhythm of nature," Banerjee tells me. The gardens "are a sea of forests with islands of tea in it. There are two tigers, four leopards, and four hundred bird species at Makaibari." This in addition to nearly sixteen hundred human workers. The harmony extends to the seven villages and the lives of the people who surround the estate. "Empower the ladies and your community thrives," Banerjee says. To that end, in partnership with the families working there, he invested in twelve hundred cows, two for each family, to increase his workers' intake of nutrition from the milk and provide methane fuel for cooking fires.

"Imagine waking at 3:00 or 4:00 a.m. every day to go collect firewood or cooking with wet wood during the monsoon. Using the methane from cows gave the ladies back four or more hours per day." The women used that time, Banerjee says, to grow vegetables in family plots, among other things, which saved funds they immediately put to use educating their older children. The younger ones, due to Banerjee's initiative, were also assured day care while their mothers worked so that the older girls were not pulled out of school to do this.

As I walk the hilly terrain at Makaibari, we pass one of the day care houses—a tidy affair with colorful blankets in piles inside along with several children at play. The tea bushes, looking like a patterned carpet from afar, are healthy and thigh-high. There are tall trees edging the fields that continue into deep forests and I crane my neck a little, not really expecting a flash of tiger or a slink of leopard but hoping for it.

Indeed, it feels as if forests wrap the steep slopes of tea bushes at Makaibari. The deep quiet and the clear air are restorative. I hadn't realized how soothing the arrangement was until we left. As we went down the mountains, I saw that each tea estate we passed had more rows of regimented bushes and near-perfect spaces between them than the last. On Makaibari's 1,573 acres, tea grows on 550 acres due to intentional planting. Insect repellents in the form of plant species unpleasant to bugs are allowed to grow along the edges and sometimes in the middle of the tea gardens.

When I spoke with Banerjee at his new location down the mountain in Siliguri, with no tea carpeting the hills in sight, I expected some reminiscences and reflections on his past truly groundbreaking accomplishments, but his robust energy is now focused on encouraging biodynamic practices with 40,000 female small tea growers of North Bengal with a venture he calls Rimpocha. His focus is soils, as it was at Makaibari, and as I can only agree from observations on my faraway Missouri farm, Banerjee sees the wealth of the planet resting in two to three inches of topsoil worldwide. He has embedded knowledge of the land and the people who work it. Large-scale tea operations seem to be the trend, but even in that environment handcrafted, gently harvested teas are still rewarded in the market as something loved.

MRS. BEETON'S TEA

TO MAKE TEA.

1814. There is very little art in making good tea; if the water is boiling, and there is no sparing of the fragrant leaf, the beverage will almost invariably be good. The old-fashioned plan of allowing a teaspoonful to each person, and one over, is still practised. Warm the teapot with boiling water; let it remain for two or three minutes for the vessel to become thoroughly hot, then pour it away. Put in the tea, pour in from $\frac{1}{2}$ to $\frac{3}{4}$ pint of boiling water, close the lid, and let it stand for the tea to draw from 5 to 10 minutes; then fill up the pot with water. The tea will be quite spoiled unless made with water that is actually 'boiling,' as the leaves will not open, and the flavour not be extracted from them; the beverage will consequently be colourless and tasteless,—in fact, nothing but tepid water. Where there is a very large party to make tea for, it is a good plan to have two teapots instead of putting a large quantity of tea into one pot; the tea, besides, will go farther. When the infusion has been once completed, the addition of fresh tea adds very little to the strength; so, when more is required, have the pot emptied of the old leaves, scalded, and fresh tea made in the usual manner. Economists say that a few grains of carbonate of soda, added before the boiling water is poured on the tea, assist to draw out the goodness: if the water is very hard, perhaps it is a good plan, as the soda softens it; but care must be taken to use this ingredient sparingly, as it is liable to give the tea a soapy taste if added in too large a quantity. For mixed tea, the usual proportion is four spoonfuls of black to one of green; more of the latter when the flavour is very much liked; but strong green tea is highly pernicious, and should never be partaken of too freely.

Time.—2 minutes to warm the teapot, 5 to 10 minutes to draw the strength from the tea.

Sufficient.—Allow 1 teaspoonful to each person, and one over.

TEA.—The tea-tree or shrub belongs to the class and order of Monadelphia polyandria in the Linnaean system, and to the natural order of Aurantiaceae in the system of Jussieu. Lately it has been made into a new order, the Theasia, which includes the Camellia and some other plants. It commonly grows to the height of from three to six feet; but it is said, that, in its wild or native state, it reaches twenty feet or more. In China it is cultivated in numerous small plantations. In its general appearance, and the form of its leaf, it resembles the myrtle. The blossoms are white and fragrant, not unlike those of the wild rose, but smaller; and they are succeeded by soft green capsules, containing each from one to three white seeds. These capsules are crushed for oil, which is in general use in China.

Isabella Beeton, who was in her mid-twenties when she published *Mrs. Beeton's Book of Household Management* in 1861, was said to be fashionable and modern, not starchy or an elder matron as her book title might imply. Still, going through her tea steps, it's hard to imagine calling her Isabella or helping to pour. She had good tea sense, for sure. I understand from tea experts that steeping a good Darjeeling tea is all that's needed; milk or sugar spoils the delicate flavor.

Back in Kolkata, within hours of leaving the mountains, I am cranking up fans to combat the heat. "Winter-schminter," I say, as I begin to be warm again after four days of mountain chill. I did not wear my multipiece sequentially layered Darjeeling outfit again.

In addition to early tea expertise, Kolkata owes another tip of the culinary hat to China. Chinese street food vendors and sit-down restaurants alike have influenced the modern palate throughout the city and created something that is uniquely Chinese and Indian. After my first taste of chili chicken at a corner stall, I go in search of more details.

Monica Liu seems like a kindly grandmother in her comfortable flowing patterned top. I meet her at Beijing, one of her five restaurants in Kolkata, and from the soft tapering at the end of her words when she speaks English, her conversation feels unassuming and kindly. That she sometimes breaks into more staccato Hakka Chinese or Hindi with passing staff doesn't change this impression. The stories about her being the mafia don of Tangra appear far-fetched.

Monica began her restaurant businesses with Kim Ling in Tangra, the historically Chinese section of the city. Then, building on that success, she opened Beijing, also in Tangra, Tung Fong on Park Street, Mandarin on Sarat Bose Road, and Mandarin on Lake Avenue. Though an unstoppable drive and pressing schedule must have propelled her to this point of five thriving restaurants, her manner seems to say that she has time for this conversation, time to discuss the past. Her phone rings, waiters stop to check details with her, and in between she encourages me to sample her dishes, orders more as I begin to wind down, and asks in gently rounded vowels if I prefer rice or noodles.

We sit at a table near the front. Monica thinks about my questions before answering, her eyes steady and calm. When I ask about her family and grandchildren, her whole face lights up in a smile. One grandchild, going to an exceptional school in the city, is an athlete, and as I talk with Monica, she stops by our table in her school uniform. I think of Monica's life and wonder at how much can shift in a generation.

The restaurant features white and gold tablecloths, a dragonfish worth 65,000 rupees (nearly $900) inside a large bubbling tank, and a sweeping open feel. As I hear her tale unfold, my first impression shifts slightly. Monica's soft voice pairs with a practical no-nonsense nature. When real-life goons in Tangra tried to coerce her to give them free meals in 1991, she didn't let it pass: she drove them away in person. And more: when a fight broke out among her first staff, which led to an employee bearing a broken beer bottle, she waded in. "I just went in there, caught one, two slaps. Caught another, two slaps."

These people really didn't know whom they were dealing with. All this spunk had to come from somewhere. And, indeed, it did.

The 1962 Indo-China War changed Monica's life forever. As James Griffiths writes in the *Atlantic*, the Leong family, along with other Chinese families living in Shillong, were abruptly shipped to the Deoli internment camp in Rajasthan, more than thirteen hundred miles away in western India. Guards came to their house and led them to the train cars, some with the word "enemy" scrawled across the side. Monica was nine years old.

Three thousand people were taken to Deoli. Each and every person on those train cars was part of the fabric of the culture of India, until they were not. Fear of spies was the reasoning behind the Defense of India Act of 1962, which was eerily similar to the U.S. reaction to and subsequent internment of Japanese Americans two decades earlier and half a world away during World War II. People who had a Chinese last name or just looked Chinese were suspect. The border dispute lasted thirty days, but the Chinese families in Deoli were not released for nearly six years.

Shillong, forested and hilly at 5,000 feet above sea level, was a far cry from the dun-colored and flat desert vista of Rajasthan at less than a thousand feet above sea level. The heat alone was astonishing to the people from the mountains. But more distressing, there was no school for the children and no work for the adults. The Leongs remained in the camp over five years until Monica, then fourteen, sent a petition to the Indian home minister that finally led to their release. Her instinct to be counted and make her place in the world was born. "They had forgotten about us."

Waiters place a plate of Monica's chili chicken on the table in front of us, and aroma lifts immediately. The succulent pieces glisten slightly. Monica's recipe adds a long, finely sliced Chinese vegetable that she says you can find at Chinese groceries in tins, though she couldn't recall its name in English. I take a tentative bite and am hooked. A small amount of sugar is dissolved into the sauce that clings to the chicken, creating a gamut of flavors—green chili heat, earthy garlic, tangy lemon, all with that balancing slight sweetness. I take many more bites.

"Have a little more," Monica encourages warmly.

After a year of the COVID-19 pandemic and more tension with China that again makes Chinese Indians wary, I study the mostly friendly relations between China and India through the 1950s. In the early days, India reassured China that it had no designs on the territory of Tibet, annexed by Beijing in 1950, but when the Dalai Lama fled to Dharamsala in India in 1959 after a failed uprising, things turned less cordial. China claimed over 60,000 square miles of Indian territory, and there followed years of military skirmishes until, in 1962, the People's Liberation Army forcefully occupied the territory. James Griffiths writes that the "Line of Actual Control" that existed pre-1959 was marked off, though China retained de facto ownership of Aksai Chin. This outcome still chafes India and may nag at the former residents of the Deoli camp in ominous ways.

I am remembering my conversation with Monica as I make chili chicken in my Missouri kitchen. Since some people avoid monosodium glutamate, I increase the amount of sea salt, although MSG adds that umami taste to foods much like the free glutamate in Parmesan cheese or tomatoes or mushrooms.

It turns out beautifully. The sauce clings lovingly to the chicken, cilantro brightens the end result on the plate, and aroma rises. I make it again and double the number of serranos, and it begins to taste closer to Monica's splendid version. She had warned me, after all: "What I am cooking and what you make will never be the same."

Kolkata Chili Chicken

Recipe with slight adaptations courtesy of Monica Liu, chef and owner of Beijing,
Kim Ling, Tung Fong, Mandarin on Sarat Bose Road,
and Mandarin on Lake Avenue, Kolkata
Serves 2–3

If you prefer a dish with sauce, Chef Monica says to add more water to the last stage
of the recipe and serve with rice. For a family member who is vegan, I tried this
dish with fried tofu and it worked well. You won't need to fry the tofu as long as the
chicken, but otherwise follow the same steps.

1 pound boneless chicken, cut into ½-inch pieces
2 green chilies, seeds removed (I used serrano peppers)
1 teaspoon sea salt (Chef Monica used ¼ teaspoon MSG and
    ¼ teaspoon sea salt)
2 ½ tablespoons cornstarch
Peanut oil for frying
1 teaspoon minced garlic
1 tablespoon tomato sauce
½ teaspoon sugar
Juice of ½ lemon
2 tablespoons water
2–3 tablespoons cilantro, chopped

Rinse the chicken pieces in warm water and drain. Mash the chilies into a
paste and set aside. In a bowl, add the sea salt and cornstarch to the chicken
and mix until all the pieces are coated. Next, in a wok or pan, heat enough
peanut oil to deep-fry the chicken. Fry the chicken pieces until they are
golden brown. Set the chicken aside on a paper towel to drain. Remove all but
1–2 tablespoons of the oil from the wok or pan and add the chili paste, garlic,

➤

tomato sauce, sugar, lemon juice, and water. Stir and fry to dissolve the sugar. Add the chicken pieces and 1–2 tablespoons of the cilantro. Stir and fry to mix well. Sprinkle the rest of the cilantro over the top of the chicken and serve hot. Excellent as an appetizer or main dish.

There are many ways to lose history. Collectively, we forget the small stories that inhabit individual lives; willfully, governments or our own minds may pick a side to amplify. Everywhere there are instances of this loss, as any minority culture can tell you, but sometimes those tales are simply idling, waiting to be lifted into view. Or simply looking down might clarify them: history is visible on the plate.

In Kolkata, where you can find chili chicken and chow mein everywhere from street stalls to indoor restaurants in every neighborhood, you can see that the flavors of China are popular and in demand. The Kolkata-China food trail began in street food stalls in 1985, Monica says, and they began because seven decades or so ago, a sugar mill owner, Tong Atchew, brought in workers from China to the area of the city now called Achipur. Earlier, in the late 1700s, Chinese immigrants were largely silk traders, dentists, carpenters, and tannery owners. Monica's Tangra neighborhood had tanneries and the Chinese to run them, including her husband later in the migration. A Chinatown in the Bowbazar area of central Kolkata also formed in the later eighteenth century with Cantonese, Hakka, and a smaller number of Fujianese.

"In those days, Chinese in India cannot afford to go out to eat," Monica tells me. "But Chinese food is booming." Looking at this, Monica's keen mind formed the idea for a restaurant of her own.

Chinese immigration to India, though beginning in the late 1700s, started in earnest in the middle 1850s when the British recruited people from Hong Kong and Guangdong to work on the tea plantations. At one point there were 20,000 people of Chinese origin living in Kolkata, though their numbers have dwindled to less than 5,000 today. The Deoli camp, Monica's six-year internment home, was courtesy of the Brits as well, who originally set it up to house prisoners of war in the 1940s.

The Hakka people, their very name meaning "guest families," know the story of being foreign. According to the Asia Society, they have been called other things: gypsies, nomads, barbarians, outsiders, even Mongolians, though their settlements pre-date Genghis Khan's invasions. Today, it is thought that the Hakka are largely northern Han Chinese who progressively migrated south, fleeing war, poverty, and chaos. The diaspora of Hakka Chinese is one of perpetual migration: they moved from the northern part of China in the twelfth century to the southeast and even farther to Shillong, to Kolkata, to Toronto, Queens, or Melbourne. Each movement becoming a layer that never completely fused with the one before, leaving its trace in the margins, in recipes, in cooking techniques.

Hakka migrations would put my small visa annoyance in its place—the Hakka movements were an exercise of centuries. Their first exodus from lands north of the Yangtze River, according to the Asia Society, came circa 400 as a result of tribal invaders. They made inroads into Hunan and Jiangxi Provinces for five hundred years, but at the close of the Tang dynasty, around 900, peasant uprisings made them move again, many going farther south to coastal Fujian. At this point, they lived in relative seclusion for nearly four centuries. It must have been a time for ripening cultural traditions and food innovations to match their new lands. "Hakka" grew to be a term of self-identity during this era, not merely a word to designate being an outsider.

However, Genghis Khan's invasions drove the Hakka to move once more, this time to Guangdong Province. Meizhou and its environs became a center for Hakka life there. And when the Ming dynasty fell, the Hakka moved to settle the newly deserted lands in Sichuan, Hunan, Hubei, and Taiwan. There were fights over the lands they settled, and in the mid-1850s 100,000 Hakka died in clashes, and others migrated to work in Bengal.

That long history of movement that brought Monica to Tangra is lost on most. But it shows in her ability to create a life from a patchy start at Deoli. Trying to find out who the Hakka are leads me to who Monica Liu is, and historical data are only part of the story. The Asia Society refers to the Hakka as a people embodied by the dandelion, a flower that will thrive under trying conditions, surviving many obstacles.

I ask about the overlapping flavors of Indo-Chinese food on Monica's menu.

"What is Indo-Chinese? It's just Chinese."

In the U.S. or Canada, she says, she can see that when you dine at a Chinese restaurant, you aren't exactly served Chinese food. "Foreigners like certain things. So there they make food for all types of people. Here, we don't have to make food for all types of people. We make food for only Bengali people. Bengalis know how to eat Chinese food. They love it."

Monica traveled to Sichuan to sample foods there. She tried Chinese foods in North America and elsewhere. Always, Monica thought of the palate of her customers in Bengal. She created a tasty version, better than others, of chili chicken using the green chili with care and confidence. Chinese food in India does have its distinct flavors, though, often spicier versions of chicken and noodles or Sichuan (spelled Schezwan in India) recipes that use dried red chilies as a substitute for Sichuan peppercorns. Indian ingredients like garlic, ginger, and green chilies are added to dishes. Chinese noodles, referred to as chow, and newer fusion foods such as golden fried prawns, Schezwan dosai, masala-filled chili chicken, and more dot the food landscape. This flavor profile is popular all over India, but its roots have always been in Kolkata.

In 2020, another time of conflict both in health precautions and along the Chinese border, Monica's Beijing restaurant in Tangra is shuttered. It's the pandemic, but it's also the military incidents, and again the idea of foreignness rises. For decades the Chinese have been shaping the history of Kolkata and its palate, but once more it is time for wariness and a certain protectiveness of what is one's own.

"It's actually Chinese food. You see, we fought to survive. We should have something."

Chapter Twelve

AT THE TABLE OF
DISAPPEARING FOOD TRAILS

…do bring some rosy mangoes in a cane-basket covered with a silken
kerchief, / And some prosaic food as well—sandesh and pantua prepared
by lovely hands, / Also pilau cooked / with fish and meat, / For all these
things become ineffable when imbued with loving devotion.

—Rabindranath Tagore, 1935

AT THE TOP OF the world, or so it seems, I stand at the plate glass window
of Anthony Khatchaturian and Brunnel Arathoon's home at the time, overlooking what used to be wetlands. The Urbana NRI Complex here has seven
residential towers, two with forty-five floors and five with forty floors, mani-
cured green spaces, and plans for three more towers. The complex's brochures
say that ecofriendly water recycling is managed here. You can see open fields
from the Khatchaturians' living room window forty stories up as well as how
the city lies within its plain.

I've never been at ease with heights like this and look outward, not down,
while standing at their window. Now is an ideal time for the weights of

my two nations to keep me grounded. In fact, they are doing so—the final **NOREPLY** word from the consulate is that I may obtain a ten-year tourist visa but not the one that designates me as being of Indian origin. I think of Rainer Maria Rilke's *Sonnets to Orpheus*: "The trees you planted in childhood have grown / too heavy. You cannot bring them along. / Give yourselves to the air, to what you cannot hold." And I do. I let it go.

In the end, I take a quick peek downward from the Khatchaturians' window. Immediately, the true badness of this small daring makes itself known. Instead of heeding Rilke and giving myself over to the air, the lesson evaporates and I step back swiftly. The view is so beautiful from a few feet back.

Bengal is a sweeping land. I breathe in deeply with that thought. India is vast in so many ways—so layered culturally and historically, rich in so much— but I had not considered its lush offerings in sheer space. In the West, we see images of dense crowds; India many times is branded as a place of poverty and need. Its wildness has been forgotten. For a land with so many ties to the natural world embedded in religious lore, this seems strange. In today's parlance, this needs hashtag clarification: #junglegreen #notmotherterasasindia #vastnature.

The open space pushes away from the city and surprises me, rolling south and east without impediment. The vista appears a deep lush jade, and from up here there's a tangible hush. None of the street sounds in the city center where I live permeates the height of these buildings. Visually, it's another matter. Looking toward Kolkata's center, I see smog rolling across the thousands of buildings, large and small, from one location clearly seen from this far up.

"The city dump," Anthony says, "they burn there twice a day."

Considering what might be in the trash—single-use plastics, packages with all manner of old chemicals, metal tins, innumerable scraps of things I am too leery to view closely when I walk by collection points near my apartment—I am appalled; the piles gathered on street corners for daily pickup do not look breathable. But standing here, I see a new, cleaner India possibly gaining ground. There are blue skies above the rolls of pollution. One year later, the pandemic lessens traffic and clear skies command the view: with pollution slashed, cerulean becomes even more visible from the photoworthy view at the Khatchaturians' home.

Armenian Bengalis may not be your first thought when you think of India: yet another citizenry that brought their foodways and culture and, like a drop of water into an ocean, blended with the whole. But the exodus of these people from Armenia, their settlement in Persia, and finally their entry into India over seven hundred years ago affect how Kolkata feels tangibly on the street—landmark buildings—how its people think of its history—influential trade dealings—and, less noticeably, what Bengalis eat.

The day I visit Brunnel, we cook Armenian dolmades, which involves great sheaves of vegetable greens, rice, and delectable additions like allspice, cayenne, cilantro, dill, and almonds. The meal is delicious, tasty in ways of conversation as well as palate. In the warm bustle of Brunnel's kitchen, a lovely meal spins into being.

A few weeks later, in a talk Anthony gives at the Victoria Memorial, "The Armenians of Calcutta," he jokes with the Bengalis in the room. "You've stolen one of our foods, the Ottoman dolma," he says to chuckles erupting in the room. To Persian Armenians, the dolma was wrapped in the leaf of the grape plant. "Of course, coming out here, no grape plants were available, so we used the cabbage leaf. But then Bengalis took it one step further, shoved it into potol, and you have potol dolma."

Anthony's avid listeners loved this reference to their beloved potol, a striped summer squash, delicious stuffed. While I help prepare Armenian dolmades, I can see the resemblance to the potol version, but these are a treat on their own.

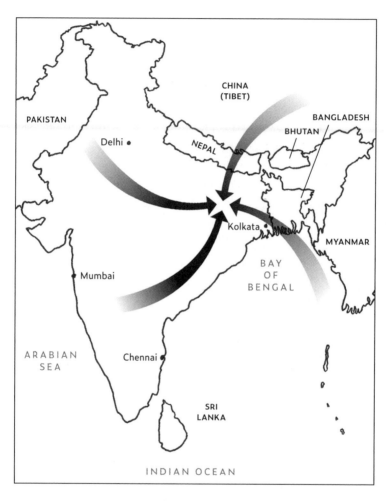

India's food trails.

Kolkata Armenian Dolmades

STUFFED CHARD

Recipe courtesy of Brunnel Arathoon

Serves 6–9

WRAP

5–6 full bunches medium to large chard leaves or other greens
    such as young grape, cabbage, or beet leaves

FILLING

1 cup long grain rice

10 tablespoons butter or vegetable oil

3 medium onions, finely diced

2 pounds ground beef or meat of your choice

3–4 tablespoons tomato sauce or tomato paste (Brunnel used
    last summer's roasted tomato and garlic puree)

½–1 teaspoon allspice

½–1 teaspoon cayenne or to taste

Handful of parsley, chopped

1 cup cilantro, chopped

½ cup dill, chopped (optional but tasty in the finished dish)

Handful of almonds, chopped into small chunks

1 teaspoon salt or to taste

Pepper to taste

SIMMERING LIQUID

½ cup lemon juice

½ cup olive oil

2 cups warm water

4 cloves garlic, mashed to a paste

Salt

➤

Fill a deep pot with water and bring to a boil. Cut the extra stalks off the green leaves and dunk them into the boiling water until softened, 30 seconds to 3 minutes depending on the kind of leaf. Drain the leaves on clean kitchen towels and pat dry. Set aside. Parboil the rice for 5 minutes, rinse well under cool water, and set aside to drain. Next heat the butter or oil in a large frying pan, and sauté the chopped onions and then the ground meat. When the meat has browned, remove the pan from the heat and add the drained rice, tomato sauce or tomato paste, allspice, cayenne, parsley, cilantro, dill, almonds, and salt and pepper to taste. This works best if you mix it with your bare hands to ensure that the juices mix well.

Carefully place each leaf on a clean flat surface. Add 1–2 generous spoonfuls of the rice-meat mixture and carefully roll up each leaf, tucking them like an envelope to prevent the filling from leaking out. Line a large heavy-based pot with more of the leaves. Next place the filled dolmades in one layer in the pot. They should fit snugly. In a saucepan, blend and heat all ingredients of the simmering liquid. When hot, pour slowly over the dolmades. If you are making a large batch—this recipe will likely make 1 ½ layers depending on the size of your pot—separate the layers with more leaves and pour the simmering liquid over the dolmades prior to covering the final layer. Cover the dolmades with more leaves or a disk of wax paper or parchment paper cut to the size of the top. Add an upturned plate to weight down the dolmades. Cover the pot with a lid and simmer on low heat for about an hour.

If you want to reduce the fat in this recipe: I made these delicious dolmades in Missouri without all the butter—I used only 2 tablespoons—and it worked well.

While the dolmades cook, Brunnel shifts her attention to the Armenian harisa we are to make. After living in North Africa years ago, I think of harissa as a tasty paste of red chili peppers and garlic that wakes up the palate, but this is quite different: not only is there just one *s* in the spelling, but the end result is a kind of soothing porridge made of boned and stewed chicken and coarsely ground wheat.

Armenians often make this dish on Easter Sunday, but it is also a historic dish. Brunnel tells me that harisa is very special and powerful. In Armenia today, it is made every year to commemorate the Musa Dagh resistance in Musaler during the genocide by Ottoman Turks in 1915. Hundreds of people gather in the Armenian region of Armavir every third Sunday of September to sing patriotic songs and dance to celebrate the victory of the resistance as well as pay tribute to all the innocent Armenians killed during the genocide.

This delicious and filling dish is made with two simple ingredients: meat and peeled wheat—wheat berries with the hulls removed. Traditionally, it was made with sacrificed lamb, which was later blessed by a priest and served to the people. As simple as it is, harisa also requires a good amount of time, stirring, patience, and love. It is a warm, thick comfort made with simple ingredients: a balm.

Kolkata Armenian Harisa

PEELED WHEAT AND CHICKEN

Recipe courtesy of Brunnel Arathoon

Serves 4–6

5–6 pounds whole chicken

1 pound peeled wheat

Salt to taste

Ghee or butter for serving

Fill a large pot with water and bring to a boil. Add the chicken and boil until tender. When it is cooked, separate the chicken meat from the bones and save the broth. If desired, fill a separate pot with water and add the chicken bones to make more broth. Next wash the wheat, place it in a pot, mix in the chicken meat and saved broth, and cook on medium heat, stirring as needed. As the chicken and wheat simmer, add more broth made with the chicken bones or simply add boiling water to cover. Cook for 4–5 hours, stirring occasionally to prevent sticking, until the chicken meat has become extremely tender and almost dissolved in the wheat. The mixture should be the consistency of a thick and heavy porridge. Salt to taste. Heat the ghee or butter to drizzle over the top, and serve. Pickled veggies are a traditional and delicious side dish.

The cuisine of the Armenians of Kolkata is not apparent on menus in the city, and you would be hard-pressed to find Brunnel's version of dolmades or harisa anywhere in Kolkata. But on the streets of the city, especially in its center, Armenians have had a lasting impact. Whether you know the city or are just learning it, the remarkable structures Armenians built are hard to miss: Queens Mansions, Nizam Palace (earlier known as Galstaun Park), Stephen Court where the iconic Flury's is, Park Mansions where today Starbucks and the Hard Rock Cafe are housed, the building currently occupied by the Oberoi Grand hotel, which had as its first entrance a lobby completely clad in jade, now disappeared, and Stephen House in Dalhousie Square. "An astonishing 350 buildings," Anthony says at his Victoria Memorial talk, were either built by J. C. Galstaun, an ancestor of Anthony's, or passed through his hands at one point or another. Another relative, Sir Paul Chater, did remarkably well in Hong Kong, seeding over sixty companies, including the HSBC international bank and Hongkong Land, and building the magnificent Marble Hall as his residence. Though he made his fortune in the Far East, Chater never forgot Bengal, where he was raised. His financial rescue of his alma mater, La Martiniere school, in the 1920s is still commemorated by the school.

"We love our paras"—neighborhoods—"and paralok"—neighborhood people—Anthony says at his talk, "and I like to think of Park Street as being an Armenian para." There were at one time thirty-seven Armenian millionaires and billionaires in Kolkata, Anthony says, several coming over after the 1915 genocide. Others came earlier. "The story starts with Akbar," the third Mughal emperor, 1556 to 1605. It seems that Armenians were always liked, perhaps because they never had any interest in converting or accepting converts to their churches. When I think about their roles in Indian history, however, things get complicated.

An Armenian, Abdul Hai, was Akbar's chief justice; another, Juliana, was a doctor for his harem whom Akbar later gave in marriage to a member of the French royal family; and then there was Mariam, whom Akbar married.

In 1688, it was an Armenian ancestor of Anthony's, Phanoos Kalandar, who introduced the then unknown Company of Merchants of London Trading into the East Indies—later the East India Company—to the Mughal court after brokering a profitable contract for "the Armenian nation." Being able to pinpoint the original British access to power in India is astonishing in itself.

Going forward, Armenians worked as financiers and intermediaries between company officials and locals, earning healthy commissions in the process. During the time of the East India Company, Peter Arathoon marshaled forces for the likes of Major-General Robert Clive, the first governor of the Bengal presidency under the British, while his brother, Gregory—later known as Gorgin Khan—rose from selling cloth in Hooghly to being commander in chief of Mir Jafar's army in Bengal. Even Bodh Gaya was affected by an Armenian, Joseph Bedlow. Bedlow, a public works official, and Alexander Cunningham were the two people who excavated the holy site where Buddha attained enlightenment under the Bodhi Tree.

Today, fewer than forty Armenians who were baptized in the national church, attended the Armenian school, and speak the language are left in Kolkata, and there are probably fewer than eighty across India. "Within a hundred years, there won't be any of us left," Anthony says. Others, like Brunnel, perhaps five thousand across the subcontinent, were baptized Catholic and slowly amalgamated into the Anglo-Indian community. After Armenia's independence in 1991, many Armenians, like the Jewish community when Israel was established, chose to return to the homeland of their ancestors, though the diaspora remains eight times as large across the world as in the home country. Today in India there are still Armenian churches standing in each major city, though the majority of Armenians in India live in Kolkata.

At the Victoria Memorial, the audience is engaged, asking questions. The community, Anthony says, takes pride in being the first Christian nation on earth, stemming from St. Gregory the Illuminator, whose enormous statue stands behind St. Peter's Basilica at the Vatican and commemorates his conversion of everyone in the Armenian region.

"Do Armenians have a particular feeling for India?" an audience member asks, and I sense a wistfulness in the question. "They are completely ignorant" of their history with India, Anthony responds. And this, to me, seems like a history that repeats itself. India has had such an impact around the world, but rarely are people aware of it outside the country.

Then Anthony adds a last note, which returns to me after I leave the hall. "There was a fourth-century Armenian historian named Zenob," he says in a story that begins in 149 BCE with two princes from India being banished for plotting to kill a maharaja. Zenob said that "the Armenian king back then was very impressed with them and their level of education, so he gave them the governorship of a province called Taron." The princes and their entourage, though foreign, thrived, settling into their new land about 150 years before the birth of Christ.

"At the peak, there were five thousand Hindus in Armenia." But unlike other instances of assimilation, this one did not take. A visitor with other ideas about foreigners came through. "All of them, in about two weeks, were wiped out by St. Gregory the Illuminator," Anthony says, "after which he decides to name Armenia the first Christian nation on earth." Could it, he poses, have been the first Hindu nation instead?

~~~~~~

The Armenians, a people who prospered and served as intermediaries during great moments of history under the Mughals and the British, are now woven into the Indian tapestry. Unlike this history, a nation and a cuisine that make more inroads today than in India's past—America—had a shaky start. While food trends from the West are easy to spot—in a food history presentation, *Adda Bites*, I did with the U.S. consulate in Kolkata and Ranjini Guha of the University of Calcutta, she cooked a potato-cheese soufflé to represent trendy foods today—others are hiding in plain sight.

No doubt this causes unease, which is not new when it comes to America. The first U.S. ships to arrive in India caused warnings to erupt as early as the

1780s. This from a "Well Wisher of the East India Company," February 1782, as reported by Holden Furber in his 1938 article, "The Beginnings of American Trade with India, 1784–1812": "I am certain from what I have seen of the Americans that … to send them amongst the quiet Gentoo Natives of Indostan, whom I have also seen, I can only compare to the Devil sowing the Tares amongst the Wheat."

An alarming image, but it becomes apparent that the calamitous vision was spawned because there was no specific East India Company policy regarding trade with America and its effect on the company's monopoly. Despite the dire predictions, American ships were tolerated at the ports. America's increasing trade with China, of which India was an ancillary stop, concerned the company more. But nothing appreciable was done.

From the U.S. side, too, there was trepidation. Holden Furber writes that the first ship bearing U.S. colors to Indian waters stopped outside of Pondicherry one day after Christmas 1784, thinking the port was in the possession of the French. It was loaded with tobacco, Virginia ginseng, copper, miscellaneous hardware, and a "considerable sum in dollars. The ship, the *USS Philadelphia*, carried four hundred tons, forty men, and Thomas Bell, master. They were headed for China via Mauritius but had acquired wine in Madeira and sought a profitable market for it.

Given the possibility of a poor reception from a British port so soon after the American Revolution, French Pondicherry seemed a prudent place to show the Stars and Stripes first. The English, however, had yet to transfer Pondicherry back to the French despite the Treaty of 1783, a surprise to Bell, but his ship nevertheless received a cordial reception. Rumors about American interests ran rampant, but trade was permitted. An Irish sailor on board was even allowed to stay in India and hire a warehouse in Pondicherry.

The first American ship to slip down the Hooghly River to Calcutta with its surprising flag was met with somewhat less cordiality. The ship, the *Hydra*, was formerly a British frigate commanded by John Haggy, once first mate of the East Indiaman *Royal Henry*. His supercargo, William Green, owned her in partnership with "Mr. Champlain of Rhode Island" and some merchants in England. There were some complications—the ship was refitted in the Thames and cleared for Madeira and Rhode Island but actually went from Madeira to India. In June 1785, it arrived in Calcutta with American colors. Green had a French as well as an American commission and caused consternation among the British port authorities. They resolved their uncertainty by allowing the *Hydra* to dock after the thirteen stripes were lowered and the French flag was hoisted.

For Bengal, imports from America increased between 1795 and 1804 from 840,000 sicca rupees—rupees issued in Bengal prior to 1836 and weighing more than the rupee of the British East India Company—to over 4.5 million rupees, and exports on American ships increased from 1.9 million rupees to 6.7 million rupees. American trade with India, for the ten years after 1795, outpaced that carried by other Continental European flags by a full 25 percent.

The British again tolerated the American ships, this time because they were selling their own goods. Furber writes that Sir Francis Baring said, rather coldly, in September 1807: "If an American is successful, and thereby increases his consumption of luxuries, those luxuries are again Indian or British manufactures. In his Sunday cloathes, he is covered with them, as well as the inside of his house. Reduce them to their original poverty, and like their red neighbors, their only consumption would be blankets, and for those, we should get ill paid."

Others such as Charles Grant, who wrote the company's official dispatches, opposed this approach, but this and other administrative disputes had little influence on the actual course of events. Jefferson's embargo halted most American shipping, and the War of 1812 and Napoleonic decrees created such an effect that foreign exports from Bengal dropped tremendously from 10 million rupees in 1807–08 to just under 600,000 in 1808–09.

As I look over the history of American trade with India between the American Revolution and the War of 1812, it appears to have pursued its course virtually unhampered by political regulation. This friendliness toward Americans was not all due to the expediency that moved Sir Francis Baring. Two other aspects were to hand: "In the first place, there was a constant desire to accommodate the Americans at British ports lest hostility, especially when British shipping was greatly affected by the war, should drive the Americans to foreign ports; and secondly, the small British European communities exiled in the East naturally welcomed American sea-captains and supercargoes in a friendly manner. They were glad the Jay Treaty had put Americans on a par with British subjects."

Furber says the records give the impression that Americans were never thought of as foreigners as long as their trade did not appear to be an immediate menace to Anglo-Indian prosperity. The authorities stretched the law as far as it would go, sometimes farther, in favor of American ships. "Throughout the period, a most fortunate series of circumstances fostered American intercourse with India, the country from which, above all others, the late rebels against His Britannic Majesty's authority might have expected to be promptly and rigorously excluded."

All this friendliness on the part of Britain to the U.S., so soon after losing the colonies in the revolution, amounted to an initial welcome that paved the way for the food trails of today. Ranjini's potato-cheese soufflé is not what first comes to mind when I think of U.S. foods, but the French fries, birthed of the potato that traveled to Europe and initially saved people from famine, that Jefferson touted and brought back to Virginia, and more since might have been the warning shots of the Devil sowing the Tares amongst the Wheat come true.

Chapter Thirteen

FOOD OF THE GODS

All beings, that exist on earth, are born of food; then they
live by food, then again to the food they go at the end.
So verily food is the oldest of all creatures.

—Second Anuvaka, *Taittiriya Upanishad*

AT BELUR MATH, ON THE WEST BANK of the Hooghly River in Kolkata, the temple kitchens are quiet at the time of day I visit. The cauldron-like stainless steel rice cookers are gleaming and ready for the next meal preparation, the floors are spotless. The room is large enough that it echoes a little now that the cooks have left. In the dining hall, the visitors are already finishing meals sent out on rolling trays that are pushed down long rows of tables. I talk with a monk assigned to take me through the kitchens. His other work as an agricultural biologist focuses on ecologically friendly pest control for rice in the region.

I want to understand the supply chains needed for such a vast food operation. I remember a visit to the Tirupati Temple in Andhra Pradesh in 2007 with my father. We were on a temple tour, a small one to accommodate the time we had to visit, but I was struck by not only the vast feeling of openness I had at the top of the hill where the temple sits but by the fact that over 70,000 laddus—lentil-based round sweets—were given out daily. This feat took three tons of urad dal, six tons of sugar, and two and a half tons of ghee, plus a lot of raisins, cashews, and cardamom. For one sweet. For one day.

The food supply manager at Belur Math, also a monk, has an office in a long row of offices with front walls that open onto an inner courtyard. I get a sense of a busily humming city of professionals running a smooth system. Squawks of crows try to interrupt our talk, but we are engrossed. Most of the rice, short grain and aromatic, is sourced in Bengal. I see hand-tallied columns for rice, dal, some vegetables, and dairy for payasam—rice pudding—and buttermilk. Hundreds of people come daily, rain or shine, and the supply chain runs nonstop.

Even more, maybe 15,000 more, come for special festival days, and everyone is fed. The monk's cell phone finally does what the crows did not and pulls him away for more urgent needs. These and other monastics run the vast Ramakrishna Mission network of temples, educational and agricultural training programs, and social service activities throughout India and the world.

When I spoke with the principal monk, Swami Shastrajnananda, earlier in the offices at the attached college, the stately Ramakrishna Mission Vivekananda Educational and Research Institute, we sipped tea and nibbled biscuits together across a wide wooden desk while I got a clear sense of a typical day here. While there is continual spiritual work, much of the daily physical work of the mission involves procuring, prepping, and cooking food followed by cleaning the kitchens and dining hall after serving it.

At 4:00 or 5:00 a.m., depending on the season, the temple opens with aarti, morning vespers, after which the aesthetics meditate until 5:30 or 6:00 p.m. At midday, cooked food such as tasty rice, lentils, vegetables, fruit, and usually a sweet—maybe payasam or perhaps suji halwa, a pudding made with semolina—is offered to all who come. The evening aarti is timed with the sunset, and typically a large number of monastics, the sadhus or renunciates, as well as lay visitors join in. Evening food is offered around 8:30 p.m.

The routine, familiar to those in India, revolves around the offering of food to God, done privately by a priest in the inner sanctum, and the return of it to people, who at Belur Math file into the room with the long rows of tables. The monks eat separately but from the same preparations. If the bhog, the food offered to the deity, is given with genuine spiritual seeking, it is said that God is satisfied and returns the food for the seeker to take it as prasad, blessed food.

After an offering of prasad in a room adjacent to where the monks eat, I look around, surprised that four hours have passed. People here to seek blessings or wait for the evening aarti mill about the grounds or stand waiting to get inside the great temple hall. Construction sounds create a sort of white noise to everything going on as building maintenance to the graceful buff-colored sandstone and concrete architecture is underway. An occasional piping voice of a child rings out as young families pass by. Behind these the Hooghly River, a branch of the Ganges, flows turgidly past. The steps to the water have bathers standing on them as well as debris bumping them. It could be any year, any time, yesterday or five hundred years ago.

There is a lot said about food in ancient Indian texts. If food helps us analyze an entire community, not just its tables, then the ancient writings in India lead us deeply into the culture's consciousness. The *Taittiriya Upanishad* (*I Am Food*), likely composed in the sixth century BCE, uses food as a lens powerfully.

Food is a cosmic and symbolic entity and, according to Signe Cohen, associate professor of South Asian religions at the University of Missouri, the text famously identifies five different layers of atman, the self: the self made of food, the self made of life breath, the self made of mind, the self made of perception, and the self made of bliss. In one section, it "tells of a man named Bhrigu who is the son of Varuna. Bhrigu arrives at an initial realization that the highest *brahman* is food, and that all beings are born from food and return to food upon death. But he then proceeds to discover even higher truths: that all beings come from the life breath, the mind, perception, and finally bliss." It seems that food represents something like the physical part of the self, Cohen tells me, "a source of life and nourishment."

This is an Upanishad I can relate to. As preoccupied as I am by all things culinary, I wish I would have understood all this better in elementary school.

Anyone could have predicted that answering the questions of second graders in Kansas about my church with a shrug might cause much discomfort all around. I would have loved an actual answer.

Even so, it would have been hard to explain that feeding the gods—any of the many avatars of God in India—is part of daily piety. It is generally agreed that the human body in India is transformed by giving and receiving. Food is given to and taken in by the gods and returned for human nourishment in an essential, innermost cycle revealing that God and humans are one. Vivekananda taught it this way: you may invent an image through which to worship God, but a better image already exists—the living human. He went further and said that you may build a temple in which to worship God, and that may be good, but a better one, a much higher one, already exists—the human body.

Could all the images I see in Kolkata, the street corner shrines, the bells, the festooned carts pulled by horses with brilliant colors and decorated with wreaths and flowers and tinsel upon which a bride or maybe a god might sit, could all the everyday devotion I witness in India add up to this? Offering and eating, feasting and fasting. An intimate round.

Somehow I am soothed by this, though the fragile connection could break at any moment. How to explain hunger for some, feasting for others? What about depleted soils and climate catastrophes that destroy crops? What about inept or corrupt leaders and failed food systems? The sacred cycle is not always assured. If only stamping my foot in frustration would do the trick and make things right.

I have to say the writer in me appreciates the lines in the *Taittiriya Upanishad*: "I am food, I am food, I am food! I am the eater of food, I am the eater of food, I am the eater of food! I am the poet, I am the poet, I am the poet!" I try to be that poet. In one sense, I succeed: I join my two culinary cultures, and though I know now that I will never be bureaucratically Indian, in this vision inclusion is already so. I am in your hands, you are in mine. We are all poets who join together the world we envision. There is not much more to add up.

Utsa Ray in *Culinary Culture in Colonial India* writes that the culinary culture of Bengal is unlike any haute cuisine because it has always been tied emphatically to a spiritual world. Food and darshan, from the Sanskrit word "darsana" meaning "sight" or "vision," at temples offer an exchange of perspectives between devotee and deity. Like food, this exchange is visual, tactile, and olfactory. It is irresistible grace. Whether the celebrants are Hindus, Muslims, Christians, or followers of other religions, food is central to any festival in India.

Food, too, with all its sensory notes, is marked by time in the sacred places of India. The earliest health diets, in the *Caraka Samhita* and the *Susruta Samhita*, the founding texts of Ayurveda first written down around the first century BCE, are records that to this day determine what is foreign and what is not. These texts are palimpsests, folding in the many peoples and foods of the subcontinent up to the point they were written down. The foods that came later are forever ambiguous—sometimes making it easier to assimilate them, sometimes causing exclusions.

Foreign foods such as potatoes, tomatoes, chilies, and more, now everyday fare for many, have an entrance date, forever noted at traditional temples. In the six food offerings made daily at the Jagannath Temple in Puri, in meals shared for more than five hundred years (with more than 4.2 million visitors in 2019 alone), culinary newcomers such as the tomato or cauliflower are never in any of the dishes. Nor, in the ancient texts of Ayurveda, are these and other newcomers like the potato mentioned. The chili, though a newcomer, too, so intrigued the Ayurvedic physicians that it made the cut.

Black pepper was replaced with chilies in many remedies. Though Ayurvedic physicians used both the long pepper, *Piper longum*, and the small round *Piper nigrum* for patients with phlegm and wind, the long pepper was also used to increase semen and treat severe fevers. Greeks and Romans used both peppers for similar medical purposes (to cure impotence, for example), Lizzie Collingham says in *Curry: A Tale of Cooks and Conquerors*, and they greatly valued peppers for flavoring meat and fish. Chilies, though new to combating these ills, were helpful in treating cholera and were found to offer an inexpensive way to add Vitamin C to diets. Ayurvedic doctors couldn't resist.

From the Ayurvedic perspective, to be a doctor is to be a cook. Choosing foods with complementary reactive properties in the body suited to the time of year—to keep the body in a state of equilibrium within itself and with its environment—is the goal. Ayurvedic prescriptions mean different foods depending on where you live and the seasonal climate—hot dry plains require much different foods than cool marshy areas. In general, during hot weather when the body needs to conserve energy, cold foods and milky gruels are recommended. When it's cold, a richer diet of fatty meat and even wine and honey is suggested.

But there is another dimension. If to be a doctor is to be a cook, then at temples and in home kitchens in India, to be a cook is the work of grace. Food isn't just about ingredients and techniques, it's about energy. The flavor of food comes not just from the quality of the local ingredients, the water, and the slow cooking but also from the purity and intention of the cooks. The aggressive chefs sometimes celebrated in Western television shows are the antithesis of this approach—thoughts have power over food and digestion in India. The mood and character, the intention and love, of the cook make all the difference.

Ayurvedic classifications have a template: two principal food divisions (hot or cold), are subdivided into six principal rasas or tastes: pungent, sour, salty (hot foods such as meat and peppers), sweet, astringent, and bitter (cold foods such as milk and most fruits). Hot foods can be dangerous indeed, promoting thirst, exhaustion, inflammation, and accelerated digestion. Cold foods promote cheerfulness and a contented, calm mind. In Ayurveda, chilies are considered rajastic foods—potent, creating passions and feelings of anger and hatred—as opposed to sattvic foods such as the cereals and pulses, fruits and vegetables thought to encourage moderate behavior and feelings of peace.

To test what it feels like to eat with this intention over a period of time, I visit Ayurdara, an Ayurvedic healing and lifestyle clinic, and stay at Albin's Glory guest house in Kochi. Though the recommendation is to stay for twenty-one days if possible, I can manage ten with my schedule. Even so, the focus and pace seep into my system.

The foods offered under a thatch roof near the Kochi backwaters are light, refreshing, filling. I sleep soundly, waking without an alarm. The early-morning sun washes between palm fronds as I do yoga outside. Church bells ring. The chants of Hindu monks rise. There is a hum in the air from the waking pollinators and the tender lapping of water against stone walls. I find myself coming into a never-before-felt equilibrium. I make plans to return, not predicting the pandemic ahead or its effect on all things travel.

The profile I receive from the retreat tells me I am to eat most vegetables but, oddly, not my favorites of eggplant, mushroom, tomato, and onion; I can have most any sweet fruits but should avoid sour ones; I learn that fresh cheeses and chili peppers are not my friends. I compare this to a workup I receive a year later from my doctor in Missouri and it mostly lines up. I begin to follow the directives for a pitta-vata or a specific carbohydrate diet, whichever you prefer to acknowledge, and over eight months I see a huge drop in cholesterol, my unseen yet worrisome interior inflammation is gone, and I feel lighter, more energetic.

~~~~~

The night I leave India, I am in a car heading to the airport. My roots and routes have come to an intersection. The ride has no interruptions, there are no traffic jams. Other days I have been caught in Ubers for long intervals while children pat the windows looking for alms on one side and hijras, transgender people dressed in saris with thick makeup on their faces, make louder demands on the other. Not today. I am breezing through streets with medians that have cloth and cardboard huts in the service areas. Residents there sit on pallets cooking, eating, chatting, bathing, gazing blankly, and sleeping. A young entrepreneur walks down the shoulder with fantastic balloons that have lights in their centers bobbing in his hands.

The car passes the beginnings of the Gariahat Market with its stalls of socks, sweets, tea in small clay cups, T-shirts, apparel for Hindu deities, underwear, jute baskets, flowers, nuts, saris, salwar kameez, bangles, earrings, towels, bed-spreads, and more, all swinging slightly at the intersections of roads, many items hanging over the walk blocking what breeze there may be, up and down the sidewalks. Vendors splash water across their patch of sidewalk to cool it and reduce dust, people mill about, choking the sides of the road. But my car blows by with nothing slowing us. I look back and see men stepping out of sweetshops holding enticing small cardboard boxes tied with twine, but even that great temptation does not slow us. Then we're on the flyway, scoot-ing faster than could be imagined on the lower streets. A stall seller looks up briefly as the car accelerates, then turns to hand over a paper-wrapped packet of fried nimki to a customer. Though I can't smell it from my seat, I imagine the slightly salty crunch of the snack and its sesame spicing. In the Hindu idea, reaching God can be sensory: touching, tasting, sensing radiant love all through the body. It's here on the street, that idea. Life. We madly race on.

It's so easy to see India as the great assimilator as I speed away. It has pulled in all sorts of traditions, goods, ideas, foods for so long. Whose history is the true story of India, of the United States, of any place? The narrative appears to be blossoming, assimilating, fermenting, roiling along. As it always has.

Chapter Fourteen

EATING INDIA

My friend, a great deal has been said already / By many men
on the art of cookery, / So either tell me something new yourself, /
Unknown to former cooks, or spare my ears.

—Athenaeus, *The Deipnosophists*, third century

A RECENT DISCOVERY TRACES turmeric, ginger, and garlic on old crockery
back 4,500 years to the sophisticated urban centers of the Indus civilization.
This finding, Shaan Merchant says in "A Colonized History," makes curry the
longest continuously eaten food in the world. Variations of this style of cooking are found, but it's the word "curry" that's a bit strange: a colonized version
of the vast repertoire of India's specific dishes. A sweeping term, you might
say, that pushes a lot under the rug.

It happens this way throughout history. Colonization takes over foodways
and alters them. Cultures absorb what comes ashore, and then they move
along. Rarely, though, has an entire complex cuisine been minimized to a
word and a singular style in such a way. When the Portuguese came through,
they most likely mispronounced the Tamil word "kari," referring to a savory
dish or perhaps only to the black pepper used to make it, and began calling

all food in India "carel." Merchant goes on to say that the British then mashed up it further to "curry," deemed almost anything eaten in India as such, and packaged their blander version of the fresh spices of India into a mix, curry powder, which they sent around the world.

Shoddy interpretations of curry then proceeded to grace the pages of many cookbooks—from *Mrs. Beeton's Book of Household Management* to New World cookbooks of the day—and curries became stews thickened with cream featuring ingredients such as apples and meat flavored with the prepared powder, Merchant says. The cuisine of India was reduced so that even Victorian women could neutralize the threat of the Other. In much the same way that fourteenth-century English cooks prepared Turk's Head pasties, sweet-and-sour meat pies shaped and decorated to resemble the features of a stereotyped Saracen during the times of the Crusades, British people ate India. But first they overran its cuisine and branded it—or blanded it, if you will allow me to say so.

You won't find that here. I have collected many delightful recipes from my interviews in Bengal and from family and friends who cook there. One and all, delicious and called by their actual names. A complete roundup of these would fill an entire cookbook, but here are some you'll like. Try them and see if that's not so.

Mutton Chaap

SUCCULENT LAMB AND GOAT MEAT WITH YOGURT

Recipe courtesy of Susmita Mookerjee

Serves 4–6

My husband, Terry, could not stop noshing on this dish created by Susmita Mooker-jee, who is my cousin's wife. In her welcoming Kolkata home, we happily ate this chaap alongside sliced red onions and a bit of lime among a table full of tasty choices.

2 pounds lamb chops or 1 pound mutton (goat) and 1 pound lamb chops,
    cut into pieces
1 cup plain yogurt
1 tablespoon salt
1 tablespoon black pepper
2 medium onions, cut into slender rings
2 tablespoons vegetable oil

Marinate the meat in the yogurt, salt, and pepper for 6 hours or more—the longer you marinate it, the more tender it is in the finished dish. Cook the marinated meat in a pressure cooker until tender, about 12–15 minutes, or in a slow cooker for 6 hours, or cook it on the stove top on very low heat in a covered heavy pan, stirring occasionally, until tender. On the stove top, the meat usually cooks in its own juice, but you may have to add a little water or chicken stock to prevent it from drying out. In a separate skillet, fry the onions in the vegetable oil until transparent, about 3–4 minutes. Add the fried onions to the cooked meat, mix well, and cover the pan with a lid until you are ready to serve. The finished dish is succulent but not saucy.

Bhuni Khichuri

FRIED RICE WITH VEGETABLES

Recipe courtesy of Suchitra Mukherjee

Serves 4–6

One delightful day, my cousin Suchitra Mukherjee, didi to me, walked me through her mother's bhuni khichuri. It tasted light, refined, on the tongue and carries the mark of a cook who cares. Her recipe drops the usual lentils and lightly fries the rice prior to using a pressure cooker for a tempting meal. That evening we talked and sampled the tastes of my family as the city began to settle: the table, food, and company such bright sweet cheer in the gathering dusk.

½ cup fresh or frozen green peas

½ cup cauliflower pieces

1 cup Gobindobhog or another short grain rice

2–3 tablespoons ghee

1–2 bay leaves

5–6 whole cloves, ground

¼ teaspoon ground cardamom

1 cup warm water

2 teaspoons fresh ginger, mashed to a paste

2 teaspoons ground cumin seeds

½ teaspoon ground coriander

1 green chili, chopped

1–2 teaspoons salt or to taste

Soak the peas and cauliflower in enough water to cover for about 10–15 minutes, then drain. In the meantime, wash the uncooked rice several times, then drain it. Heat the ghee in a frying pan; when hot, add the bay leaves. Next add the ground cloves and cardamom and fry for 3–5 seconds. Add the rice and stir until a light aroma rises. Add the peas and cauliflower. Stir and fry for 3–4 minutes. In a pressure cooker, add the warm water. Make a paste with the ginger, cumin, and coriander and add that to the pressure cooker as well. Add the green chili and salt. Add the stir-fried rice and spices and mix well. Set the pressure cooker for about 10 minutes (two whistles in India). Remove, fluff with a fork, and serve warm.

Maacher Kalia with Potatoes and Cauliflower

~~~~~~

FISH WITH POTATOES AND CAULIFLOWER

Recipe courtesy of Anuradha Banerji, New Delhi, as learned from Rani Banerji

Serves 4

In a conversation with my baro mamima, my mother's oldest brother's wife, Anuradha Banerji, I learn about Rani's fish. Her maacher kalia is a saucy dish with ginger, garlic, cayenne, turmeric, and a little sugar, essential to many Bengali dishes. Here she adds potatoes and cauliflower.

4 rui or carp fillets

1 teaspoon turmeric

1 teaspoon salt

1 teaspoon ground coriander

1 teaspoon ground cumin seeds

½ teaspoon cayenne

2–3 tablespoons vegetable oil

2 medium potatoes, cut into chunks

2 cups cauliflower florets

½ teaspoon cumin seeds

2 bay leaves

1 small onion, mashed to a paste

½ inch fresh ginger, grated

1 small tomato, finely chopped

½ teaspoon sugar

½ teaspoon garam masala

1 tablespoon ghee (optional)

Wash the fish fillets and pat them dry. Sprinkle ½ teaspoon of the turmeric and ½ teaspoon of the salt on the fish and set aside for 10 minutes. Mix the ground coriander and cumin, cayenne, and the rest of the turmeric and salt in a little water (about 1 teaspoon) in a small bowl; set aside until needed or for at least 5 minutes. Heat 2 tablespoons of the oil in a pan and fry the potatoes until they begin to soften but do not brown. Remove the potatoes from the pan and set aside. Do the same for the cauliflower pieces, remembering not to brown them. Set aside. Fry the fish fillets until they soften but do not brown and set them aside as well. Next add a little fresh oil to the pan and heat; when hot, add the cumin seeds and bay leaves. After the cumin begins to sputter (a few seconds), add the mashed onion and ginger. Stir well. Add the coriander, cumin, cayenne, turmeric, and salt paste. Stir and fry, adding a little water if needed. Add the chopped tomato. Stir and fry for 5–7 minutes. Add the sugar and stir. Add the potatoes, cauliflower, and fish. Cook until the potatoes are done, 5–7 minutes, stirring gently so you do not break the fish into pieces. Take the pan off the heat and add the garam masala. In a small pot, heat the ghee, if using, and pour it over the top before serving. Excellent with rice.

Green Mango Pickles

Recipe courtesy of Mohan and Sheila Banerji and friends
Makes about 1 ½ quarts

My uncle and aunt, Mohan and Sheila Banerji, in their home near London retrieved this recipe for green mango pickles once they heard of my search for Rani's recipe. While this is not sweet-sour-hot like my grandmother's, it's delicious as a palate sweeper. Another tasty option for those who like a good mystery, getting to the bottom of things by trial and error, and pungent Indian pickles. The mangoes should be green, and ideally their seeds will still be soft, not hard like they are in ripe fruit.

2 cups underripe mangoes, unpeeled, seeds removed, diced
1 teaspoon slaked lime
1 tablespoon ground cumin seeds
1 tablespoon ground coriander
½–1 teaspoon cayenne or to taste
3 cups high-quality mustard oil
1 teaspoon panch phoron (Indian five-spice blend)
1 teaspoon asafetida
1 teaspoon salt
1 teaspoon sugar or to taste (optional)

Begin by adding enough water to a shallow dish to cover the mango pieces. Add the slaked lime and stir. Set aside overnight. After 8–12 hours, rinse the mangoes well, drain, and spread them on paper towels to dry. Next mix the cumin, coriander, and cayenne in a bowl with enough water to make a runny paste. Set aside. In a medium-sized heavy pan, add 2 cups of the mustard oil and heat on medium-high until it just begins to smoke. Turn the heat to low and add the panch phoron. As soon as the seeds stop sputtering (about 5 seconds), add the asafetida. Immediately add the mango pieces and the salt. Turn the heat to high and stir frequently. When the mangoes begin to change color and are slightly brown, add the cumin-coriander-cayenne paste. Stir well and cook until the water evaporates. Adjust the salt. If desired, add the sugar now. Once all the water has been cooked out and the mangoes are soft but not mushy, turn off the heat and add the rest of the mustard oil. When completely cool, store in airtight jars in the refrigerator or can with a pressure cooker for longer storage.

Korola and Begun Subji

STIR-FRIED BITTER GOURD WITH EGGPLANT

Serves 2–3

I never thought I'd say this, but as an adult I've come to relish the Bengali specialty of bitter gourd with mixed vegetables. One Saturday at my local Missouri farmers market, I looked down and there it was: the squash my father and I called blood purifier as a joke when I was growing up (haha! Ayurveda might be a serious health regime, but we made good fun of one of its cherished ingredients). Korola is at its savory best if you slice it thin and let it get slightly crispy.

3 tablespoons vegetable oil

1 dried red chili, broken into pieces

1 ½ cups bitter gourd, cut lengthwise into 4 pieces, then into
   ¼-inch slices ⅛-inch thick

1 cup eggplant, cut into small cubes

½–1 teaspoon turmeric

½–1 teaspoon salt or to taste

Heat the vegetable oil in a medium-sized pot. When hot, add the red chili pieces and let sizzle for 10–20 seconds. Add the bitter gourd. Stir and fry for about 5 minutes. Add the eggplant. Stir. Add the turmeric and salt. Stir-fry until the eggplant is tender and the gourd is soft.

Kosha Mangsho

MUTTON WITH ONIONS

Recipe courtesy of Kastura Bandyopadhyay and Sandhya Singh

Serves 4

My neighbor in Kolkata, Kastura Bandyopadhyay, a tremendous cook, made this as a special treat, which we devoured. Her hospitality is well remembered. Mutton in India often means goat meat. In this dish, other meat substitutions such as lamb work as well. Sandhya Singh, Kastura's able cook as well as mine for the time I was in Kolkata, was much appreciated.

5 cloves garlic, mashed to a paste
1 inch fresh ginger, peeled and grated
1 teaspoon salt
1 teaspoon cayenne
1 cup plain yogurt
1 pound mutton, cut into cubes 1–2 inches square
3 tablespoons vegetable oil or ghee
1 bay leaf
2 small white onions, finely chopped
1 small white onion, grated
½–1 teaspoon turmeric
½ teaspoon sugar
1 cup water
½ teaspoon garam masala

Combine the garlic and ginger in a small bowl. Mix half of this with the salt, cayenne, and yogurt in a large bowl. Add the cubed meat to this and marinate for 2 hours. Heat the oil or ghee in a heavy pot. When hot, add the bay leaf and after a few seconds add the chopped onions. Fry for 3 minutes, then add the grated onion and the remaining garlic and ginger. Fry for 2–3 minutes.

➤

Add the turmeric. Stir. Taste for spice level and add more cayenne if desired. Then add the mutton cubes with their marinade. Continue to stir and fry. Add the sugar. If needed, add more salt to taste. Add the water to the now-empty yogurt bowl, swish, and pour this into a pressure cooker. Continue to stir-fry the meat until the oil begins to separate from the sides of the pan, about 15–20 minutes. Place the meat mixture in the pressure cooker. Add a little water to the pan used to fry the meat and swish it around to get all the spices and sauce, then add it to the pressure cooker as well. Sprinkle in the garam masala. Start the pressure cooker and cook the mixture for about 10–15 minutes. Serve in a bowl with rice or Indian bread.

Maacher Shorshe Jhol

MUSTARD FISH

Recipe courtesy of Sandhya Singh

Serves 4

As I have noted throughout this book, Bengal is a region full of fish specialties, far too many to list comprehensively here. One that I especially appreciate for its stand-out pungent flavor is mustard fish. The cook who fed us during my stay in Kolkata, Sandhya Singh, patiently let me watch while she cooked our meals. She was efficiency itself, moving through the kitchen with grace before heading off to the other kitchens she managed.

4 tilapia fillets, about 1 pound

1 ½ teaspoons salt

1 teaspoon turmeric

½ teaspoon black mustard seeds

½ teaspoon yellow mustard seeds

5 green chilies

½ cup mustard oil

½ teaspoon sugar

Rub the fish fillets with ½ teaspoon of the salt and ½ teaspoon of the turmeric and set aside. Grind the black mustard seeds, yellow mustard seeds, and 2 of the green chilies in a spice grinder or with a mortar and pestle. Add enough water to make a very runny paste. Next heat the mustard oil in a pan. When hot, place the fish in the oil and fry for about 3 minutes on each side. Remove the fish and set aside.

Add the remaining salt, turmeric, and chilies and the mustard-chili paste to the oil in the pan. Add the sugar. Once the sugar has dissolved, return the fish to the pan. Bring to a boil, then keep at a hard simmer for 3–5 minutes. The sauce will thicken slightly. Pour into a bowl to cool and keep the fish from continuing to cook. Serve with rice.

Pitha Patishapta Narole Gur

~~~

EGGLESS CREPES WITH COCONUT AND JAGGERY

Recipe courtesy of Priyadarshini Ghosh Shome and Srikanta Pramanik

Makes 10–12 crepes

No recipe collection is complete without at least one sweet offering. The classical dancer Priyadarshini Ghosh Shome invited me to her Kolkata home to learn about patishapta, a Bengali delicacy that hits my comfort zone square in the solar plexus. I visited in December, and nolen gur—a winter syrup made from the sap of the date palm tree—was part of this special concoction. In Priyadarshini's kitchen, I witnessed a choreography of motion and aroma by her cook, Srikanta Pramanik, as the crepes, dense with jaggery, coconut, and cardamon, flavored the air. They were delectable.

Oil or butter to cook the crepes

BATTER

2 cups all-purpose flour

1 ¼ cups water or enough to cover flour

½ teaspoon salt

FILLING

1 ¼ cups jaggery, broken into pieces (brown sugar will do in a pinch)

1 ¼ cups freshly grated coconut

½ teaspoon ground cardamom

TOPPING

¼ cup jaggery

½ cup milk

Put the flour and salt in a large bowl, add enough water to cover, and set aside for 30 minutes. In another bowl, mix the jaggery and grated coconut with your hands until well combined. Add the cardamom. Put this mixture into a skillet and heat and stir for 7–10 minutes or until aroma rises and the mixture is dense and begins to pull away from the edges. Take off the stove to cool. In the meantime, stir the water and flour mixture with a large spoon. It should be the consistency of a thin batter. Heat a large flat griddle on the stove to medium-hot. Add a little oil or butter to the surface. Pour a ladleful of the batter onto the pan, spreading it into a circle about 5–6 inches in diameter. Cook for 2 minutes, then flip. Cook for another minute, being careful not to let it get too brown. While the crepe is still on the pan, place a spoonful of the jaggery-coconut-cardamom filling on it and roll the whole patishapta into a log. Heat through, rolling and slightly flattening the filled crepe.

Mix any remaining filling with the ¼ cup jaggery and ½ cup milk and heat for 5 minutes over medium heat. Pour this sauce over the top of your patishaptas and serve—or drizzle with nolen gur syrup if available.

Patishaptas are often made with rice flour. To try this version, replace the flour with 1 cup all-purpose flour, ½ cup rice flour, ½ cup semolina, and 1 tablespoon sugar. Mix this with a little salt and let the mixture soak in 1 cup warm milk instead of water for 30 minutes prior to following the rest of the steps.

As I gather my notes after my nearly nine months in India, I see so many foods coming into and going out of the subcontinent to consider. My thoughts go to the onion. The poet Naomi Shihab Nye wrote aptly about its virtues, first quoting Emma Bailey's 1972 *Better Living Cookbook*: "It is believed that the onion originally came from India. In Egypt it was an object of worship—why I haven't been able to find out. From Egypt the onion entered Greece and on to Italy, thence into all of Europe."

> When I think how far the onion has traveled
> just to enter my stew today, I could kneel and praise
> all small forgotten miracles,
> crackly paper peeling on the drainboard,
> pearly layers in smooth agreement,
> the way the knife enters onion
> and onion falls apart on the chopping block,
> a history revealed.
> And I would never scold the onion
> for causing tears.
> It is right that tears fall
> for something small and forgotten.
> How at meal, we sit to eat,
> commenting on texture of meat or herbal aroma
> but never on the translucence of onion,
> now limp, now divided,
> or its traditionally honorable career:
> For the sake of others,
> disappear.

The onion. Such a thing to overlook! In India, besides adding flavor to dishes, the onion has long been important as a paste to thicken sauces, unlike the Western technique that might use a roux of wheat flour and oil. Other techniques for thickening in India involve ground almonds or coconut cream, but in my mother's kitchen it was always the onion. As well as doing the heavy lifting to create the right texture in sauces, the piquant addition of onion to cuisine can tease out a high degree of savory pleasure. The food trail of the onion—and others no doubt—all but disappears for us eaters in the joy of the moment of aroma, texture, and taste.

In the town I grew up in, Pittsburg, Kansas, I can look down at a plate of the local specialty of fried chicken from restaurants hailed for generations there and see the settlement story of the region: vinegary potato salad and coleslaw (Balkan), fried chicken (southern U.S.), and spaghetti (Italian). This alone can tell you the tale of the backgrounds of the people who came to southeastern Kansas to work in the coal mines. This alone can tell you that they ate together, at the same restaurants, and that their foods touched on the plates. This alone can give you an idea of how foreignness was once handled in the Midwest.

When I consider the ongoing debates regarding food appropriation, I know that acknowledgment of the ingenuity of the people who took a wandering ingredient and made it their own in tasty ways is the sticking point. Let's own the history. Let's celebrate it. Food history is a world heritage story that has all the drama of a tense thriller or maybe a mystery. Whose food is it? Who gets to tell its tale? If there's respect for a food's history and origins, maybe the issue of appropriation is less of a concern, especially when it comes to taste and health.

The cuisine within Bengal throbs with regional diversity. The entire region, including Bangladesh, is oriented to rivers, and fish is central to diets. Sharanya Deepak in "A 'Forgotten Holocaust' Is Missing from Indian Food Stories" describes Bengal's staple foods thus: rui fish cooked in briny yogurt, the beloved hilsa, rich and succulent and steamed in banana leaves, vegetables often as center stage of the meal, banana flowers laboriously peeled and roasted with coconut, fleshy eggplants sliced and fried into slim slivers. Yes, I think. This captures my idea of Bengal.

I agree with Chef Anumitra that we are all archives of the sensory world we have experienced, often at the table. Some of what's on the plate in Bengal has aged into its claim to heritage by stealth, tastiness, and the imagination of the people it touched. Cuisine everywhere is a result of change, foreign ingredients, and, as Utsa Ray says, the importation of ideas. Those sneaky impostors like the chili, tomato, and potato from South America (or that tasty cocoa we all love), okra and coffee from Africa, citrus, mango, sugar, and black pepper from India, and so many other foods found their way everywhere when the Columbian exchange exploded in the first globalization of food. I see this is so in Missouri. When I taught food-writing courses in Italy, it was so clear. Clues have always been right there on the plate in plain sight.

Whittling the scope of the world's food story down to my kitchen recipe books, I look at a page and see my family in scribbled notes. Sachin likes less cayenne in lamb chaap, Rich hates peas! (punctuation mine circa 1989) in Missouri seven-layer salad, Sipra's yearning for a taste of Bengal in 1975 Kansas hued an easier way to make rosogolla. A specific history emerges. These recipes—marking the history of women, available foods, agriculture, trade, and colonial power—are also codes to the behind-the-scenes story of us. My particular family and the women like my grandmother, who passed on recipes and sensory memories of good tastes and comfort, come alive to me as I look in the margins. There she is again. Finding Rani all along *was* a kitchen story. This is why her green mango chutney recipe means so much.

Then, shaking myself out of the circuit of foods, people, ingenuity, and terroir, sighing a little, I pause. It's time to eat. My plate will again speak to me. My taste buds, however, will not differentiate among the lands of origin, self-centered as they are, honing in only to flavor, texture, and temperature. Trying to emulate that poet of the Upanishads, I will endeavor to connect.

METRIC CONVERSION CHART

APPROXIMATE CONVERSION OF QUARTS TO LITERS

To convert quarts to liters, multiply the number of quarts by 0.95.

1 qt	1 L
1 ½ qt	1 ½ L
2 qt	2 L
2 ½ qt	2 ½ L
3 qt	2 ¾ L
4 qt	3 ¾ L
5 qt	4 ¾ L
6 qt	5 ½ L
7 qt	6 ½ L
8 qt	7 ½ L
9 qt	8 ½ L
10 qt	9 ½ L

APPROXIMATE CONVERSION OF OUNCES TO GRAMS

To convert ounces to grams, multiply the number of ounces by 28.35.

1 oz	30 g
2 oz	60 g
3 oz	85 g
4 oz	115 g
5 oz	140 g
6 oz	180 g
7 oz	200 g
8 oz	225 g
9 oz	250 g
10 oz	285 g
11 oz	300 g
12 oz	340 g
13 oz	370 g
14 oz	400 g
15 oz	425 g
16 oz	450 g
20 oz	570 g
24 oz	680 g
28 oz	790 g
32 oz	900 g

APPROXIMATE CONVERSION OF POUNDS TO GRAMS AND KILOGRAMS

To convert pounds to kilograms, multiply the number of pounds by 453.6.

1 lb	450 g
1 ¼ lb	565 g
1 ½ lb	675 g
1 ¾ lb	800 g
2 lb	900 g
2 ½ lb	1,125 g, 1 ¼ kg
3 lb	1,350 g
3 ½ lb	1,500 g, 1 ½ kg
4 lb	1,800 g
4 ½ lb	2 kg
5 lb	2 ¼ kg
5 ½ lb	2 ½ kg
6 lb	2 ¾ kg
6 ½ lb	3 kg
7 lb	3 ¼ kg
7 ½ lb	3 ½ kg
8 lb	3 ¾ kg
9 lb	4 kg
10 lb	4 ½ kg

APPROXIMATE CONVERSION OF INCHES TO CENTIMETERS

To convert inches to centimeters, multiply the number of inches by 2.54.

¹⁄₁₆ in	¼ cm
⅛ in	½ cm
½ in	1 ½ cm
¾ in	2 cm
1 in	2 ½ cm
1 ½ in	4 cm
2 in	5 cm
2 ½ in	6 ½ cm
3 in	8 cm
3 ½ in	9 cm
4 in	10 cm
4 ½ in	11 ½ cm
5 in	13 cm
5 ½ in	14 cm
6 in	15 cm
6 ½ in	16 ½ cm
7 in	18 cm
7 ½ in	19 cm
8 in	20 cm
8 ½ in	21 ½ cm
9 in	23 cm
9 ½ in	24 cm
10 in	25 cm

SELECTED BIBLIOGRAPHY

GREEN CHILI AND OTHER IMPOSTORS follows the movement of particular foods around the world with India as the nexus. I gathered my information on this subject from a wide array of print and online sources including books, peer-reviewed journals, websites, and news articles. In addition to in-person interviews and deep consultation with my taste buds while on location in India, I have synthesized research from these sources. I relied most often on K. T. Achaya, Jayanta Sengupta, David Burton, and Colleen Taylor Sen for general colonial culinary history, Utsa Ray for the cultivation of rice in Bengal, John McPhee for the history of citrus, Lizzie Collingham for the story of curry, Andrea Wiley for an understanding of the cultures of milk, and Jael Silliman for Jewish-Indian history. I am indebted to their expertise and the many sources that they consulted as well as to the expertise of the others listed.

~~~~~

Achaya, K. T. *A Historical Dictionary of Indian Food.* New Delhi: Oxford University Press, 1998.

———. *Indian Food: A Historical Companion.* New Delhi: Oxford University Press, 1994.

Ackerman, Diane. *A Natural History of the Senses.* New York: Vintage Books, 1990.

Albala, Ken. *Beans: A History.* New York: Berg, 2007.

———. *Food: A Cultural Culinary History.* Audiobook. Chantilly, Va.: The Great Courses, 2013.

———, ed. *The Food History Reader: Primary Sources.* London: Bloomsbury, 2014.

Allámí, Abul-i-Fazl. *The Ain-i-Akbari.* Trans. H. S. Jarrett. Kolkata: Asiatic Society of Bengal, 1894.

Balachander, Vidya. "On Knafeh and a Vision of the World without Borders: What a Beloved Dessert Reveals about Cultural Appropriation." *Literary Hub*, January 6, 2020. https://lithub.com/on-knafeh-and-a-vision-of-the-world-without-borders.

Baruah, Pradip. "Tea Drinking: Origin, Perceptions, Habits with Special Reference to Assam, Its Tribes, and Role in Tocklai." *Science and Culture* 77, nos. 9–10 (2011): 365–472.

Beeton, Isabella. *Mrs. Beeton's Book of Household Management: Comprising Information for the Mistress, Housekeeper, Cook, Kitchen-Maid, Butler, Footman, Coachman, Valet, Upper and Under House-Maids, Lady's-Maid, Maid-of-All-Work, Laundry-Maid, Nurse and Nurse-Maid, Monthly Wet and Sick Nurses, Etc. Etc.—Also Sanitary, Medical, and Legal Memoranda: With a History of the Origin, Properties, and Uses of All Things Connected with Home Life and Comfort.* London: S. O. Beeton Publishing, 1861.

A Book for a Cook: Being a Collection of Certain Recipes and Other Things Which Every Good Cook Knows. Minneapolis: Pillsbury Company, 1905.

Braudel, Fernand. *Civilization and Capitalism, 15th–18th Century.* Vol. 1: *The Structures of Everyday Life.* Trans. Siân Reynolds. London: William Collins Sons and Co., 1981.

Brown, Patricia. *Anglo-Indian Food and Customs.* New Delhi: Penguin Books India, 1998.

Burton, David. *The Raj at Table: A Culinary History of the British in India.* London: Faber and Faber, 1993.

Carney, Judith. *Black Rice: The African Origins of Rice Cultivation in the Americas.* Cambridge, Mass.: Harvard University Press, 2001.

Collingham, Lizzie. *Curry: A Tale of Cooks and Conquerors.* Oxford: Oxford University Press, 2006.

DasGupta, Minakshie. *Bangla Ranna: The Art of Bengali Cooking.* Calcutta: Jaya Chaliha, 1982.

Dash, Mike. "The Secret That Preceded the Indian Rebellion of 1857." *Smithsonian,* May 24, 2012.

Deepak, Sharanya. "A 'Forgotten Holocaust' Is Missing from Indian Food Stories." *Atlas Obscura,* September 17, 2020. https://www.atlasobscura.com/articles/indian-food-writing.

Dursun, Sukru, Fatma Kunt, Zeynep Cansu Ozturk, and Blerina Vrenozi. "Global Climate Change Effects on Ecology." In *Proceedings of the 2nd International Conference on Sustainable Agriculture and Environment.* 2 vols. Konya, Turkey: Selçuk University, 2015.

Fisher, Mary Frances Kennedy. *The Art of Eating.* Hoboken, N.J.: Wiley, 2004.

Flint-Hamilton, Kimberly B. "Legumes in Ancient Greece and Rome: Food, Medicine, or Poison?" *Hesperia: The Journal of the American School of Classical Studies at Athens* 68, no. 3 (1999): 371–385.

Fontes da Costa, Palmira. *Medicine, Trade and Empire: Garcia de Orta's "Colloquies on the Simples and Drugs of India" (1563) in Context.* New York: Routledge, 2016.

Forster, E. M. *A Passage to India.* New York: Harcourt, Brace and World, 1924.

———. *Where Angels Fear to Tread.* London: William Blackwood and Sons, 1905.

Freedberg, David A. "Ferrari on the Classification of Oranges and Lemons." In *Documentary Culture: Florence and Rome from Grand-Duke Ferdinand I to Pope Alexander VII: Papers from a Colloquium Held at the Villa Spelman, Florence, 1990.* Bologna: Nuova Alfa Editoriale, 1992.

Freedman, P. "Health, Wellness and the Allure of Spices in the Middle Ages." *Journal of Ethnopharmacology* 167 (2015): 47–53.

Furber, Holden. "The Beginnings of American Trade with India, 1784–1812." *New England Quarterly* 11, no. 2 (1938): 235–265.

Ghosh, Deepanjan. "Forgotten History: How the Last Nawab of Oudh Built a Mini Lucknow in Calcutta." *Scroll.in,* August 6, 2020. www.scroll.in/magazine/869214.

Griffiths, James. "India's Forgotten Chinese Internment Camp." *Atlantic,* August 9, 2013.

Hanusz, István. "Magyar Fűszerszám" (Paprika). *KL* 11: 13–17 sz. k., 1896.

Hensley, Tim. "A Curious Tale: The Apple in North America." Brooklyn Botanic Garden, June 2, 2005. http://www.bbg.org/gardening/article/the_apple_in_north_america.

Heyd, Wilhelm. *Geschichte des Levantehandels im Mittelalter*. Vol. 1. Stuttgart: J. G. Cotta, 1879.

Hourigan, Malcolm. "Holding On: Anglo Indian Settlement in McCluskiegunj." *Probashi Bengal*, February 6, 2015. http://www.probashionline.com/holding-angl o-indian-settlement-mccluskiegunj.

Jacobs, Rita D. "English Trifle: Serious Dessert." *New York Times*, March 27, 1988.

Johnston, Paul F. "The Smithsonian and the 19th-Century Guano Trade: This Poop Is Crap." National American History Behring Center, May 31, 2017. www.american-history.si.edu/blog/smithsonian-and-guano.

Juvenal, Decimus Junius. "Satires V and XL." *The Satires of Juvenal, Persius, Sulpicia and Lucius*. Trans. Lewis Evan. New York: Harper and Brothers, 1881.

Kenney-Herbert, Arthur Robert. *Culinary Jottings for Madras, Or, A Treatise in Thirty Chapters on Reformed Cookery for Anglo-Indian Exiles*. Madras: Higginbotham, 1878.

Krondl, Michael. *The Taste of Conquest: The Rise and Fall of the Three Great Cities of Spice*. New York: Ballantine Books, 2007.

"Lakshmi Revealed." *Deccan Herald*, October 10, 2009.

Liu, YuQiu, Emily Heying, and Sherry Tanumihardjo. "History, Global Distribution, and Nutritional Importance of Citrus Fruits." Institute of Food Technologists, October 16, 2012. https://onlinelibrary.wiley.com/doi/pdf/10.1111/j.1541-4337.2012.00201.x.

Lo, Vivienne, Paul Kadetz, Marianne J. Datiles, and Michael Heinrich. "Potent Substances: An Introduction." *Journal of Ethnopharmacology* 167 (2015): 2–6.

Mann, Charles. "How the Potato Changed the World." *Smithsonian*, November 2011.

McNeill, William H. "How the Potato Changed the World's History." *Social Research* 66, no. 1 (Spring 1999): 67–83.

McPhee, John. *Oranges*. New York: Farrar, Straus and Giroux, 1966.

Meghvansi, M. K., S. Siddiqui, Md. Haneef Khan, V. K. Gupta, M. G. Vairale, H. K. Gogoi, and Lokendra Singh. "Naga Chilli: A Potential Source of Capsaicinoids with Broad-Spectrum Ethnopharmacological Applications." *Journal of Ethnopharmacology* 132 (2010): 1–14.

Merchant, Shaan. "The Violent Rise of Curry." OZY Media Company, March 25, 2021. https://www.ozy.com/true-and-stories/the-violent-rise-of-curry/425914.

Mohan, Urmila. "Dressing God: Clothing as Material of Religious Subjectivity in a Hindu Group." In *The Social Life of Materials: Studies in Materials and Society*, ed. Adam Drazin and Susanne Kuchler, 137–152. London: Bloomsbury, 2015.

Monardes, Nicolás. *Historia medicinal de las cosas que se traen de nuestras Indias Occidentales que sirven en medicina.* Ed. J. M. López Piñero. Madrid: Ministerio de Sanidad y Consumo, 1989.

Moran, Daniel, Keiichiro Kanemoto, Magnus Jiborn, Richard Wood, Johannes Többen, and Karen C. Seto. "Carbon Footprints of 13,000 Cities." *Environmental Research Letters* 13, no. 6 (2018): 064041.

Mukerjee, Madhusree. *Churchill's Secret War: The British Empire and the Ravaging of India during World War II.* New York: Basic Books, 2010.

Nag, Arindam. "A Milk-Curdling Tale." *Society,* February 1989.

Nealon, Tom. "A Zest for Life: How Lemonade Saved Paris from the Plague." *Boston Globe,* June 26, 2017.

Newbery, John. *The Original Mother Goose's Melody, as First Issued by John Newbery, of London, about A.D. 1760.* Introductory notes by William H. Whitmore. Albany, N.Y.: Joel Munsell's Sons, 1889.

Nosrat, Samin. *Salt, Fat, Acid, Heat: Mastering the Elements of Good Cooking.* New York: Simon and Schuster, 2017.

Nye, Naomi Shihab. *Words under the Words: Selected Poems.* Portland, Ore.: Eighth Mountain Press, 1995.

Pillai, K. G. Sankara, E. V. Ramakrishnan, and K. M. Sheriff. "The Trees of Cochin." *Indian Literature* 37, no. 5 (1994): 41–45.

Quaisar, Ahsan Jan. "The Indian Response to European Technology and Culture (AD 1498–1707)." *Bulletin of the School of Oriental and African Studies* 47, no. 2 (1982): 373–374.

Ramón-Laca, L. "The Introduction of Cultivated Citrus to Europe via Northern Africa and the Iberian Peninsula." *Economic Botany* 57, no. 4 (2003): 502–514.

Ray, Utsa. *Culinary Culture in Colonial India: A Cosmopolitan Platter and the Middle-Class.* Cambridge: Cambridge University Press, 2015.

Robinson, Simon. "Chili Peppers: Global Warming." *Time,* June 14, 2007.

Roy, Pratap Chandra, ed. *The Mahabharata of Krishna-Dwaipayana Vyasa.* Calcutta: Bharata Press, 1894.

Scholes, Mary C., and Robert Scholes. "Dust to Dust." *Science,* November 2013.

Scora, Rainer W. "On the History and Origins of Citrus." *Bulletin of the Torrey Botanical Club* 102 (1975): 369.

Sen, Colleen Taylor. *Curry: A Global History.* London: Reaktion Books, 2009.

———. *Feasts and Fasts: A History of Food in India.* London: Reaktion Books, 2014.

———. "Tracing India's Food Journey." *Live History India*, May 12, 2018. https://www.livehistoryindia.com/history-in-a-dish/2018/05/12/tracing-indias-food-journey-from-the-vedas.

Sengupta, Jayanta. "India." In *Food in Time and Place: The American Historical Association Companion to Food History*, ed. Paul Freedman, 68–94. Oakland: University of California Press, 2014.

———. "Nation on a Platter: The Culture and Politics of Food and Cuisine in Colonial Bengal." *Modern Asian Studies* 44, no. 1 (2010): 81–98.

Silliman, Jael. *Jewish Portraits, Indian Frames: Women's Narratives from a Diaspora of Hope*. Lebanon, N.H.: University Press of New England, 2001.

Sloan, Robin. *Sourdough or, Lois and Her Adventures in the Underground Market: A Novel*. New York: Farrar, Straus and Giroux, 2017.

Slow Food Foundation for Biodiversity. "Social Report 2011." https://www.fondazioneslowfood.com/wp-content/uploads/2015/06/2011_social_report_bassa.pdf.

Smith, Stephen Halikowski. "In the Shadow of a Pepper-centric Historiography: Understanding the Global Diffusion of Capsicums in the Sixteenth and Seventeenth Centuries." *Journal of Ethnopharmacology* 167 (2015): 64–77.

Sohail, Sara. "How the British Discovered Tea in Assam." *Madras Courier*, February 5, 2019. https://madrascourier.com/insight/how-the-british-discovered-tea-in-assam.

Spanbauer, Tom. *Faraway Places*. Portland, Ore.: Hawthorne Books, 1988.

Tagore, Rabindranath. *Collected Poems and Plays of Rabindranath Tagore*. New York: Macmillan, 1937.

Tewari, Rakesh, R. K. Srivastava, K. K. Singh, K. S. Saraswat, I. B. Singh, M. S. Chauhan, Anil K. Pokharia, A. Saxena, V. Prasad, and M. Sharma, "Second preliminary report of the excavations at Lahuradewa, District Sant Kabir Nagar, UP: 2002–2003–2004 & 2005–06," *Pragdhara* 16 (2006): 14.

United Nations, Food and Agriculture Organization. "What Is Happening to Agrobiodiversity?" http://www.fao.org/docrep/007/y5609e/y5609e02.htm.

University College London. "Debating the Origins of Rice." https://www.UCL.ac.uk/rice/history-rice/debating-origins-rice.

Van der Veen, Marijke, and Jacob Morales. "The Roman and Islamic Spice Trade: New Archaeological Evidence." *Journal of Ethnopharmacology* 167 (2015): 54–63.

Wagner, Kim A. *The Great Fear of 1857: Rumours, Conspiracies and the Making of the Indian Uprising*. Oxford: Peter Lang, 2010.

Wiley, Andrea S. *Cultures of Milk: The Biology and Meaning of Dairy Products in the United States and India.* Cambridge, Mass.: Harvard University Press, 2014.

Yule, Henry, and A. C. Burnell. *Hobson-Jobson: A Glossary of Colloquial Anglo-Indian Words and Phrases, and of Kindred Terms, Etymological, Historical, Geographical and Discursive.* New Delhi: Rupa and Company, 1886.

INDEX

260